Lust, Violence, Religion

Life in Historic Waco

Compiled by Bradley T. Turner

Publishing

ISBN 978-1-934302-69-9 (softback)
ISBN 978-1-934302-74-3 (hardback)

TSTC Publishing
Texas State Technical College Waco
3801 Campus Drive
Waco, Texas 76705
http://publishing.tstc.edu/

Publisher: Mark Long
Project manager: Grace Arsiaga
Sales manager: Wes Lowe
Marketing manager: Sheila Boggess
Cover design: SoroDesign, sorodesign.com
Page layout: Stephen Tiano, steve@tianodesign.com
Editors: Carly Kahl & Kayla Allen
Indexing: Michelle Graye, indexing@yahoo.com
Special thanks: Katharine O'Moore-Klopf & Dr. Jim Usery

Manufactured in the United States of America

First edition

Publisher's Cataloging-in-Publication
(*Provided by Quality Books, Inc.*)

    Lust, violence, religion : life in historic Waco / compiled
      by Bradley T. Turner. -- 1st ed.
        p. cm.
        Includes bibliographical references and index.
        ISBN-13: 978-1-934302-69-9
        ISBN-10: 1-934302-69-4

      1. Waco (Tex.)--History--19th century. 2. Waco
    (Tex.)--History--20th century. I. Turner, Bradley T.

    F394.W12L87 2010   976.4'284
                    QBI10-600047

For the people of Waco: Past, present, and future

Table of Contents

Introduction   **5**

Chapter 1: We Will Look for You: The Legacy of the Circuit Rider
   by Bradley T. Turner   7

Chapter 2: Waco Undressed
   by Amy S. Balderach   21

Chapter 3: The Apostle of Personal Protest: William C. Brann and the *Iconoclast* in Waco
   by Richard H. Fair   41

Chapter 4: The Sins of Our Fathers: Lynching in McLennan County Before 1920
   by Richard H. Fair   55

Chapter 5: Sending in the Second String: A Brief History of Camp MacArthur and Rich Field
   by Bradley T. Turner   77

Chapter 6: The Approaching Storm: The 1942 World War II Home Front in Waco
   by Bradley T. Turner   113

Chapter 7: "Lord Have Mercy": The Horrific Tornado of 1953
   by Bradley T. and Andrea R. Turner   139

Chapter 8: A House Divided: A Concise History of Integrating Commercial Waco
   by Bradley T. Turner   181

Chapter 9: For the Pleasure of Which People? Race in William Cameron Park, Waco, Texas
   by Mark E. Firmin   203

Chapter 10: What Are They Fighting For? Reaction to the Vietnam War in Waco
  by Bradley T. Turner   227

Index   255

Acknowledgments   313

About the Authors   317

Introduction

The essays in this book offer the best critical examinations to date of the rich and complex history of Waco and McLennan County, Texas. Unlike other major Texas cities, Waco has garnered relatively little serious scholarly attention, largely because the other cities eclipsed Waco during the latter half of the twentieth century—and the reasons conjure up bitter debates even today, during Waco's recent renaissance. But these essays represent a major leap toward correcting the neglect and explaining the problem. Most of all, they illuminate Waco's history as colorful, controversial, violent, and often tragic.

Recent products of the Baylor University History Department graduate program, the authors include Bradley T. Turner, who deserves much credit for conceiving and editing the book. Each essay reflects impressive research and sharp interpretations of Wacoans' clashes over social and political power, particularly along the persistent fault lines of race, class, gender, and religion.

Such outstanding scholarship will encourage future historians to continue analyzing and interpreting Waco's past in critical ways. Like the authors of these essays, they can profit greatly by conducting research in the Baylor Texas Collection (see: http://www.baylor.edu/lib/Texas), a superb special library devoted to the study of Texas history and culture.

For basic background information, anyone interested in Waco history should also examine the following: Roger N. Conger, *A Pictorial History of Waco*, Second Edition, Indexed and Updated by Kari Vanhoozer (Waco, TX: Texian Press, 1998); Patricia Ward Wallace, *Waco: A Sesquicentennial History* (Virginia Beach, VA: Donning Company, 1999); Patricia Ward Wallace, *Waco: Texas Crossroads* (Woodland Hills, CA: Windsor Publications, 1983); and the Waco History Project website (see: http://www.wacohistoryproject.org).

T. Michael Parrish
Department of History
Baylor University

We Will Look for You:
The Legacy of the Circuit Rider

by Bradley T. Turner

We expect soon to pass down side by side and rest awhile in the church graveyard and wait for your coming; and finally when the Master calls we will get up, body and soul united, and attended by beloved kindred, we will part no more forever, but in the home of the good we will live, love, and be happy always. We will look for you.

—Rev. Thomas and Lemerles Stanford[1]

Introduction

Someday, when you travel on Highway 6, exit at Imperial Drive and follow the four-lane road past Texas Central Parkway and Old Hewitt Drive. Continue on, past the bump and dip of the Hewitt Drive intersection, and watch as Imperial Drive changes into Chapel Road, morphing into a two-lane rural road that eventually winds its way along a j-curve to the intersection of Old Lorena Road and Spring Valley Road, between Lorena and Moody. While traveling on Chapel Road, about one-quarter mile past Ritchie/Richey/ Richie Road (spelled differently on various road signs) stop at the chain-link gateway announcing "Stanford Chapel: 1875"—Chapel Road's namesake—and investigate the seemingly forgotten area. The gate marks the entrance for the old Stanford Chapel, named after a local Methodist circuit rider, who developed the spot into a churchyard and cemetery during the late nineteenth century. Though many people regularly drive past the gates, few people know the history of Stanford Chapel or what the tiny tract of land represents to local heritage.

In the times between the American Revolution and the settling of the American West, the general public's value of individualism grew at a rapid pace. Along with social individualism came religious individualism in the form of Christian evangelicalism—an idea that religion should reach out to the people instead of the people reaching out for religion. The concept of evangelicalism became synonymous with individualism, because evangelicalism represented the process of taking religion to an individual level and promoting the idea of a personal relationship with

Entrance to Stanford Chapel Grounds, 2009. *Photograph by Bradley T. Turner.*

God and Jesus Christ, a concept orthodox European dogma generally considered too liberal. In the American South, few examples embodied the new evangelical approach to religion better than the circuit rider. Circuit riders provided ministry and religious activities in rural environments, far removed from the downtown commercial centers of urban American developments. The riders constantly ventured into the deep back country of America and brought civil order, religion, and culture to previously neglected peoples.

Circuit riders traveled specified routes designed to provide preachers with the ability to minister to nearby families once a month. Congregations rarely organized churches in the dense back country of America because of the limited availability of church members. Instead, well-established churches and organizations sponsored circuit riders to organize satellite churches and recruit local families for attendance. Each circuit commonly consisted of either four to five small churches or one large church encompassing about 100 church members, along with any recluse families in areas along the circuit.[2]

Many personal descriptions of circuit riders depict single, young males riding and sleeping about the countryside, spreading the gospel of Christ.[3] But the life of a circuit rider was not commonly met with ease and carefree weekdays. It was a difficult lifestyle riddled with nomadic characteristics. One scholar documents that of 737 circuit preachers who died before 1847, 203 of them were under thirty-five years of age. Longevity was not common among riders. If the riders managed to survive into old age, most congregations awarded the riders with retirement to permanent churches in various agricultural villages.[4]

Following the turn of the twentieth century, personal accounts and journals concerning circuit preachers began to disappear. Few reasons for the decline of circuit riders exist, but perhaps transportation improvements provide the best explanation for gradual extinction. After the Civil War, better roads and rail lines became prominent across America as settlers developed various terrains. When transportation systems improved, farmers could then travel farther distances in shorter times, providing the circuit rider with less responsibility and fewer stops along the circuit. Membership levels remained steady, but since people could travel farther distances, many churches merged into one body. The circuit rider then either became tethered to a more permanent location or ventured to fewer meeting places, since smaller populations combined into larger congregations.

Setting the Stage for the Riders

"As you go, preach this message: 'The Kingdom of Heaven is near!'"
—Matthew 10:7[5]

"Do all the good you can, in all the ways you can, to all the souls you can, in every place you can, at all the times you can, with all the zeal you can, as long as ever you can."—Rev. John Wesley[6]

Around Waco, Texas, while most individuals consider Baptist the dominant Protestant denomination, Methodism emerged as the most frequent choice for the riders because of its national popularity. Methodists targeted slaves, freedmen, immigrants, and native whites across the country in an effort to broaden the church's membership base. The consensus remained among Methodists that all peoples, regardless of origin, ethnicity, gender, or economic status, possessed souls and the availability for salvation—an issue not related to political rights or status.

The theology surrounding Methodism originated in England in 1703 and the church officially organized in 1739 under the direction of John Wesley. The Methodist Church initially used an internal structure comparable to that of the Anglican Church and developed a popular following in America because of a high level of tolerance.[7] By 1760, large numbers of Methodists began arriving in the middle British-American colonies and the demand for Methodist ministers rose.

During the nineteenth century, a theological debate over slavery raged through the church, and by 1844 the Methodists had divided into Northern and Southern constituencies over the nullification and promotion of slavery. The question of how to treat black Americans was not a new issue for the church, however. In 1816, the Method-

ists established the African Methodist Episcopal (AME) church to minister to slaves and freedmen.[8] White ministers presided over the services for the AME church, but the institution represented one of the few sects addressing religious questions of race. Matthew Simpson, a circuit rider from Indiana, declared the United States' Constitution presented a clear criterion for solving the problem: all men are created equal. The same man stood resolved on the same principle during the Civil War—that the Constitution protected the rights of the rebels who took up arms in opposition.[9]

Throughout the late nineteenth century, the Methodist church lacked the human and financial resources needed to supply each area with proper attention because the American countryside was simply too large for any one denomination to adequately reach all of the people.[10] Though the rural populations numbered few, the miles between the people numbered many and most families could not financially afford to cease farm production weekly for attendance at a distant church.

Americans needed a religion that could come to each of them individu-

ally, where the ministers would come to the people as authority figures to promote the concept of an individual relationship with God and Jesus Christ. The circuit preacher provided a systematic attempt by the Methodist church to reach the difficult rural areas. Over time, the traveling reverends created a religious unity in rural areas and provided country families with other social activities following church services. These activities might represent the only opportunities for rural individuals to find a spouse or converse with neighboring friends since most of their time was spent toiling on family farms.

The circuit rider provided remote locations with a scheduled activity for scattered peoples and served as a local and national milestone toward unity and the building of a national identity during a critical time in American development. Another important advantage Methodism held over other denominations presented itself in the form of both a church hierarchy and elected bishops. This structure allowed the church to maintain a sense of unity, while introducing democratic methods to religious doctrine—an aspect of Methodism located solely in America during this era.[11]

Today, historians and theologians believe the first official Methodist circuit rider was an Irish immigrant named Robert Strawbridge who served during the 1760s mostly in the areas around Maryland, Virginia, and Pennsylvania—some of the most religiously diverse British colonies. Even decades after his death in 1781, the legacy of Strawbridge remained steadfast through his reputation as a firebrand and as a benchmark in comparing the effectiveness of his successors.[12] Strawbridge provided the Methodist church with the template of expectancy for all circuit riders and confidence in the realistic possibility of building a thin network of riders able to minister to a large population.

Life on the Circuit

"Those who had been scattered preached the word wherever they went."
—Acts 8:4[13]

"When you set yourself on fire with enthusiasm people will come for miles to watch you burn." —Rev. John Wesley[14]

Around the era of the American Revolution, an almost-fatal accident changed Freeborn Garrettson's life when, during a normal horseback ride, Garrettson's horse became wild and threw him onto the ground. Believing his injuries to be fatal, Garrettson remained on the ground waiting for assistance. He began to despair when no help arrived, and began to plead for his life with God, asking that he be spared and that God show him mercy. In return for staying alive, Garrettson vowed to dedicate his life to spreading the gospel. Soon thereafter, a traveler appeared and Garrettson, ecstatic about the sighting, called the incident a miracle of God. In response, Garrettson, once a wealthy plantation owner, freed his slaves, converted to Methodism in 1775, joined a circuit route, and began a preaching career that spanned decades and distances ranging from New York to Pennsylvania.

The most unique aspect of Garrettson's preaching style originated from his perseverance and charisma. On numerous occasions, Freeborn Garrettson preached to less than ten people in a sitting to make the sermon personal.

Garrettson's journal lists twenty-five years of daily entries riddled with stories of his evangelic adventures and his interactions with individuals. Garrettson's desire to interact with rural families simultaneously provided the Methodist church with the ability to extend into remote areas. The charisma, concern, and stamina of the intrepid rider created the image of a wilderness preacher that lasted beyond his death in 1827 and continued on throughout the nineteenth century.[15]

Francis Asbury represents another nationally reputed circuit rider who later became the first bishop of the evangelical American Methodist Church. Circuit riders led lives filled with diversity and hardship. In a career that took him to almost every community on the Atlantic Coast between the mid-1770s and 1815, Asbury wrote that in the course of one average day he had breakfast with a friend and explained the death of both the friend's wife and daughter as being "asleep in Jesus," mended his gear at noon, rode through the countryside in the afternoon, and ordained a deacon in the evening at the opening of a new chapel.[16] Throughout Asbury's journal, similar schedules reveal the intense stress and complexity of the circuit rider's life in the early nineteenth century. When Asbury died in 1816, his family interred him adjacent to Robert Strawbridge in Baltimore, Maryland.[17]

The vastness of the frontier and the sparse populations of the back country frequently caused gaps in the availability of circuit riders and an overextension of clergy. On occasion, the Methodist church assigned entire territories (Missouri and Illinois) as one monthly circuit, preaching at noon every day except the Sabbath (Sunday), the opposite of contemporary custom. Circuit riders did not typically receive high wages and many riders with families either left the ministry for higher wages or struggled to provide for their families. Around 1810, one rider, Benjamin Lakin, requested a raise in his salary to support his wife and children to which the committee responded: "it is therefore our opinion that it is ungenerous in him to bring a demand on Conference; and seeing there are other more needy, it is our judgment that he ought not have anything."[18] Though demo-cratically elected, the Methodist church leaders did not tolerate many questions involving their authority and decisions.

The Methodist church held each rider accountable for administering the holy sacraments of the Lord's Supper and baptisms four times a year along each route. The sacraments generally required two days for proper administration and ended on Sunday to honor the Sabbath. Services for large audiences began on Saturday mornings with two sequential sermons and a third in the evening, sometimes led by a junior rider or local church elder. On Sundays, the congregation feasted around 11:00 a.m. and enjoyed lighthearted fellowship. Sometimes these traditional customs adapted to seasonal weather and the varying assignment of circuit riders who might control massive circuits and routes.[19]

Perhaps the most common thread was loneliness. A Catholic circuit rider named Adolf Bakanowski frequently complained of loneliness during his long rides through the Texas Hill Country and befriended a dog he called Lamurck to help abate his sadness. Bakanowski's writings indicate a sense that his congregations sometimes appeared apathetic concerning his personal emotions and private life.[20] Though he found excitement in his works and travels, the constant grind of daily travels and nightly changes appears to have slowly eroded the sense of belonging common in people with permanent establishment. Loneliness represents a realistic and common theme that likely rode with the riders along their extensive routes.

Local Circuit Riders and their Legacies

"He came as a witness to testify concerning the light, so that through him all men might believe."—John 1:7[21]

"And when you read endeavor to realize this thought: 'These dear old ones of long ago when writing these words were thinking and talking of us children.'" —Rev. Thomas and Lemerles Stanford[22]

As time passed and needs changed, the circuit rider evolved into a stationary preacher who still preached a circuit but also opened a permanent chapel that acted as the rider's base for ministry work. Waco experienced this gradual shift in the Methodist church as the closing of the nineteenth century approached.

In 1842, Thomas Stanford sat down at the kitchen table with his wife, Lemerles, in their home in Arkansas and told her that he felt called to join the traveling circuit conference of the Methodist church. Lemerles turned slightly pale and slowly began to cry,

Thomas Stanford, 1872. *Photograph courtesy of A. Frank Smith, Jr., Library Special Collections, Southwestern University, Georgetown, Texas.*

saying, "I am not surprised: I have been expecting it."[23]

Thomas Stanford represents one of the best examples of a Methodist circuit rider in the area surrounding Waco, Texas, during the late nineteenth century. Stanford was born in 1813 in Lincoln County, Tennessee, the oldest son of a circuit preacher from South Carolina.[24] Stanford followed many other American settlers who slowly moved west. Stanford's American roots ran strong, back to the American Revolution where his ancestors fought the British at the battle of Camden, South Carolina. Stanford became a Christian at twenty-six and a minister at twenty-nine. During the years of his career as a circuit rider, he estimated he moved thirty-three times over a forty-six year period, while providing for a large family of ten or more at most times.[25]

Stanford preferred circuit routes in either Arkansas or Texas because he enjoyed life in the South. At the beginning of the Civil War, Stanford held a post in Fayetteville, Arkansas, but transferred to Central Texas to remove his family from the conflict.[26] Stanford remained in the area sur-

rounding Waco, Texas, following the Civil War until his death in 1892.

As the national turmoil of the Civil War and Reconstruction dissipated, Stanford received a five-acre land donation from his son-in-law to build a school, church, and cemetery in the area of the Richey Switch, roughly five miles west of Waco, Texas. Stanford, along with the family of Rev. E.R. Barcus, Sr., framed the chapel around 1875.[27] Believed to be the first Methodist church in the area, Stanford Chapel grew as a permanent location for cultural development and fellowship servicing the Hewitt, South Bosque, and Lorena communities because of its ability to provide steadfast religion.[28] Contemporaries described the church as a white building with an extremely high steeple. The grounds also included an arbor or tabernacle with a shingled roof, a raised platform-pulpit, wooden benches, and a floor consisting of straw and dirt.[29]

Another local Methodist circuit rider who preached in the Waco area during the end of the nineteenth century was E.R. Barcus, Sr. Born in Ohio in 1825, Barcus rode a circuit in

Stanford Chapel, about 1900. *Photograph courtesy of the Stanford Cemetery Association.*

Arkansas at the same time as Stanford and immigrated to Texas in about 1874.[30] Barcus organized several local Methodist churches ranging from the Lorena United Methodist Church in 1881 to the First United Methodist Church of Temple in 1882 and preached at numerous others in the area. When establishing the Lorena United Methodist Church, Barcus originally used the Lorena Baptist Church for religious services and assisted in organizing a construction committee to erect a permanent sanctuary in 1886.[31] Barcus and Stanford grew to be close friends on the circuit together. In fact, their families inter-married and Stanford even requested that Barcus fill his circuit in 1886 when Stanford retired.[32]

At Stanford Chapel, most religious activities occurred on Sunday morning. Morning Bible schools filled the church grounds with the primary sermon given at 11:00 in the morning. Each child learned a scripture or hymn before playing on Sunday afternoons. After each weekday on the farm, the locals gathered in the evenings for prayer meetings and fellowship.[33]

The annual summer camp meeting represented the biggest celebration for Methodist revival and development in the church grounds. At Stanford Chapel, the meeting commonly lasted for ten days in the middle of August and housed families venturing from many miles away. Clergy instructed visitors not to stake their tents within 300 feet of the church in order to demonstrate the proper respect. Authorities also divided the sleeping arrangements of the camps according to gender with the men and boys on the west end of the grounds and women and girls on the north. The average meeting encompassed two Sundays and people brought adequate food to supply their families for the extended summer stay. Meals of canned goods (a semi-rare item at the end of the nineteenth century) consisting of potted ham, salmon, peaches, pears, and strawberries became commonplace for summer meeting participants with an occasional first-day feast of perishable cakes and pies.[34]

Circuit riders of rural McLennan County used these events to draw straying individuals back into the religious congregation and conduct any formal

E.R. Barcus, Sr., about 1880. *Photograph courtesy of the McEachern and Barcus Family Archive.*

business the church required. Clergy worked long, diligent hours at revivals, praying at sunrise, preaching throughout the day, singing in the afternoon, and preaching again when the sun abated. The first sermons generally revolved around preparing for revival, with the main sermons encompassing heaven, hell, sin, and grace.[35]

Education represented one of the most crucial values of importance to Thomas Stanford.[36] Before moving to Central Texas, one resident of Greene

County, Arkansas, remembered that Stanford carried an English spelling book he read during any spare moments throughout the day, demonstrating his fervor for learning.[37]

A circuit rider possessed time while traveling and most riders commonly used travel time for studying as each preacher required an above-average education to fulfill other church duties involving literacy and general academics. In fact, Stanford Chapel served a multitude of functions in service to both God and the community by sponsoring religious activities and public school lessons where Mary Frances Barcus (E. R. Barcus' wife) served as the main school teacher.[38] A multi-functioning building, however, did not always represent the best solution for providing education and religion. Stanford feared that a multi-functioning church building may have too little floor space, and most congregation members typically backed out of any project to expand the building because of the increased cost associated with such a task.[39]

Primary education did not present the only academic concern for Stanford. Out of respect, Stanford's colleagues elected him a curator for Southwestern University in Georgetown, Texas, a position he held for twenty years (1872–1892).[40] The university provided local rural and agricultural areas with an opportunity for a collegiate education, bringing yet another source of culture to the area. Stanford's vocation and reputation as a strong, intelligent circuit rider and clergyman gave him the tools required to educate locals, connect to people, and assist in the development of a university.[41]

In one experience, John Barcus (the son of E.R. Barcus, Sr.) hitched a ride with Thomas Stanford to Georgetown, Texas, for his first semester at Southwestern University. After two days of travelling, Stanford stopped the buggy near the San Gabriel River, overlooking the city, and told the young Barcus, "Yonder is where you are to lay the foundation for your future greatness."[42]

E.R. Barcus, Sr., also held a strong emphasis on the importance of education. Initially, it was the Methodist Conference that requested Barcus relocate to Central Texas to serve as a music teacher at Waco Female Academy in about 1875, where he decided to farm

and preach instead of teach.[43] One of his sons, J. Sam Barcus (known as one of the "Preaching Barcuses"), eventually became president of Southwestern University in Georgetown, Texas.[44]

For the circuit rider, preaching did not stop with the scattered congregation—a true clergyman stood by virtue wherever he physically stood. In one instance, Stanford boarded a train from Georgetown to Waco, via the Richey Switch, and shared a train car with an unnamed Waco attorney and former Texas governor. The former governor offered Stanford a cigar, but Stanford declined by saying he only saw sin in something that partook of so much money and caused such little good.[45] The abrupt manner of Stanford's response to a political figurehead demonstrates his commitment to his values as well as the personal demeanor of the old circuit rider.

Around 1880, Stanford purchased a hundred-plus acre farm, believed to be near the chapel grounds. Today, the location may be in a residential development known as Stanford Oaks. A tax appraisal of the complete Stanford assets varied between 1875 and 1900, but

Thomas Stanford, about 1885–1890.
Photograph from Stanford's Sermons, *1892.*

generally floated around $2,000. The Stanfords owned, on average, one to two buggies or wagons, one to four horses or mules, a half-dozen cattle, and, on occasion, some hogs. Naturally, the life of the traveling minister prevented Stanford from developing a large farm—instead he generally produced enough to satisfy basic needs. After Stanford's death in 1892, Lemerles slowly sold the animals and wagons, only owning the original acreage at the time of her death in 1900.[46]

The relatively small amount of Stanford's assets differs from those of his circuit colleague, Rev. E.R. Barcus, Sr. Initially, Barcus met the idea of farming with skepticism, but after discussing the concept with local farmers (one of these being his colleague Stanford), Barcus bought his first land in Central Texas at $2 per acre for 110 acres. He ended up owning between 335 and 1,220 acres in McLennan County.[47] Upon his arrival, Barcus experienced a tough economy and Stanford gave Barcus a cow and calf, a pig and piglets, a chicken and chicks, and a hive of bees for honey to assist in the development of his neighbor's new farm.[48] Barcus worked as both a farmer and minister, leaving specified work details for his sons before traveling on a circuit.[49] In 1885, the year before Stanford retired and the year Barcus organized the Lorena United Methodist Church, Barcus owned some thirteen horses or mules, two dozen cattle, and nine hogs—a large fortune for a Methodist circuit rider.[50] Barcus claimed he never earned over $1,000 annually preaching and instead relied on his large family and farm to provide significant

profits.[51] In 1896, E.R. Barcus, Sr., died and was interred in a family plot in Stanford Chapel Cemetery directly behind the gated graves of Thomas and Lemerles Stanford.

Overall, Thomas Stanford and his little chapel represent the icon of individualism in the developing rural areas west of Waco, Texas. Barcus' and Stanford's vocation reflects the central theme of American individualism and evangelism—taking religion to all the people on a personal level. As transportation systems improved and populations became better established, people began to venture to permanent establishments for religion, allowing the circuit rider to travel to fewer locations. The newer religious sites also housed better facilities and provided adequate locations for greater amounts of people. Improved transportation, growing populations, and permanent facilities combined to serve as the primary model for the modern American evangelical church. Stanford maintained his circuit after the construction of his chapel, but did not experience the same difficulty as he had on previous routes because the new circuits did not require the same

level of intensity.

The Stanford Chapel congregation disbanded in 1912 and some previous Stanford Chapel worshippers relocated to the First United Methodist Church of Hewitt in 1922, some eight miles away from Stanford Chapel.[52] A total of 35 marriages, 155 infant baptisms, and an estimated 468 people attended functions at Stanford Chapel between 1884 and 1910.[53] Sometime during the 1920s, Stanford Chapel hosted a homecoming celebration, where Rev. Thomas Stanford Barcus spoke to the descendents of Stanford and Barcus as well as to the former governor of Texas, Pat Neff.[54] Fire destroyed the original church structure around 1945, but a perimeter of brick still traces a polygon in the dirt and small pieces of broken stained-glass also rest nearby. Vandals broke several tombstones during the 1970s and again one evening in 2007, but the cemetery still serves the community today. The State of Texas acknowledged the five-acre tract with a historic marker in 1997, ensuring the preservation and maintenance of the chapel grounds in the future.

ENDNOTES

1. Thomas Stanford, *Stanford's Sermons* (Nashville, TN: Barbee and Smith, Agents, 1892), 4.

2. William Warren Sweet, *Methodism in American History* (Nashville, TN: Abingdon Press, 1953), 165.

3. Nathan O. Hatch and John H. Wigger, *Methodism and the Shaping of American Culture* (Nashville, TN: Abington Press, 2001), 88.

4. John O. Gross, *The Beginnings of American Methodism* (Nashville, TN: Abington Press, 1961), 71.

5. Mt. 10:7, *NIV*.

6. "John Wesley Quotes."

7. James E. Kirby, Russell E. Richey, and Kenneth E. Rowe, *The Methodists, Student Edition* (Westport, CT: Praeger Publishers, 1998), 255.

8. Kirby, et al., *The Methodists*, 90.

9. David L. Kimbrough, *Reverend Joseph Tarkington: Methodist Circuit Rider* (Knoxville, TN: University of Tennessee Press, 1997), 133.

10. Ibid., 171.

11. Hatch, *Methodism*, 11.

12. Frederick E. Maser, *Robert Strawbridge: First American Methodist Circuit Rider* (Rutland, VT: Strawbridge Shrine Association, Inc, 1983).

13. Acts 8:4, *NIV*.

14. "John Wesley Quotes."

15. Robert Drew Simpson, ed., *American Methodist Pioneer: The Life and Journals of the Rev. Freeborn Garrettson, 1752–1827* (Rutland, VT: Sharp Offset Printing, Inc., 1984), 39–41.

16. Francis Asbury, *The Journal of the Rev. Francis Asbury, Bishop of The Methodist Episcopal Church from August 7, 1771, to December 7, 1815* (New York: N. Bangs and T. Mason), 3:279.

17. Maser, *Robert Strawbridge*, 59–61.

18. William Warren Sweet, *The Rise of Methodism in the West being The Journal of the Western Conference 1800–1811* (Dallas, TX: Smith and Lamar, 1920), 45–46.

19. Ibid.

20. Marion Moore Coleman, ed., *Polish Circuit Rider: The Texas Memoirs of Adolf Bakanowski* (Cheshire, CT: Cherry Hill Books, 1971), 10–19.

21. Jm. 1:7, *NIV*.

22. Stanford, *Stanford's Sermons*, 3.

23. Ibid., 10–11.

24. *A Memorial and Biographical History of McLennan, Falls, Bell, and Coryell Counties* (Chicago, IL: The Lewis Publishing Company, 1893), 784–85.

25. Stanford, *Stanford's Sermons*, 5–13.

26. Ibid.

27. John McFerrin Barcus, *My Personal History*, Barcus Family Papers, 13.

28. *A History of Stanford Chapel*, Barcus Family Papers.

29. Frank Miles Locke, "Action on Bull Hide Creek, 1897–1908," (privately printed, 1971), 84–88.

30. "A brief summary of the Barcus family history compiled by Anne Stratton Barcus McEachern for the Barcus family gathering, Thanksgiving 1996," McEachern Family Papers.

31. Lorena United Methodist Church Historical Marker; First United Methodist Church of Temple Historical Marker.

32. Stanford, *Stanford's Sermons*, 10.

33. "Barcus Family is Famous for its Preachers," *Dallas Morning News*, 13 October, 1925.

34. Ibid.

35. Ibid.

36. *Barcus/Barkhous Family History*, Southwestern University Archive, Georgetown, TX.

37. B.H. Crowley, *History of Greene*

County, 1906, http://www.usgennet.org/usa/ar/county/greene/2nd.htm [accessed 23 March, 2009].

38. *A History of Stanford Chapel.*

39. Stanford, *Stanford's Sermons*, 291–92.

40. Thomas Stanford comments found throughout Southwestern University minutes from 1872–1892.

41. Ibid., 10.

42. "Barcus Family is Famous for its Preachers," 14.

43. Ibid., 12.

44. "Barcus Family is Famous for its Preachers."

45. Stanford, *Stanford's Sermons*, 182–84.

46. McLennan County Tax Records, 1875–1900, http://www.co.mclennan.tx.us/arc/taxrolls.aspx [accessed 20 March, 2009].

47. "Barcus Family is Famous for its Preachers," 12.

48. "Autobiography of Sam Barcus," Southwestern University Archives, Georgetown, TX, 5.

49. "Barcus Family is Famous for its Preachers," 12.

50. McLennan County Tax Records, 1885.

51. "Barcus Family is Famous for its Preachers."

52. First United Methodist Church of Hewitt Historical Marker, 2000.

53. *A History of Stanford Chapel.*

54. "Homecoming Services to be Held at Stanford's Chapel Sunday Morning," unknown newspaper clipping between 1925–1932, Barcus Family Papers.

Waco Undressed

by Amy S. Balderach

Oh, I wish I was a fascinatin' lady.
My past would be fast and my future would be shady.
I'd live in a house with a little red light.
I'd sleep all day and I'd work all night.[1]

The Triumph of Capitalism

Across the Brazos River, linking downtown Waco to its eastern portions, stretches the historic suspension bridge created by the city's residents in the 1870s. While not presently used, save as a walkway and photograph opportunity for curious tourists, the bridge was essential to Waco's economic past. The city was a significant thru-way on the famed cattle drive route of the Chisholm Trail, and Waco's leaders constructed the link in the nineteenth century to ensure easier travel for cattle drivers. Today, the area around the historic landmark enjoys a convenient location near Waco's convention center, hotels, and a pristine walkway that memorializes Vietnam veterans. At the intersection of Washington Street and University Parks Drive, a few yards past the bridge, motorists momentarily halt and proceed through the four-way stop, perhaps noticing the bridge's symbol of bygone Texas days. Without a doubt, however, what each driver does not know is that a very different kind of business once existed in the same area: prostitution. Prostitution, however, did not simply exist in Waco; the trade thrived in a designated area known as the Reservation, or Two Street, from the 1870s to the early 1920s.

Waco was a city that contained both Old South and Old West characteristics when prostitutes began to populate the area close to the suspension bridge. By the late nineteenth century until the early twentieth, cotton was king in Waco and the crown prince was cattle. The "rough and tumble" life of the cattle boomtown often coexisted with a genteel and conservative society. Using the Brazos River as a means for transportation, depots for cotton merchants and

The Reservation Site, 2009. *Photograph by Bradley T. Turner.*

cattle drivers sprouted up along the waterway in Waco after the Civil War. The small town was soon an epicenter for the two key Texas economies.

Spurred by cotton and cattle, the late nineteenth century was a period of immense economic growth in Waco—the kind of growth that brought new residents to a town and redefined racial and ethnic lines. And with such changes, new social problems developed. They were changes brought about by the city's evolving economies, and they occurred throughout the country as American cities and towns dealt with the drawbacks of an increasingly industrialized and urban society. Following cattle and cotton industries, other businesses blossomed in the legitimate quarters of the city, but brothels also sprang up near them along the Brazos River.

The city's growing economy was integral in forming its red-light district; prostitutes simply went where the money was. And they flocked to Waco in droves. By the 1890s, Waco's red-light district housed more than 200 prostitutes and several successful madams.[2] Women's bodies became one

of Waco's largest draws, and the sex trade was a cash crop in its own right. At the same time, however, city officials felt the heat from a growing movement that began to take hold across the country: progressivism. Under the aegis of progressive reform, white Americans called for improvements in workers' conditions and food regulatory laws. Reformers also rallied around ideas of "social purity" and "social hygiene." This meant that they wanted to clean up American cities, curb venereal disease (in an age before penicillin), and ensure that white, Protestant citizens remained "pure," or untainted by immigrant or minority blood. By calling for social control, these reformers ultimately hoped to deal with problems of urban life and maintain the country's demographic status quo. And one of their biggest causes was the abolition of prostitution.

In many ways, Waco experienced trends in prostitution that occurred in other colorful Texas cities. Most of the state's largest cities contained red-light districts: Austin's Guy Town, El Paso's Utah Street, Fort Worth's Hell's Half Acre, Galveston's Post Office Street, and San Antonio's The District, among

others. Literally existing in the shadow of its more "legitimate" past (signified by the suspension bridge across the Brazos River), Waco's district was called Two Street because of the street bordering the Reservation to its south and west: North 2nd Street. After Fort Worth's Hell's Half Acre and San Antonio's The District, Waco's Two Street was the state's next most infamous red-light district.[3]

The Ladies of Two Street

The Reservation symbolized Waco at its lowest, and it was an embarrassment to the city's clean-cut image. Available records show that more than 200 prostitutes came and went between 1889 and 1895, not to mention the remaining years of Two Street's operation.[4] Crime and venereal disease among prostitutes were vital challenges in Waco, and the city attempted to contain these problems in a restricted zone. Lawmakers assumed that by allowing Two Street to remain open, rowdy behavior was prevented from entering more respectable areas. At the same time, the city took further measures by regulating the practice under strict guidelines. First, any woman operating as a prostitute had to register with the city. Second, prostitutes had to pay fees for prostitute and bawdy house licenses every three months. Third, in order to maintain their licenses, these same working women had to undergo monthly medical examinations. Similar systems were enacted in other Texas cities, but Waco experienced the greatest longevity in both its official and unofficial policies toward prostitution and, by some luck, its bawdy register still survives.[5]

The fact that 200 women once populated the Reservation during the period of licensing (1889–1895) alone indicates that commercialized sex thrived over the course of several decades in Waco. Plying their trade near Waco's downtown, prostitutes did business with men of all stripes. Several madams owned real estate and enjoyed unparalleled entrepreneurial success. Nevertheless, the women who sold their bodies on Two Street were also outliers of respectable Waco society. The owner of a flourishing

Looking down Two Street, 2009. *Photograph by Bradley T. Turner.*

brothel simply did not enjoy the same status as even the city's least successful businessman. Their being undesirables aside, prostitutes were a large part of Waco's history, and their lives were no doubt more colorful than the average woman who lived in a very different, more "respectable" part of the city.

Throughout Two Street's history, Waco had its own legendary, infamous madam at the height of its prostitution: Mollie Adams. Today, the majority of Waco's residents are hardly aware of the fact their city once maintained a bustling red-light district adjacent to downtown Waco. Thus, the name Mollie Adams holds little meaning for them. Nevertheless, in the early 1900s, Mollie Adams was an infamous name throughout Waco. Said to be a beautiful madam, Adams was a financial success story by the turn of the twentieth century.[6] She was a woman with many connections throughout Waco, even though she was likely shunned by "polite" society. At times, this private rapport with officials allowed her more liberties than were allowed to other madams on Two Street. In fact, Adams occasionally left the Reservation and

A painting of Mollie Adams, composed during a trip to New York City. *Photograph courtesy of The Texas Collection, Baylor University, Waco, Texas.*

hired public hacks to take her brothel's inmates on an annual picnic outside of Waco.[7] And, by 1900, she was wealthy enough to journey northward to sit for a formal portrait in New York City.[8]

Adams' local repute resulted from her longevity as a Waco resident. The reason for her arrival in Waco is a mystery, but she remained there from at least the mid-1880s until her death in 1944.[9] Portions of Adams' history in

Waco can be traced in the city directories of the period. By 1886 she lived on 130 Bridge Street, between 1st Street and the Square. At first, Adams did not operate her own bawdy house. Her employer remains a mystery, but in that year, she lived with two other bawds, Dot Daggett and Maggie May, both Caucasian.[10] By 1890, Stella Nolan employed Adams at 116 North 1st Street, very close to the Brazos River.[11] Nolan was the owner of Waco's largest brothel and entertained customers in a nine-room house.[12] Only two of Nolan's prostitutes, May Townsend and Ella Fisher, were registered with the city.[13]

Adams' entrepreneurship can further be traced in Waco's bawdy register. As stated previously, she first appeared during the initial years as simply a prostitute, but as the years progressed, she slowly acquired a brothel.[14] The initial indication of her evolution into the role of madam was in November 1891, when she was listed as owning a bawdy house with three rooms.[15] A year after her employment at Nolan's bordello, Adams was financially capable of running her own establishment. And by April 1893, Adams doubled the size of her house and paid the city a fee for a seven-room establishment.[16] By then, the madam had moved her sporting house to 126 North 1st Street, on the corner of Washington, and had registered two of her workers, Maggie Alexander and Myrtle Jones.

The structural plans for Mollie Adams' brothel illustrate the typical design of a successful bordello in Waco. By 1910, Adams had moved her establishment to 408 North 2nd Street.[17] Portions of the plans show Adams had the latest technological devices installed in her new house: indoor plumbing, complete with additional toiletry services for the men, and electrical wiring.[18] Each room was connected to a bell system, allowing for more discretion when a customer rang for a specific room. The plans also show the house had two parlors, a dance hall, a bar near the fireplace in the dance hall, and several bedrooms.[19] To an unsuspecting reader, the plans might draw suspicion as to why a single woman needed so many specific plans for several rooms designed for mass entertainment. But since Adams was a well-known madam, the plans do reveal that, by

1910, Mollie Adams had become a success in her adopted town of Waco.

The architectural specifications of Adams' house illustrate another aspect of prostitution's existence in Waco. The firm that designed Adams' bordello was one of the most established in Waco. Milton W. Scott designed some of the most notable buildings in the city, including the Artesian Manufacturing and Bottling Company, which currently houses the Dr Pepper Museum in Waco. Four years before creating the structural specifications of one of Waco's most infamous bordellos, Scott had designed a monument of Christian faith—the First Baptist Church. Scott's skills as an architect and his respectable reputation in Waco allowed him to design some of the community's most famous landmarks. His reputation, however, did not prevent him from offering his services to women of ill-repute. Waco's businessmen evidently were sometimes not concerned with the source of their profits.

While Adams' business flourished, her establishment was not the only bordello operating in Waco by the late nineteenth century. Other madams

achieved similar, if not more, financial success. In 1886, at least three madams operated brothels. Edna Elmore employed at least two women, Alice Edwards and Ella Fisher, on the corner of South 1st Street at 106 Jackson. At 130 Bridge, on the corner of South 1st and the Square, three registered prostitutes plied their trade. Stella Nolan kept her house at 130 Jackson. At 642 North 2nd Street, Eva Thompson employed ladies of ill-repute.[20] Although located within a general area, the brothels were not confined or concentrated specifically on Two Street within the Reservation. In fact, the only house operating on North 2nd Street was that of Eva Thompson.

During the period from 1889 to 1895, other women served Waco as madams. In November 1889, Hattie Tyree paid a $25.20 fee to operate an eight-room bawdy house.[21] Located at 101 Washington,[22] her business continued to grow as she later paid $34.65 every three months for the fees on an eleven-room house. In financial terms, Tyree was the most successful madam. Nonetheless, Tyree's establishment also became rather infamous.

Mollie Adams' house in the early 1960s before urban renewal. *Photograph courtesy of The Texas Collection, Baylor University, Waco, Texas.*

In August 1890, one of Tyree's workers was murdered during a fit of jealousy, and a trial soon followed. Lilly Murphy, a twenty-five-year-old mother of two and sister of Tyree, had resided as a prostitute at her sister's brothel. Tyree removed her sister from the house because of the latter's penchant for disruption. Jealous of her boyfriend's infatuation with Eva Clinton, a twenty-year-old prostitute at Tyree's house, Murphy threatened to kill Clinton. When she finally forced a confrontation, a scuffle ensued that resulted in Murphy's death from a stab wound received from Clinton.[23] The negative attention afforded to this crime of passion diffused Tyree's popularity. Two years after the incident, Tyree left Waco and closed her sporting house, evident in her disappearance from the bawdy register after May 18, 1892.[24]

Madam Tyree's story exemplifies various aspects of the Reservation's social conditions. First, her disappearance from Waco's register illustrates how madams' successes ebbed and flowed with the tides of public apathy or social concern. Second, the Reservation was a profitable but dangerous place to operate. Prostitution was a business, but the workers and customers often could not suppress the violence that resulted from jealous passions and flaming tempers. Sex was a risky business that sometimes involved emotional attachment. Still, Waco continued to allow the area to remain, and other women profited from careers as brothel-keepers.

While women like Kate Cleveland (alias Kate Coleman), Winnie Clark, Madge Middleton, Josie Tweedy, and Belle Pence also claimed their place as longtime madams in Waco's sexual underworld, other women were not nearly as successful. Until they were too old to sell their bodies at the ripe age of twenty-eight, some prostitutes simply worked for a madam. Success in the sex industry was not the rule; it was the exception. Many times, prostitutes found great difficulty in climbing the

Rough location of Mollie Adams' house, 2009. *Photograph by Bradley T. Turner.*

proverbial ladder simply because their debt to a madam was too high and the madam's cut out of their earned income was too great—and madams relentlessly demanded payment. After all, the bond between madam and prostitute was based on money. Thus, the relationship between madam and prostitute did not always evince unerring loyalty in a form of a "lost sisterhood." In fact, business was business on Two Street, and sometimes the wheels of commerce needed to be greased with the intervention of Waco's own civil law system.

A case involving Mollie Adams and one of her former inmates, Pearl Miller, exemplifies the business-like relationship between madam and prostitute. Miller, a prostitute from Alabama, arrived in Waco in 1893 and was employed by Adams for five months. Shortly after her arrival, Miller became ill and Adams paid the doctor's fees. Adams claimed Miller gave her a pair of diamond earrings as security for what she owed the madam in rent and doctors' fees. Not staying in Waco and not knowing where her final destination would be, Miller left her trunk with Adams under the belief that her former

employer would send it to her within four days after receiving communication from her. Miller arrived in Houston and sent for her trunk, but Adams refused to send it unless Miller forwarded her $186. Stating she had owed Adams five dollars but "not a cent more," Miller filed suit for her trunk and earrings, both having a value of $233.90, which is a present-day amount of $5,000.[25] Within a year, however, the McLennan County court ruled in favor of Adams.[26]

The case between Miller and Adams reveals various aspects of the bawdy lifestyle. Miller's migratory patterns support a long-held assumption that prostitutes were transient, repeatedly moving between towns. Miller resided in three different cities within six months, eventually ending her travels in Galveston. On her doctor's bill, Miller's illness is termed a "specific disease."[27] Miller likely suffered from venereal disease, a conclusion further supported by the fact that another doctor treated her after her recovery from the first incident. The doctors' care for Miller shows that at least some of Waco's physicians treated prostitutes. And while madams were prepared to seek medical care for

their employees, they were not willing to provide the fringe benefits of free medical attention.

A perusal of the contents of the trunk, mentioned in Miller's deposition, offers a glimpse into what a prostitute working on Two Street owned. Some articles are unassuming and warrant little suspicion as to Miller's profession: one large white hat, one small pink hat, one woolen dress with velvet trimming, one tan cashmere dress, one blazer suit, one tan cloak, one blue silk sash, and one silk necktie. Other clothes appear slightly stereotypical of the garments of prostitutes: one crepe dechine dress with silk trimming, one black silk dress with black velvet trimming, one red cashmere dress, six lawn chimese, six lawn dresses, and red satin slippers. Miller also owned six nightgowns, an unusual number for the period.

The trunk also contained two family photographs. Although transient and "fallen," ladies of the night evidently did not forget about their ties with relatives.[28] Perhaps they acknowledged that while they shared a common career bond with other brothel inmates, they were not family. The relationships formed in brothels were built around sexual solicitation and a shared identity on the outskirts of society, not nurturing love. As the case between Miller and Adams shows, that nurturing love between madam and prostitute only went as far as securing one's own financial assets.

Another case also revealed the downside of debt in a madam's business. In May 1895, W.E. Dupree, owner of Agricultural Implements, Vehicles, and Grain on North Bridge Street and resident of South 4th Street,[29] rented a house on 1st Street to Viola Burton. Dupree leased the house to the madam for fifty dollars a month in May, June, and July and later for seventy-five dollars a month. In April 1895, Thomas Goggan & Bro. sold Burton an Emerson upright piano, stool, and scarf for $350.00, the fee of which would be paid in monthly increments of ten dollars. By October, Burton owed Dupree $122.00 in past rent and had only paid forty dollars to Goggan & Bro. for the piano. When the case arrived in the county court two years later, Dupree wanted his $122.00 plus an additional $75.00, declaring that Goggan & Bro.

were *in pari delicto*, in equal fault, for the contractual problems with Burton. The county court decided in favor of Dupree, ruling that Burton pay him $197.00 with six percent interest and that his landlord's lien entitled him to the possession of the piano.[30]

By 1898, the city continued to witness court cases generated by problems between property owners and brothel keepers. J.C. Birkhead, head salesman at W.E. Dupree and whose father owned Waco Cider Extract, rented a house on 110 North 1st Street to Madge Middleton.[31] The house was leased to Middleton on a month-to-month basis, the rate being fifty dollars a month. Birkhead claimed that he later believed that her use of the house was for an immoral and unlawful purpose and wished to terminate Middleton's agreement. Not wanting to follow Birkhead's written demand to leave the house, Middleton refused. Birkhead quickly brought a suit for forcible detainer to the city court, which, in turn, ruled in favor of Middleton. Birkhead appealed to the county level, suing for the furniture that he had also rented to the madam. The county court decided in his favor.

Birkhead's appeal to the county court in September 1898 offers clues to the interior of a Waco madam's brothel. Valued at $936.75, the property included: a conversation chair, a leather couch, a cloth couch, eight parlor chairs, seven rugs, a willow settee, three rocking chairs, nine dining chairs, a hat rack, a side board, five wardrobes, five dressers, six wash stands, six beds, twelve pairs of lace curtains, twenty-one window shades, two parlor carpets, a back parlor carpet, two hall carpets, five bedroom carpets, eight pillow shams, five china pitchers and bowls, eight slop basins, five chamber pots, five soap stands, five toothbrush holders, and a few other articles. Indicated by the number of wardrobes and beds, one can deduce that five inmates lived in the brothel. The list further describes what furnished Middleton's bedroom: one white maple bedroom suite consisting of a bedstead, dresser, washstand, and wardrobe. The eight slop basins specify that the madam often had company, a number high enough to need eight spittoons. Further, the other furniture evidences that the brothel was moderate in size, with six bedrooms and a front and back parlor.

In its judgment, the county court had ruled that Middleton pay Birkhead fifty dollars each month that she continued residing at the dwelling. But the madam's attorneys noted that an area real estate agent had testified that the practical value of the property, if used "for legitimate purposes," was fifteen dollars a month. Birkhead clearly gained from renting the house to a madam, as he charged her over 300 percent of what the rental was valued. Wacoans who rented property to brothel keepers in the Reservation profited from the sex business. As a consequence, madams frequently moved, possibly due to the high rates of their rent fees. Some madams, however, reaped the same benefits that men like Dupree and Birkhead enjoyed. These madams did not hold leases to the locations of their brothels—they owned their dwellings.

In 1912, Mollie Adams rented her house on 404 North 2nd Street to Belle Pence. Pence fell behind on her rent, which was fifteen dollars a week ($1,128.53 in modern currency), and she refused to vacate the premises. Claiming that Pence was forcibly detaining her property, Adams took her suit to the county court in 1915. The jury quickly ordered that Pence return the plaintiff's property and pay her twenty-five dollars, with six percent interest. Nevertheless, both Adams and Pence were unsatisfied with the court's ruling. Adams contended that the defendant owed her $225.00, which was more than the sum ordered by the court. On the other hand, Pence appealed the decision, saying that Adams had leased the house to Pence knowing her lessee was using the property solely for prostitution and would be using a portion of her profits reaped from "immoral and illegal purposes" to maintain her business and pay her rent.[32] After the last appeal in 1915, however, the McLennan County court sustained the previous rulings in favor of Adams.[33]

While the previous cases inferred that madams were sometimes victimized by the economic system of real estate businessmen, the Adams case shows two counterarguments. First, madams could also profit from the commerce of other madams. Second, even though they were largely confined to Two Street's boundaries, madams could use the justice system to protect their assets and regain property. Respect and recognition for loose women was uncommon outside of the red-light district, but the benefits of the judicial process, although sometimes biased, were still obtainable.

Another incident reveals that Waco's madams strove to join in public policymaking, albeit to a small degree. In the early 1890s, Meyer Adams peddled goods around the district and lived at 327 North 2nd Street, in the heart of the Reservation.[34] By 1907, Adams wanted to open a retail beer store at 413 North 2nd. Following legal procedures and after receiving the permit from the comptroller of public accounts in Austin, Adams applied for a malt license in Waco. In order to be a licensed dealer, though, the former peddler needed to obtain the signatures of homeowners in the block or square where his store was located. He found no objections from the block's residents, and they signed his petition for the license as follows: Mollie Adams, Annie Vickers, Anna Tucker, Florence Young, Anna Wood, Ella Miller, Maude Riley, Grace Summers, Katie Cleveland, Liza Jones, and Ophelia Vickers.[35]

Nevertheless, one Waco citizen did object. Attorney Pat Neff, future governor of Texas and president of Baylor University, filed an ex parte with the county court during its July term in 1907. He insisted on attaining "strict proof" of Adams' claim.[36] The outcome of Neff's complaint against Meyer Adams remains unknown due to incomplete records. Still, his objections to the license procurement reveal a significant trend in the ideological convictions of progressivism: the belief that liquor and lewd behavior often coalesced into immoral and illegal actions. Neff particularly objected to the petition's facts, yet those who signed it were clearly home owners in the retailer's proposed location.

Where Have You Been? Where Are You Going?

Perhaps the largest reason that Pat Neff fought against the liquor license was that the Reservation and its surrounding streets did not simply house prostitutes. The Reservation also maintained diverse populations of working-class residents, many of whom were not part of the commercialized sex business. There

ways, the Reservation separated the rest of Waco from migrant workers, blacks, Hispanics, gamblers, saloonkeepers, and prostitutes. And the one definite trend of this social landscape was that it was always in flux. From the 1870s until after World War I, the characteristics of Two Street's inhabitants would change considerably. Nevertheless, as the Federal Census from this period indicates, the one constant in that fluid landscape was the existence of women who sold their bodies for cash.

The Reservation's demographics indicate that many prostitutes were transient. Many of these women stopped in Waco on a brief sojourn, looking for work. In 1870, the only prostitute listed in the census was Margaret Burger, a nineteen-year-old mulatto from Alabama.[37] Burger lived alone but near possible relatives, Maria and Sarah Burger. Although the Alabama woman was the only prostitute officially listed in the census, one

must assume that other bawds resided in Waco at the time. Perhaps they maintained prostitution as a secondary outlet for earning money, choosing to be registered as laundresses, servants, or as "keeping house," all of which were the usual occupation listings for women in Waco during the period. Job variety was nonexistent for women, yet they began to mobilize in the job market by Burger's appearance in the census.[38]

By 1880, women who lived on North 2nd and 3rd Streets registered as prostitutes with the census, showing a rise in public acknowledgment of the practice but also indicating an influx of women from other areas. Bawds hailed from several states: Indiana (1), Illinois (1), Pennsylvania (1), Missouri (2), Texas (4), Virginia (1), Arkansas (3), Louisiana (3), Georgia (2), Mississippi (1), and California (1). They also emigrated from foreign countries such as Germany and Ireland. Most were listed as "white" in regard to race and belonged to a range of age groups.[39] None of the prostitutes registered with the census were over thirty or younger than eighteen.

The age trends of the prostitutes in 1880 show the typical maturity of prostitutes in the late nineteenth century. On average, few stayed in the business longer than their middle twenties, and many began prostituting before age eighteen. Other young girls were forced into the profession through unwanted pregnancies resulting from an adolescent seduction or rape. A number entered prostitution because of economic circumstances that a philandering husband or widowhood brought. Many also continued to embrace a familiarity with social deviance, such as alcoholism or abuse. The majority, however, joined the ranks of bawds simply because the money was better than working in jobs considered more respectable and suitable for women at the time: factory girl, schoolteacher, or domestic. Some women chose these traditional roles but also decided to supplement their incomes with sexual solicitation.

Despite their reasons for entering the sex trade, most prostitutes remained in the business for six years, at the most. During that time, few resided in the same city, let alone the same brothel. Some left the business for a period but returned for various reasons. A select

few became madams and did continue to operate in the same city for the majority of their lives, as in the case of Mollie Adams. Others eventually married, started homes for fallen women, or spent the remainder of their aged career still plying their trade in small shanties called cribs. Some committed suicide.

The 1880 census reveals more than the general age patterns and locations of the prostitutes, however. As was true with Hildy Brown's hotel-brothel, sporting girls lived and mingled with laborers and other members of the working class. Well diggers, farm hands, boot blacks, carpenters, and painters were a few of the occupations chosen by men who lived with their families among the scarlet women. Some men, sharing a love of way-faring common with most bawds, were gamblers who boarded with households located within the general area of Two Street.[40] This ilk of men had plenty of opportunities to try their luck in the saloons and back alleys that flanked the Reservation, and their choices of residence are no significant surprise.

Workers also lived close to their jobs, and the blocks around what

became the Reservation abounded with businesses. As previously noted, the red-light district was less than a block from Waco's public square, and some houses of ill-repute were even located across the street from the suspension bridge.[41] While Waco's red-light district was morally ostracized from the community, it was by no means entirely separate, economically or residentially. Most of the other residents in the Reservation, though, experienced their own sense of separation. The location there of several working class families likely resulted in part from race and not by choice, since most of the neighborhood's residents who were not prostitutes were black or mulatto.[42]

From the 1860s through the 1880s, the Reservation witnessed an interesting blend of interracial mingling. In his study of Los Angeles interracial relationships between prostitutes, Mark Wild has argued that prostitutes' social standing in the sex industry in Los Angeles from 1880 to 1940 allowed for greater integration between races, both in customer-bawd and bawd-bawd affiliation.[43] Waco's Two Street in the Reservation was similar in the sense that the district contained mostly blacks who lived in the same area as white prostitutes. As mentioned earlier, the first prostitute to register with the Federal Census was Margaret Burger, a mulatto from Alabama. Prostitutes in later decades, however, were primarily whites living next to, with, or near black residents. In 1880, Lucy West, a twenty-two-year-old white prostitute, boarded with Hildy Brown and Alice Franks, both mulattos living on Two Street. On the same street, Kate Collins, also a mulatto, boarded with a black farmhand and his family. [44] Although the majority of prostitutes were either mulatto or white and lived among black laborers, other races resided in the area, including Minnie Perry, a nineteen-year-old Native American from the Indian Territory. Perry lived with Thomas Heart, a white clerk, also nineteen, from Louisiana.[45] Perry and Heart illustrate a significant deviance in the period's racial composition, but they were not the only ones living around the Reservation who showed interracial compatibility.

By 1900, the area around Two Street was similar in demographic composition to that seen twenty years before, yet slightly different. While most blacks hailed from southern states other than Texas in 1880, the majority of them were native Texans by 1900. Another aspect that was slightly different in 1900 was that black husbands in the Reservation were not the only individuals in the household who worked. By 1900 their wives were earning supplementary incomes through jobs as washwomen or laundresses. A few took up jobs as cooks and chambermaids.[46]

The Reservation's non-prostitute population reflected other changes in Waco's demographics at the turn of the twentieth century. Confirming national trends of immigration patterns, the vicinity around Two Street experienced a moderate influx of Southern and Eastern Europeans, as well as some from the Middle East. Syrian and Italian families resided on North 3rd Street.[47] Two Jewish families, also from Syria, lived on North 2nd and North 1st Streets, and a Syrian on North 1st Street provided board to two other Syrian males.[48] Similar to the area's blacks, a large portion of these immigrants belonged to the working class. One Syrian worked as a salesman at a dry goods store; other immigrants peddled food items like chicken and fish.[49] The presence of other ethnic groups, coupled with the existence of a black laboring class on North 2nd Street, demonstrates that the red-light district continued to include working-class families among the working girls of Two Street.

Significantly, prostitutes populated the Reservation in far greater numbers in 1900 than they had in 1880. By the turn of the century, the scarlet women were confined to the area around North 2nd and North 1st Streets. On Washington Street (one of the lanes bordering the district), Sallie Wiley and Ella Miller operated brothels. Two other women worked independently, likely in cribs, on the same thoroughfare.[50] While no prostitutes on 2nd Street registered with the census, the majority were located on North 1st Street, closer to the Brazos River. Winnie Clark and Mollie Adams, listed as married to unnamed men, both continued to operate their sporting houses. Each of their venues housed seven bawdy women. Ray Douglas, a thirty-three-year-old white female from Kentucky, established a bawdy house in the same vicinity as well. Seven other bawds worked out of two saloons owned by Will Humphries and George Walker.

Altogether, sixty-two women were registered as prostitutes or inmates in the census of 1900. Because of the ladies' transient migratory patterns, however, their exact number is impossible to deduce. Still, the census offers a significant portion of that unknown number. Women continued to hail from various states and countries: Illinois, Tennessee, Texas, Kansas, New York, Missouri, Indiana, Vermont, Mississippi, Arkansas, Montana, Colorado, Ohio, Virginia, South Dakota, Georgia, Ireland, Kentucky, and West Virginia, to name a few. Overall, these women and the families who lived near them contributed to the hustle and bustle of Waco's business district at the turn of the twentieth century.

Trends that existed in the red-light district during 1880 and 1900 continued in 1910. Building on the previous decade, more immigrants continued to settle in areas near or next to Two Street. North 3rd Street, once home to some of Waco's prostitutes, now mostly housed immigrants from Russia and

Germany, as well as Romania and Austria. A unique ethnic element that was more pronounced in Texas was also beginning to present itself: Mexican immigration. What was barely existent in the previous federal survey was now hard to ignore as Mexican residents began to outnumber other ethnicities and, significantly, the black population. In fact, the number of black residents around the Reservation was fewer than in previous decades. On the other hand, the population of white immigrants, white Americans, and Mexicans living in and close to the red-light district continued to rise.[51]

Even though the racial and ethnic composition altered slightly among non-prostitutes in the Reservation, the bawdy women's situation also changed. The previous decade showed that prostitutes gradually left North 3rd Street but continued to live on North 1st and in nearby alleys. But by 1910, scarlet ladies were confined to that thoroughfare with which the Reservation had become synonymous: Two Street, or North 2nd. Maude Riley had the largest business during that year with eight girls. Mollie Adams con-

tinued to serve the sexual needs of the male community with the aid of her six prostitutes, one of whom was her sister Rosa. Lula Rice and Sallie Gray both ran bordellos with five prostitutes apiece. Josie Tweedy ran a four-inmate establishment, while Katy Schwartz, a thirty-year-old from Russia, oversaw the same, but with three inmates. Della Smith, Irene Riley, Isabella Thomas, and Myrtle Harris all operated slightly smaller brothels with two inmates each. Three women were not employed by a madam, however, and they solicited sex independently from the larger operations. Overall, fifty-seven women registered with the census as operating sex businesses on North 2nd Street.[52]

The fewer numbers of prostitutes and the smaller area of operations reflect how some changes occurred on Two Street. Certain aspects remained the same, including the longevity of Mollie Adams. The various origins of each prostitute, who continued to migrate to Waco from many states and countries, revealed a similar trend. Nevertheless, significant evidence of racial segregation is prominent: absolutely no black or mulatto prostitute registered in the Reservation for the 1910 census. Although some outliers must have existed in the census, changes had clearly occurred from 1880 to 1910, as racial barriers had apparently permeated throughout even the moral outcasts of society. The shrinking landscape of the district also illustrates that the Waco community began to decrease prostitution's influence.

In the years before Two Street closed, the area around the red-light district had already begun to experience the effects of Hispanic immigration. In 1913, North 1st Street, once a significant thoroughfare for brothels, witnessed a growth in its Mexican population. Out of twenty-three residences listed in the street directory between Washington and Jefferson Streets, eleven were Hispanic households, ten were black, and three were white.[53] In the same block on North 2nd Street, the ratio of prostitutes to minorities was far greater. Twenty-two brothels were owned by white women and seven operated by unregistered black madams. Across from Washington Street, near the public square, several black and Hispanic

citizens owned commercial businesses such as a livery, drugstore, doctor's office, and restaurants, one being owned by Ysabel Rodriguez.[54] Across Jefferson Street, to the west of the Reservation, the homes of approximately twenty black residents, mixed with vacant buildings, bordered the red-light district.[55] Although pockets of minority businesses and homes bordered Two Street, the area within the designated zone was still dominated demographically by white prostitutes in 1913.

Turn Out the Lights

Waco was slow to surrender its sex trade. In fact, the area was only ready to close Two Street's brothels when Secretary of War Newton Baker threatened to close its new military base, Camp MacArthur, if Waco did not shut down the Reservation by 1917.[56] The threat was powerful enough, and the potential earnings from the military encampment sufficient enough, to impel the city of Waco to officially board up the brothels' doors. And, as such, the demographics changed dramatically.

In 1916, the year before the district closed, the demographics of home

owners listed in the street directory for North 2nd were similar to those of the previous three years. Madams operating brothels still represented the majority, as women like Winnie Clark, Stella Nolan, and Mollie Adams, along with newer generations of brothel owners, continued to operate.[57] Across Jefferson Street, in the block west of the Reservation, the same number of black residents owned property as had three years before then. However, numerous vacant buildings were also evident. These would later appeal to Mexican families looking for homes after the close of Waco's red-light district.[58]

Between 1917 and 1918, many residences were inhabited by the same people who lived in them during the previous years, yet some things were changing. Even after Waco officially "closed" the Reservation, prostitutes continued to remain listed at the majority of addresses on North 2nd Street. In the block between Washington and Jefferson, twenty madams continued to rent buildings for their businesses, while six women, including the infamous Mollie Adams, remained in the residences they privately owned.[59] Still, minute changes indicated the area's social landscape was experiencing a dramatic shift. Numerous vacant lots appeared along North 1st Street.[60]

By 1919, vacancies on North 1st Street were not the only empty buildings in the area around Two Street. Although the immediate effects of Waco's abolishment of the Reservation by 1917 did not show a considerable amount of change regarding the listed homeowners in the directory, two years after the Reservation was ordered to close, the landscape was dramatically different. In the block of North 2nd Street that had been the home of so many different prostitutes over the course of four decades, vacancies took the place of once-occupied houses of ill-repute. The directory listed sixteen buildings as vacant, which were properties that had been occupied the previous year. Two bawds remained—two who had owned properties instead of renting them like the majority of madams.[61] Mollie Adams, of course, was one of these, and she continued to stay in Waco, albeit in a different residence, throughout the rest of her life.[62] Of the other lots formerly occupied by

prostitutes, five Hispanic males now rented them. The two remaining properties consisted of the Mexican Presbyterian Mission and Baptist Mexican Mission, operated by Emil Garcia and Justo Luna, respectively. In the block to the west of the former red-light district, a considerable number of the residents were black, yet ten residences were now rented by Mexicans. Various empty buildings also continued to exist as they had in previous years. Therefore, even though the area around Two Street did not experience immediate results when the district was ordered to close by the federal government in 1917, most of the scarlet ladies vacated within a year.

With the emigration of prostitutes from the red-light district, the buildings that once housed them were soon used by another group that was growing in numbers among the Waco populace. According to the directory of 1921–1922, the presence of Mexican Americans in the area, formerly a haven for the commerce of sex, was no longer marginal; Latinos had become the majority. Lots that were vacant from the exodus of prostitutes in 1918 now

housed Mexican residents. They were the only residents living on North 2nd Street between Washington and Jefferson. Mixed into the residences, which were largely rented properties, a Hispanic grocer served the block's families, and the Mrs. Caroline Miller Mexican School educated their children. Across Jefferson, several blacks had remained, but by 1921, the Mexican population clearly held the majority. Between the two blocks, two former madams remained: Mollie Adams (at her own property at 414 North 2nd near the corner of Jefferson) and Madge Middleton (at her rented property on the same street, though in the block west of Adams' place).[63] Two Street had become Waco's Mexican barrio, but Adams and Middleton remained in their former brothels because they had no other alternative but to live among Waco's newest minority population. The establishments of Adams and Middleton ultimately proved to be the swan song for the city's red-light days.

Although prostitutes' exodus from the red-light district was evident in the city directory, prostitution did not exactly end in Waco. When Two Street closed, prostitutes no longer lived in a concentrated area that the city could easily police and regulate. One resident recalled the effects of shutting down the red-light district, as well as the result of moral crusaders' activism in outlawing the sale of alcoholic beverages in the same period: "[L]iquor went out here about the time the camp come here. … They closed all that. They closed up the red light district here and tried to purify the community and I think if anything it made it worse than it ever was."[64] Liquor and loose women remained in Waco. The secret popularity of both allowed them to continue even in a municipality that became known for its religious conservatism.

The More Things Change …

Waco, like any entity of its size, continues to grapple with a social problem that was once seen as a necessity. The sex trade did not stop with the closure of the Reservation, and it continued on a smaller scale among individual sex workers during the ensuing decades. Today, streetwalkers still operate in the more disreputable areas of Waco. Many prostitutes visit local missions and soup kitchens looking for food, and locals talk about the women who ply their trade under the bridges of the city and in northern parts of Waco. At the right location, one can glimpse a business exchange at a so-called crack house as random cars pull up to a specific residence, a brief exchange of conversation is made, and one of the women jumps in the car to drive to a location to sell herself to the newly met passenger.

One wonders if cities like Waco will ever remove prostitution completely from their communities. As long as social and economic marginality exists, however, the world's oldest profession will continue. Nevertheless, the trade has long since experienced its swan song in legitimately contributing to local economies in the United States. The memory of the likes of Mollie Adams and her scarlet cohorts barely exists and remains a whisper. Nonetheless, it is a whisper audible enough to reveal that a darker side of Waco once coexisted with the obvious past of cotton, cattle, churches, Baylor, and its well-known suspension bridge.

ENDNOTES

1. Vance Randolph, *Roll Me in Your Arms: "Unprintable" Ozark Folksongs and Folklore, vol. 1.* (Fayetteville: University of Arkansas Press, 1992), 240.

2. *Bawdy House Register*, 1889–1895, The Texas Collection, Baylor University, Waco, TX.

3. Kent Biffle, "Waco Was 1st To Reserve Areas for Brothels," *Dallas Morning News*, 30 November, 1997, Home Final Edition, Texas & Southwest Section, 45A.

4. *Bawdy House Register*, 1889–1895.

5. The registry is located in Baylor University's Texas Collection. Its contents provided crucial information about the success of Waco's prostitutes, including bawds' acquisitions of bawdy houses.

6. Anna Mae Bell Warner, interview by Lawanda Ball, 16 February, 1976, The Texas Collection, Baylor University, Waco, TX, 18.

7. Margaret Davis, "Harlots and Hymnals: A Historic Confrontation of Vice and Virtue in Waco, Texas," *Mid-South Folklore*, 4, no. 3 (1970): 91.

8. Ironically, that same portrait sits in a storage room in a mansion that once belonged to C.C. McCullough, the city

mayor who initially demanded that prostitutes obtain licenses from the city in 1889.

9. Davis, "Harlots and Hymnals," 91.

10. *Waco City Directory, 1886–1887* (Waco Public Library, Waco, TX), microfilm.

11. *Waco City Directory, 1890–1891.*

12. *Bawdy House Register,* August 1889.

13. *Waco City Directory, 1890–1891.*

14. *Bawdy House Register,* September 1889–June 1891.

15. Ibid., November 1891.

16. Ibid., April 1893.

17. *Waco City Directory, 1911.*

18. Scott & Pearson, "Specifications of a Two-Story Frame Residence for Miss Mollie Adams, Waco, Texas," 17 January, 1910, The Texas Collection, Baylor University, Adams (Mollie) Item 3C410, 3.

19. Ibid., 8–9.

20. *Waco City Directory, 1886–1887.*

21. *Bawdy House Register,* 18 November, 1889.

22. *Waco City Directory, 1890–1891.*

23. Aimee Harris Johnson, "Prostitution in Waco, 1889–1917" (M.A. thesis, Baylor University, 1990), 52.

24. *Bawdy House Register, 1892–1895.*

25. John McCusker, "Comparing the Purchasing Power of Money in the United States (or Colonies) from 1665 to Any Other Year Including the Present," *Economic History Services,* 2004, 3 November, 2004, found online at http://eh.net/hmit/ppowersusd/.

26. Pearl Miller *v.* Mollie Adams, 3366, Civil Case Records (McLennan County Archives, Waco, TX).

27. Ibid.

28. Ibid.

29. *Waco City Directory, 1894–1895.*

30. W.E. Dupree *v.* Viola Burton, et al., 9575, Civil Case Records (McLennan County Archives, Waco, TX).

31. *Waco City Directory, 1896–1897.*

32. Mollie Adams *v.* Belle Pence, 8343, Civil Case Records (McLennan County Archives, Waco, TX).

33. Ibid.

34. *Waco City Directory, 1892–1893.*

35. M. Adams, ex parte, 5951, Civil Case Records (McLennan County Archives, Waco, TX).

36. Ibid.

37. 1870 Federal Census, McLennan County (Waco Public Library, Waco, TX, 23 June, 1870), microfilm p.14.

38. This is most evident in comparing the 1870 record with the 1860 Federal Census, McLennan County (Waco Public Library, Waco, TX, microfilm collection).

39. 1880 Federal Census, McLennan County (Waco, TX, 1–3 June, 1880) [accessed online at http://www.ancestry.com 23 January, 2005].

40. Ibid.

41. Digital Sanborn Maps, Waco, TX, 1889, UMI database [accessed online at http://bearcat.baylor.edu/ 12 August, 2004].

42. 1880 Federal Census, McLennan County (Waco, TX, 1–3 June, 1880).

43. Mark Wild, "Red Light Kaleidoscope: Prostitution and Ethnoracial Relations in Los Angeles, 1880–1940," *Journal of Urban History,* 28, no. 6 (2002): 720–42.

44. 1880 Federal Census, McLennan County (Waco, TX, 2 June, 1880), 9.

45. Ibid., 6.

46. 1900 Federal Census, McLennan County (Waco, TX, 13–15 June, 1900).

47. Ibid., 13 June, 1900.

48. Ibid.

49. Ibid.

50. Ibid.

51. 1910 Federal Census, McLennan County (Waco, TX, 20–21 April, 1910).

52. Ibid., 21 April, 1910.

53. *Waco City Directory, 1913*, 16.

54. Ibid., 30.

55. Ibid., 31.

56. Secretary Baker did not direct this threat to Waco alone. Reformers had finally gained a valuable political ally with Baker's appointment; before serving under President Wilson, the former mayor of Cleveland, Ohio, had his own experiences with curbing prostitution in that city. Anxieties over venereal disease within the American forces served as a huge impetus to closing down red-light districts near military encampments.

57. *Waco City Directory, 1916*, 102.

58. Ibid., 103.

59. *Waco City Directory, 1917–1918*, 105–06.

60. Ibid., 86.

61. *Waco City Directory, 1919*, 549.

62. Davis, "Harlots and Hymnals," 91.

63. *Waco City Directory, 1921–1922*, 632.

64. Francis L. Pittillo, interview by Thomas Charlton, transcript, 6–26 August, 1974, The Texas Collection, Baylor University, Waco, TX, 37.

The Apostle of Personal Protest:
William C. Brann and the *Iconoclast* in Waco

by Richard H. Fair

The Early Life of William C. Brann
Frontier justice took hold of McLennan County after the Civil War, leading to several infamous lynchings and shoot-outs, giving Waco the name "Six Shooter Junction."[1] One of the most notable incidents was the fate of William Cowper Brann, a talented writer with a penchant for attacking Baylor University. After penning several unfavorable articles regarding morality at the university in his publication, the *Iconoclast*, Brann was shot at point-blank range on April 1, 1898, dying the next day as a result of his wounds. Brann's monument at Oakwood Cemetery later became a pistol target, as animosity toward the writer took many years to fade. Around the same time period, the Lindsey brothers were lynched for horse theft on one of Waco's many "hanging trees" along the old Meridian Road, near present-day Lindsey Hollow Road. Waco's reputation for violence became so pronounced that train conductors arriving in Waco would often yell, "Waco, Texas, get your guns!"[2]

William Cowper Brann was born in Humboldt, in Coles County, Illinois, on January 4, 1855, to Rev. Noble Brann and his wife.[3] After his mother's death when he was two and a half, Reverend Brann placed his son in the care of William and Mary Hawkins, a nearby farming couple, with whom he remained for ten years. In 1868, at thirteen years old and in the third grade at school, he ran away and never returned nor received any further formal education.[4] His first job was as a hotel bellboy, most likely in St. Louis. He later learned the trades of painter and grainer, followed by printer and reporter. Eventually, Brann became an editorial writer after completing the necessary self-education.[5]

After obtaining a stable job as an editorial writer in Illinois, Brann married Carrie Belle Martin on March 3, 1877, in Rochelle, Illinois.[6] The couple had two daughters and a son. His daughter Inez committed suicide while the family lived in Houston in 1890. Brann blamed himself for her death for the remainder of his life. Frequently moving, Brann held editorial jobs in St. Louis, Galveston, Houston, Austin, and San Antonio, and gained notoriety as a vitriolic yet brilliant editorialist. While in Austin working for the *Austin American-Statesman*, Brann invested a majority of his life savings to begin publishing the *Iconoclast*, a periodical he often referred to as his "journal of personal protest."[7] Brann garnered the interest of William Sydney Porter, popularly known as O. Henry, while he was working as a drug clerk in Austin.[8] With little success in his trial run of the *Iconoclast*, Brann sold his printing press and the *Iconoclast* to Porter for $250. Porter attempted to keep the journal alive with his particular flair of journalism, but it did not fare better, failing after two issues. In 1894, Porter began another publication called

The Rolling Stone, but it too failed. Later, he became a *Houston Post* reporter before attaining literary fame.[9] Meanwhile, Brann eventually settled in Waco in the summer of 1894 as chief editor for the *Waco Daily News* after a string of editorial jobs in St. Louis and San Antonio. After obtaining permission from Porter, he revived the *Iconoclast* and reestablished its publication in 1895. This time, it obtained immediate success and attained a circulation between 90,000 and 100,000.[10]

The *Iconoclast* and Baylor University

Brann enjoyed new levels of success from his second attempt with the *Iconoclast*, boasting a readership rivaling that of many dailies and magazines of large cities. Even his most ardent detractors habitually read his work, for if they did not find themselves the focus of Brann's attacks, they wanted to know who was. As his name, and that of his paper, gained national renown, Brann took obvious delight in attacking, or "roasting," institutions and persons he considered hypocritical or overly sanctimonious.[11] One of his usual targets

Artistic depiction of William C. Brann, 1897. *Courtesy of the* Dallas Morning News.[14]

was Baylor University, which he dubbed "that great storm-center of misinformation."[12] Despite a strenuous relationship with Baylor from the *Iconoclast*'s creation, Brann said of his publication, "The *Iconoclast* makes war upon no religion of whatsoever name or origin that has fostered virtue or added aught to the happiness of the human race. It is simply an independent American journal, exercising its constitutional prerogative to say what seemeth [sic] unto it best, without asking any man's permission."[13]

Despite Brann's initial desire to print articles casting Baylor University and its administrators in a favorable light, he found himself unable to do so. He was reportedly not "one to automatically worship at the feet of college administrators merely because they cloaked themselves in the lordly garments of academia and Christian righteousness."[15] Brann's personal aversion to hypocrites, whom he observed in abundance at Baylor, and his ardent refusal to glorify the university without just cause, placed him at odds with Baylor supporters almost immediately, and even led to an official Baylor edict demanding the boycott of the *Iconoclast*.[16]

Baylor created an enemy of Brann when the university brought in a lecturer named Joseph Slattery, a former Catholic priest married to a former nun.[17] In a lecture given at Garland's Opera House on April 25, 1895, Slattery denounced the Catholic Church and its nuns, as well as Brann's *Iconoclast*, in the interest of the American Protective Association (APA). This anti-Catholic, anti-Semitic organization

from Clinton, Iowa, spread fears of a "Romish conspiracy," capitalizing on the economic and political unrest in the South. Lecturers such as Slattery were advertised as "ex-priests" and "ex-nuns" who escaped the tyranny of the Catholic Church and subsequently fought to save America from complete corruption.[18]

Responding to what he considered shocking and unforgivable slander of both his publication and the Catholic Church, Brann rose from his seat, outraged, and pointing a finger at Slattery, said, "You lie and you know it, and I refuse to listen to you." Turning and walking out of the opera house, Brann was almost mobbed by the audience of predominantly Baylor faculty and future Baptist ministers on the spot.[19]

Renting the same opera house, Brann responded to Slattery in person as well as in the pages of the *Iconoclast*.[20] Labeling the APA the "Aggregation of Pusillanimous Asses," Brann wrote of the organization, "There may be some honest men connected with the movement; but if honest they should get their heads trepanned to give their brains room to grow. They are as unable as a mule-eared rabbit to comprehend either

the broad principles upon which this government is grounded, or its political and religious history. No man—not even Judas Iscariot Slattery—is to blame for his ignorance; so we should humbly pray, Father forgive them, they know not what they do."[21] Extending his critique to Slattery's proposed "Romish conspiracy," Brann replied, "And I tell you Protestants right here, that if it be the intention of the Church of Rome to transform this government into a theocracy by fair means or foul, then the Pope is the real founder of the APA and Slattery's a Papal spy."[22]

Summing up his distaste for Slattery and the APA in general, Brann voiced his opinion concerning their place in America, stating, "If there were no better Americans than those trailing in the wake of the Rev. Joseph Slattery, like buzzards following a bad smell, I'd take a cornstalk, clean out the whole shooting match and stock the country with niggers and yaller [sic] dogs."[23]

Brann's sentiment toward blacks can be seen in the following segment from an *Iconoclast* article entitled "The Buck Negro": "I once severely shocked the pseudo-philanthropists by suggesting that if the South is ever to rid herself of the Negro rape-fiend she must take a day off and kill every member of the accursed race that declines to leave the country …"[24] Given the racially charged social culture of post-Reconstruction era Texas and Brann's personal bias, the fact that he would prefer a country filled with "niggers and yaller dogs" to Slattery's followers was an especially low blow.

Untrustworthy, Dishonest, and Boy-Crazy

Despite the initial rift between Brann and Baylor, relations between them might have been reconciled if not for an incident concerning a young female student named Antonia Teixeira. An orphan from Brazil, Antonia was taken into President Rufus C. Burleson's household at age eleven and began receiving training at Baylor to become a missionary.[25] Scandal erupted when, at age fourteen, she was discovered to be pregnant. The part of her story that captured Brann's attention, however, revolved around the injustice of her subsequent treatment.[26]

When Antonia indicated Steen Morris, the brother of President Burleson's son-in-law, Rev. Silas Morris, as the father of her child, Burleson accused her of being untrustworthy, dishonest, and boy-crazy, and implicated that she had an affair with a Negro before throwing her into the streets without making an effort to identify the real father.[27]

Brann championed the girl's defense, attacking everything from her initial place in the university to Burleson's accusations against her. In the first of two *Iconoclast* articles published on the subject, Brann said of Antonia's pre-scandal life at Baylor, "But ere long she found herself in Dr. Burleson's kitchen instead of the classroom. Instead of digging Greek roots she was studying the esculent tuber. Instead of being prepared for missionary work, this 'ward of the Baptist church' was learning the duties of the scullion—and Dr. Burleson has informed the world through the public prints that as a servant she was not worth her board and clothes."[28] In response to the injustice little Antonia received at the discovery of her illegitimate pregnancy, Brann mercilessly "roasted" President Burleson and Baylor University, stating, "Another

Baptist reverend had to have his say. He was somewhat interested in the matter, his brother having been named by Antonia as her ravisher. This reverend gentleman tried to make it appear that the father of her unborn child was a negro servant and her accepted paramour. Had this been true, what an 'ad' for Baylor University—that fourteen-year-old girls committed to its care conceived children by coons!"[29] Brann even further defamed President Burleson and Baylor with his description of the public's response to Antonia's plight: "Men about town—'publicans and sinners' such as Christ sat with, preferring their society to that of the pharisees [sic]—raised a handsome purse to provide for her and the young Baptist she was about to bring into the world, while those who should have guarded and protected her were resorting to every artifice human ingenuity could devise to blacken her name, forestall pity, prevent charity, and make an impartial trial of the case impossible."[30]

Although Antonia eventually let Steen Morris off the hook from a legal standpoint, the true father of her child remains a mystery. But Brann refused to relent in his prosecution of the incident.[31] Penning a second *Iconoclast* article on the subject, Brann said of his previous rant against Baylor, "The *Iconoclast* did not find fault with Baylor for the child's misfortune, fully realizing that accidents will occasionally occur even in the best regulated sectarian seminaries; but it did criticize Dr. Burleson for trying to shield that institution by branding as a willful bawd the fatherless little foreigner committed to its care."[32]

Rivalry Turns Violent

With Baylor suffering humiliation on a national scale from Brann's literary assaults, the relationship between the two parties was embittered beyond repair.[33] A Baylor-Brann war had been declared that would eventually turn violent and even deadly for supporters of both sides, as well as Brann himself.

Brann essentially signed his own death warrant when he published an *Iconoclast* article concerning his thoughts on the progress of Baylor University and its boasted recent increase in student population: "I note with unfeigned pleasure that, according to claims of Baylor University, it opens the present season with a larger contingent of students, male and female, than ever before. This proves that Texas Baptists are determined to support it at any sacrifice—that they believe it better that their daughters should be exposed to its historic dangers and their sons condemned to grow up in ignorance than that this manufactory of ministers and Magdalenes should be permitted to perish."[34]

Brann's enemies interpreted this as a slander against the female students of Baylor, equating them to Mary Magdalene, rather than part of the diatribe directed at Baylor administration as intended. This vile and unforgivable insult in the eyes of Brann's opponents and Baylor's supporters demanded immediate action to protect the young ladies' honor.[35]

On October 2, 1897, Brann was kidnapped from his office in the Pythian Knight building.[36] Two carriages with four to five students from Baylor University rushed into Brann's office, secured his hands with rope, removed his revolver, rushed him to the carriages, and traveled to Baylor's campus. After news of the incident reached Brann's associates, they quickly mounted buggies and horses in pursuit of the carriages from Baylor. Brann's description of his kidnapping shows his lack of compliance with his captor's intended goal:

Four young men suddenly presented pistols to my head and after forcing me into a carriage secured my arms with a cord and drove off with me. On the grounds I was presented with the alternative and preferred signing the paper to being trampled to death. The members of the faculty urged me to sign it, using arguments. I did not read the paper. I noticed it contained an agreement for me to leave town. I signed it to escape the mob. You or any man would have done the same under similar circumstances. I signed the paper, but as it was a matter of force I am not bound by its terms.[37]

Shaken by the incident, Brann and his comrades armed themselves as they went about their business in the city and vowed to kill his captors if they attempted to make a second attack.[38] Bad blood between Brann and the Baylor students continued throughout the remainder of the week as Waco police officers intensified their work to prevent a shootout from occurring.[39] Numerous arrests were made for possession of six-shooters within the city limits and several hand-to-hand fights. Students at Baylor University remained supportive of the four students who orchestrated Brann's kidnapping while faculty urged students to return to their studies and McLennan County law enforcement officials attempted to keep the peace on campus. The four boys responsible for the incident, however, remained belligerent due to Brann's comments about Baylor and attempted to resolve the situation extralegally because they believed the court system would not allow proper redress for Brann's insults. In the end, Brann declined to prosecute the students and the incident never went to court.

A mere four days after this incident, some people were furious that Brann had not yet left town as promised, and he was met with physical violence once again. One account of the event describes George Scarborough, son of

William C. Brann at his desk.
Photograph courtesy of The Texas Collection, Baylor University, Waco, Texas.

prominent Judge John Scarborough, as determined to hunt Brann down with a pistol. The Judge promised that if his son would forestall the gunplay, he would personally "deliver a horsewhipping to the Apostle."[40]

Regardless of the circumstances, Brann and the two Scarboroughs happened to meet in the hall of their office building. Young Scarborough drew his gun, and the Judge raised his cane, and in a moment they had beaten Brann down the stairway and into Franklin Street. As Brann stumbled into the street, a third attacker, one of the Baylor students from his kidnapping, joined the assault with a horse whip, shouting, "So you wouldn't leave town, eh?"[41] Risking being shot in the back, Brann made a dash for his horse a short distance away. With a broken right wrist, Brann grasped the reigns with his left hand, and before riding away shouted to his tormentors, "Truth will rise again! Truth crushed to earth will rise again!"[42]

In response to these physical attacks, Brann once again turned to the *Iconoclast* to express his sentiments. Concerning the offending parties and their methods of persuasion to see things from their point of view, Brann wrote:

I have just been enjoying the first holiday I have had in fifteen years. Owing to circumstances entirely beyond my control, I devoted the major part of the past month to digesting a couple of installments of Saving Grace presented by my Baptist brethren, and carefully rubbed in with revolvers and ropes, loaded canes and miscellaneous cudgels—with almost any old thing calculated to make a sinner reflect upon the status of his soul.[43]

Later in the same article, Brann also issued an official apology to the young ladies of Baylor University for his comment concerning "ministers and Magdalenes" directed at Baylor's administration:

A word to the lady students of Baylor: Young ladies, this controversy does not in the least concern you. The Iconoclast has never questioned your good character. You are young, however, and mischievous people have led some of you to believe that it has done so. If you so believe, I am as much in duty bound to apologize as tho' [sic] I had really and intentionally wronged you. A gentleman should ever hasten to apologize to ladies who feel aggrieved; hence, I sincerely crave your pardon for having printed the article which gave you offense. Upon learning that you read into it a meaning which I did not intend, I stopped the presses and curtailed the circulation of the October [1897] number as much as possible, proving my sincerity by pecuniary sacrifice. I would not for the wealth of this world either do you a willful injustice, or have you believe me capable of such a crime.[44]

He continued by encouraging the city of Waco to forget the whole incident: "If God neglected to bless them with brains, that is their misfortune instead of their fault. Let it go at that. They have had their say, I've had mine, and right here I drop the subject until another attempt is made to run me out of town. I make this concession, not that Baylor deserves it, but at the earnest request of the law-abiding element of this city."[45]

The Colonel and the Chairman

Brann's followers insisted the two previous attacks equaled a blow to freedom of the speech and press, stating that Baptists in Waco were enforcing a spirit

of intolerance that would not be toler-
ated outside of the city.[46] Col. G.B.
Gerald, a notable supporter of Brann,
instigated a fist fight after encountering
an individual who denounced Brann.
Gerald was arrested by the McLennan
County Sheriff's Office and posted
bond the same day. J.W. Harris, editor
of the *Waco Morning Times-Herald* and
chairman of McLennan County's Democratic Executive Committee, publically
condemned Brann and the *Iconoclast*
shortly after the incident.[47] He later
upheld the students' actions, believing
that Brann's harassment from supporters of Baylor was justified.[48]

The animosity between Gerald and
Harris grew after Gerald wrote an
article that articulated his praise for
Brann and disdain for Harris and the
Waco Morning Times-Herald.[49] After
its decline from publication at Harris'
newspaper, Gerald attempted to recover
the manuscript, which led to a fight
between the two parties that resulted
in numerous injuries and Gerald
without his manuscript. Infuriated by
this incident, Gerald published a circular that received national attention
in which he explained his disdain for

**Artistic depiction of Col. G.B. Gerald,
1897.** *Courtesy of the* Dallas Morning
News.[50]

Harris and his poor conduct regarding the submission of his previous
editorial. Describing the confrontation between the two, Gerald wrote:

*In relation to the difficulty which occurred
between myself and the editor of the Times-
Herald, about a communication left at his
office, which he refused to publish and
refused to return to me, I have this to say:
that it is the universal rule among all editors*

*to return rejected communications, if they
are demanded, the writer either furnishing
the stamps to carry them through the
mails or upon making a personal demand
for same; I will also assert, that no honor-
able editor will ever allow the communication that he rejects to willingly pass into
the hands of another ... I left him [Har-
ris] a message that I wanted it, and held
him responsible for its return to me. It was
my property, and I had an unquestioned
right to demand it, and I was determined
to have it. I was refused again and again.*

Artistic depiction of J.W. Harris, 1897.
Courtesy of the Dallas Morning News.[51]

Provoked beyond endurance, I at last told him—knowing that I was physically unable to engage in a fisticuff with him, to get his pistol, come out into the street, and we would make it a matter of life or death. He refused to do that [and we fought hand to hand]. These are the facts, and I hereby brand J.W. Harris, editor of the Times-Herald, as a liar, a coward, and a cur; as a man who has taken every advantage, who lies about difficulties that he has brought about himself, and then, like the craven cur that he is, refuses to meet the man he has wronged on equal terms.[52]

Weeks before, Dr. W.O. Wilkes spoke with Harris' brother, W.A. Harris, regarding the probable results of the escalating confrontation between J.W. Harris and Gerald. Speaking frankly, he stated, "[I told] him that, knowing Gerald as I did, either Gerald or J.W. would be killed before it was over. Gerald was old and in bad health, and soured by disappointment in his two sons and oldest daughter, and did not care for life; in fact, I heard it said that he wanted to die."[53]

Hostility between Gerald and Harris reached its breaking point on November 19, 1897, when the two parties met on Austin Avenue.[54] As Gerald crossed from North 4th Street to Austin Avenue, he spotted Harris in front of the drug store conversing with doctors H.L. Taylor and W.W. Wiles. When Harris noticed Gerald headed his direction, he remarked that "trouble was on hand and that they better get out of the way." Initiating the confrontation, Harris drew his revolver, aimed toward Gerald, and fired. Gerald quickened his pace toward Harris, drew his weapon, and fired a shot into Harris at close range. According to reports after the incident, the shot pierced Harris' windpipe, struck his spinal cord, and paralyzed him from the neck to his feet, mortally wounding him. Suddenly, Gerald was confronted by gunshots from the opposite corner as W.A. Harris began firing upon him from the Citizens National Bank. Struck

Artistic depiction of the Gerald–Harris confrontation. *Courtesy of the* Dallas Morning News.[55]

by two bullets, Gerald turned and faced his second assailant as Hunt Bellefant, a Waco police officer, attempted to quell the confrontation at gunpoint. Gerald disregarded Bellefant and continued to fire on Harris until he sank to the ground mortally wounded. Gerald escaped the deadly confrontation with a shattered arm and a wound to his hip. After the scene of the incident calmed, Shepherd Jasper, a black drayman, was ascertained to be the fourth casualty of the fray because he was struck by a stray bullet as he passed by Gerald and J.W. Harris.

Brann's Own Demise

Despite Brann's ardent and sincere apology to the young ladies of Baylor, the university's supporters still felt that the matter remained unresolved. At this point in the Brann-Baylor war, his enemies would only be satisfied by his departure from Waco or his death. A short five months after the first deaths attributed to Brann's inflammatory pen, the editor met his own death on April 2, 1898.[56]

Only a matter of days before a planned lecturing trip, Brann and Capt.

Tom E. Davis, a real estate man, engaged in a deadly revolver duel at 6:00 p.m. on April 1 in front of the Cotton Belt ticket office.[57] Brann and his business manager, W.H. Ward, were walking together in the direction of French's book store, with Captain Davis' office situated between the two locations. When Brann and Ward reached the front of the book store, Captain Davis was in front of his office. Brann and Davis exchanged heated words before drawing their weapons on each other. With daughters at Baylor University, Davis was furious over Brann's

seemingly slanderous references to the moral character of its female pupils, and many Waco citizens had long predicted bloodshed between the two men.[58]

As the battle ensued, neither man sought shelter from the other's fire, and eye-witness accounts describe Brann standing erect, aiming deliberately at Captain Davis' chest.[59] Police officers Sam S. Hall and Dave Durie, hearing the reports of the firearms, raced to stop the duel, but reached the scene too late.[60]

The *Dallas Morning News* account of the battle reported that about ten seconds of shooting left both parties

The Colt .41 Brann used to kill Davis, on display at the Red Men Museum and Library. *Photograph by Bradley T. Turner.*

Three of the pistols used in the confrontations can be seen at the Red Men Museum and Library. *Photograph by Bradley T. Turner.*

lying bleeding on the ground, while the report from the *Waco Weekly Tribune* indicates that despite three wounds, Brann remained standing.[61] Both accounts agree, however, that the firefight left Ward with a bone-shattering bullet wound in the right hand, and a musician and street car motorman with wounds in the sole of the right foot and left leg, respectively, neither injury serious.[62] Following the fiasco, Davis was immediately taken home. Brann, however, went to the police station to give a statement while still bleeding from his injuries before returning to his home. The following day, April 2, Brann died at 1:55 a.m. from a perforated left lung, while Davis lived until 3:00 that afternoon, his cause of death attributed to kidney damage.[63]

Ward was arrested after the incident, as neither the officers nor eyewitnesses knew if he had fired at Davis as well or not. The following day, before Davis died of his wounds, he accused Ward of firing on him as he lay on the sidewalk as well, resulting in an affidavit charging him with murder.[64] He was permitted to attend Brann's funeral and serve as a pallbearer under the supervision of the McLennan County Sheriff's Office.[65] Brann's final resting place included a headstone with an oil lamp and a profile of his face, his initials, and a quote that said, "Truth."

Ironically, only minutes before the fatal gun fight, one witness reported actually sharing drinks with Brann at the nearby Pacific Hotel bar, where he claimed, "I expect to get killed. But when I am, Baylor will have become a thing of the past."[66] Although Brann was correct in the prediction of his

William C. Brann's headstone in Oakwood Cemetery, Waco, Texas, 2009. *Photograph by Jean M. Fair.*

death, his assessment of Baylor's longevity was ill-founded. Brann's legacy, in a way, kept him alive along with the institution he grew to despise.

Concerning the circumstances surrounding Brann's death, while it is commonly accepted that Davis fired the first shot in the lethal duel, speculations abound that Davis opened fire on Brann while his back was still turned, striking him in the back before he could draw his own weapon and return fire.[67]

Along with the publications in Brann's *Iconoclast*, a one-man play by Jerry Flemmons entitled *O Dammit!* immortalized Brann and his distinctive, fiery language. The play was first staged in 1984, and Waco actor Les Smith took on the role of Brann at the Waco Civic Theater in 2000.[68]

Today, as at the time of his death, many varying opinions concerning Brann and his *Iconoclast* exist. Elbert Hubbard, editor of the *Philistine*, wrote an epitaph for Brann's death and legacy entitled "Brann, the Fool" that was published in the April 14, 1898, issue of the *St. Louis Mirror*. Praising Brann in a slightly unusual manner, Hubbard wrote:

have been delighted in these times of image makers so he could have had at them. Alas, he has his own icon shattered by a bullet from the pistol of an enraged politician who could take it no longer."[71]

Detail of Brann's headstone with the quote "Truth," 2009. *Photograph by Jean M. Fair.*

It's a grave subject. Brann is dead. Brann was a Fool. The Fools were the wisest men at Court; and Shakespeare, who dearly loved the Fool, placed his wisest sayings into the mouths of men who wore the motley … Brann shook his cap, flourished his bauble, gave a toss to that fine head, and with tongue in cheek, asked questions and propounded conundrums that Stupid Hypocrisy could not answer. So they killed Brann.[69]

Modern opinions of the fiery Apostle vary as much as the opinions of Brann's contemporaries. The author of a 1987 *Dallas Morning News* article described Brann as "a slouch-hatted, gun-toting, beer-drinking, woman-worshiping, hellfire-snorting, scandalmongering journalist, and, at the end, a casualty in the personal war he had declared on Baylor University."[70] A more insightful opinion captures Brann's flamboyant nature and his effect on his readers, particularly those he chose to attack, perfectly: "The Great Iconoclast would

Endnotes

1. William Robert Poage, *McLennan County, Before 1980* (Waco: Texian Press, 1981), 189–93.
2. Patricia Ward Wallace, *Waco: Texas Crossroads* (Woodland Hills: Windsor Publications, 1983), 46.
3. William R. Carr, "Remembering Brann the Great Iconoclast," *Springhouse Magazine*, Available online at http://www.springhousemagazine. com/brann.htm [accessed 25 August, 2009].
4. *Handbook of Texas Online*, s.v. "Brann, William Cowper," http://www. tshaonline.org/handbook/online/ articles/BB/fbr23.html [accessed 19 May, 2009].
5. Ibid.
6. Ibid.; Carr, "Remembering Brann."
7. Handbook of Texas Online, s.v. "Brann, William Cowper."
8. Ibid.; Carr, "Remembering Brann."

9. Carr, "Remembering Brann."

10. Ibid.; *Handbook of Texas Online*, s.v. "Brann, William Cowper."

11. Carr, "Remembering Brann."

12. *Handbook of Texas Online*, s.v. "Brann, William Cowper."

13. Charles Carver, *Brann and the* Iconoclast (Austin: University of Texas Press, 1957), 41.

14. "Editor Brann Seized," *Dallas Morning News*, 3 October, 1897.

15. Carr, "Remembering Brann."

16. Ibid.; "Editor Brann Seized."

17. Carr, "Remembering Brann."

18. Carver, *Brann and the* Iconoclast, 7–8.

19. Carr, "Remembering Brann."

20. Ibid.

21. Roger N. Conger, ed., *The Best of Brann: The Iconoclast, Selected Articles* (Waco: Texian Press, 1967), 19–20.

22. Ibid., 22.

23. Ibid., 25.

24. Carver, *Brann and the* Iconoclast, 43.

25. Carr, "Remembering Brann;" Kent Biffle, "Waco 1890s 'Holy War' Cost 4 Lives," *Dallas Morning News*, 20 January, 1991.

26. Carr, "Remembering Brann."

27. Ibid.; Biffle, "Waco 1890s 'Holy War' Cost 4 Lives."

28. Conger, *The Best of Brann*, 111.

29. Ibid., 113.

30. Ibid.

31. Biffle, "Waco 1890s 'Holy War' Cost 4 Lives."

32. Conger, *The Best of Brann*, 115.

33. Carr, "Remembering Brann."

34. Conger, *The Best of Brann*, 106.

35. Carr, "Remembering Brann."

36. "Editor Brann Seized."

37. Ibid.

38. "Editor Brann Seized."

39. "The Brann-Baylor Episode," *Dallas Morning News*, 5 October, 1897.

40. Carver, *Brann and the* Iconoclast, 151–52.

41. Ibid., 152.

42. Ibid., 152–53.

43. Conger, *The Best of Brann*, 120.

44. Ibid., 133–34.

45. Ibid.

46. "The Brann-Baylor Episode."

47. Ibid.; "A Terrible Duel at Waco," *Dallas Morning News*, 20 November, 1897.

48. "A Terrible Duel at Waco."

49. Carver, *Brann and the* Iconoclast, 159–60; "A Terrible Duel at Waco."

50. "A Terrible Duel at Waco."

51. Ibid.

52. Carver, *Brann and the* Iconoclast, 160–63. The full text of the circular can be found in the aforementioned book from pages 160–164.

53. Ibid., 164.

54. Ibid.

55. "A Terrible Duel at Waco."

56. Carr, "Remembering Brann."

57. Ibid.; "Brann Dead," *Dallas Morning News*, 2 April, 1898.

58. "Brann Dead."

59. Ibid.

60. *Waco Weekly Tribune*, 2 April, 1898.

61. "Brann Dead."

62. Ibid.

63. Ibid.; "Davis is Dead," *Dallas Morning News*, 3 April, 1898.

64. Ibid.

65. "Waco's Burials," *Dallas Morning News*, 4 April, 1898.

66. Carlos Sanchez, "Story of Waco's William Brann Needs No Hyperbole," *Waco Tribune-Herald*, 7 April, 2002.

67. Carr, "Remembering Brann."

68. Carl Hoover, "Les Smith Echoes a Famous Photograph of Waco Writer and Curmudgeon William C. Brann in the One-Man Play 'O Dammit!,' Presented for Three Weekends at the Waco Civic Theater," *Waco Tribune-Herald*, 31 March, 2000.

69. Carr, "Remembering Brann."

70. Biffle, "Waco 1890s 'Holy War' Cost 4 Lives."

71. Carr, "Remembering Brann."

The Sins of Our Fathers:
Lynching in McLennan County Before 1920

by Richard H. Fair

Violence in McLennan County

Located roughly seventy miles south of Dallas, Texas, in McLennan County, Waco represents the largest city between Dallas and Austin.[1] Built near the confluence of the Bosque and Brazos rivers, Waco's origins trace back to the founding of McLennan County and Waco Village in the early 1850s. Growing to around 750 people in 1859, Waco became an incorporated city due to the explosion of cotton along the Brazos River.

Beginning in the late nineteenth century, Waco's reputation for violence came in the form of lynching, specifically racially-charged actions against African-American citizens in McLennan County.[2] The population of blacks in McLennan County declined rapidly after the Civil War.[3] United States census reports in 1860 indicated that African-Americans represented 37.1 percent of the county. The numbers dropped almost 10 percent in 1880 to 28.3 percent, reaching 24 percent by 1900. This drop was further exacerbated by the racial violence and the rise of the Ku Klux Klan in the 1920s in McLennan County, with the 1930 census indicating that black citizens represented only 18.9 percent of the county's population.

Evolving from the context of corporal punishment, lynch law is described by historian Richard Maxwell Brown as "the practice or custom by which persons are punished for real or alleged crimes without the due process of law."[4] The punishment intensified, however, during the mid-nineteenth century as the term altered from reference to punishment in the form of lashings to one that became argumentatively tantamount with extralegal hangings. Historiographically, Texas is credited with two of the worst instances of lynch-law violence in the United States: the 1916 lynching of Jesse Washington in Waco, and earlier, the "Great Hanging at Gainesville" in 1862. The lynchings at Gainesville in northern Central Texas claimed forty lives out of the 151 Union sympathizers indicted by an extralegal jury of Confederate supporters who convicted and sentenced their neighbors within the context of pervasive fear of slave revolt. Richard Maxwell Brown, in his book *Strain of Violence: Historical Studies of American Violence and Vigilantism*, described Central Texas as a region unmatched in the United States in its long-term vigilante violence.[5]

No event in recent memory is more infamously associated with Waco, Texas, than the violent actions of the Branch Davidians, led by David Koresh, that culminated in the 1993 standoff lasting a total of fifty-one days at the cost of many lives of followers, children, peace officers, and agents of the federal government. This event became synonymous with the city of Waco, McLennan County, and Central Texas at large. Before the violent events of 1993, however, extralegal lynch mob actions

occurred on May 16, 1916, at Waco City Hall, near present-day Heritage Square. The burning and lynching of seventeen-year-old Jesse Washington, an African-American farmhand working for the Fryer family in the nearby town of Robinson, became etched in the minds of the citizens of McLennan County long after the crowd of an estimated fifteen thousand left the scene of his charred body and returned to their daily lives.[6] During the two decades surrounding the lynching of Jesse Washington, Central Texas saw an active extralegal subculture that witnessed and participated in roughly eight known lynching actions: four unconfirmed episodes and five documented cases, including Washington's.[7] Of the eight acts of vigilante violence, seven of the victims were African-American, and only one was classified as Caucasian. Furthermore, accusations of rape constituted a common denominator among the crimes attributed to the victims of extralegal violence in four out of the five well-documented cases.

Historian William D. Carrigan recently compiled charts of evidence indicating that lynch law erupted in

McLennan County during the latter third of the nineteenth century, with a total of fifty documented and unconfirmed cases of mob violence between 1865 and 1900.[8] This era saw a significant increase in racial violence as the effects of emancipation weighed on the minds of whites in Central Texas. Local leaders increased criticism regarding lynch parties that executed whites, but they granted approval to groups that hanged African-Americans in the context of the growing scourge of rape emanating from the black community.[9]

Rape in the specific instance of African-American men violating white women caused great fear in the minds of the white community, yielding an increase in participation in vigilante groups seeking to defend their homes and women from the horrendous actions of black rapists. As extralegal groups continued their mission to protect their wives and daughters, their violent actions began to receive the disapproval of respectable white leaders in McLennan County with news of events such as the bombing of the Phillips family house in neighboring Falls County, which claimed the lives of seven black citizens, including a mother and young child.[10]

This increase in mob violence in Central Texas halted between 1897 and 1905. Carrigan contends that the lack of evidence of violent mob action during this timeframe contrasts greatly with the continued organized advancement of vigilante groups in other regions of Texas and the United States. This can be explained and substantiated by a whitecapping incident in McLennan County that set a new precedent regarding the activism that local law enforcement and the county attorneys took toward these frequent, violent incidents.[11] Mob violence surrounding labor disputes was common at this time, as much of society viewed African-Americans as "troublemakers," but the instance of whitecapping in 1896 proved substantially different.

"Whitecapping" represents another phenomenon with a purpose different from lynching, but it shares a similar mob mentality that often proved as lethal. Historian William F. Holmes describes whitecapping roughly as all types of criminal acts perpetrated by whites against blacks.[12] He contends

that this type of criminal act was utilized for the purpose of attempting to forcibly remove blacks from property or homes they owned or rented. In the context of the account of whitecapping in McLennan County described in the following paragraphs, this definition holds true, with the addition that whitecappers were also influenced by potential economic competition from the black farmers they were attempting to remove.

Exploring the origin of the term whitecapping, Holmes contends that while it is somewhat ambiguous, he observes a connection with the Ku Klux Klan of the Reconstruction era.[13] While dismissing rumors that whitecappers typically wore costumes similar to the Klan, he states the term possibly originated "when Klansmen sometimes wore robes and hoods to disguise themselves; the Whitecaps, in fact, modeled themselves partly on earlier terrorist groups such as the Ku Klux Klan, Knights of the White Camelia, and rifle clubs."[14]

The Attack on "Good Colored Citizens"

In late August 1896, a group of black

men were conversing in their front yard after a day of work in the cotton fields and enjoying their evening meal when a group of masked whitecappers approached the group, drew weapons, and proceeded to beat them. One of the members of the victimized group, Anderson Vaughn, did not fully comprehend the gravity of the situation at hand, and he was described as confused and hesitant in following the attackers' directions. This resulted in Vaughn's death and the severe whipping of the other members of the group: the Robertson brothers, Evant Sandler, and Morris Davis. These men were described by local individuals as "all good colored citizens," and the surrounding farming communities reacted with pledges to support local law enforcement in the apprehension of the white men responsible for this violent murder and flogging against a group of African-Americans striving to maintain the respect of their white peers.[15]

Responding to support from the citizens of the community, County Attorney J.W. Taylor pushed this issue to the forefront of current cases and demanded the whitecapping incident receive special attention at a grand jury hearing and a thorough investigation that would bring the perpetrators to trial.[16] As the case reached the grand jury of the 54th District Court, Judge Samuel R. Scott publicly decried whitecapping and requested that the jury be "more than ordinarily diligent" in proceeding with this case and others of its kind.[17] Judge Scott later referenced the whitecapping case as the paramount blemish on the virtue of McLennan County. The grand jury's subsequent inquiry resulted in ten indictments ranging from whites such as Bruce Kendrick, a wealthy farmer's son, to Henry Downing, a married and settled man.[18]

This new step toward judicial equality in the midst of an increasingly divided color line in McLennan County contributed to new insight into the consequences of mob violence, showing that justice was apparently moving toward a new sense of color blindness in Central Texas. This impartial justice, however, was not without ulterior motives, as common knowledge indicated that the indicted Kendrick was the son of the prominent farmer, James Kendrick, who employed the victimized black gentlemen. This proved to be a key issue in the responses of the farming communities, as they viewed this event as an excuse to use violence to further limit the supply of employable black men in Central Texas and a direct strike on the legitimate commerce rights of James Kendrick.

The Texas penal code complicated efforts for law enforcement and the legal system by justifying actions of vigilantes. Changing minimally since its initial version in 1856, the code, Richard Maxwell Brown argues, "retains too much of the frontier in its treatment of firearms [and] still permits too much force on too many occasions."[19] Brown goes further to contend the Texas penal code favored the rights of individuals exercising deadly force, providing them with a significant amount of discretion in the section dealing with justifiable homicide.

Specifically, Article 1108 addressed the issue of an individual's duty to retreat before responding with deadly force, stating, "The party whose person or property is so unlawfully attacked is not bound to retreat in order to avoid the necessity of killing his assailant."[20]

Article 1091's subsequent clause, pertaining to those charged with the duty of the execution of a convict, afforded ambiguity to the culpability of a peace officer (and possibly another avenue for justification of mob violence), stating, "By officers in the performance of a duty, and by other persons under certain circumstances."[21]

Summing up the complexities that the Texas penal code presented in the early twentieth century for the prevention of mob violence, Brown quotes Henry P. Lundsgaarde stating the need "for police, judges, juries, and any form of third party authority [is practically eliminated] as long as one can convincingly establish that the killing was a response to a threat against person or property."[22] In conjunction with ambiguous laws concerning mob violence, such acts remained a primary method for lower class white citizens to exert power and flaunt what little status they could attain.

Sank Majors (1905)

The reprieve in organized mob violence ceased in 1905 with the extralegal lynching of Sank Majors, an African-

American man from Waco, ending the eight years of silence from the vigilantes in McLennan County.[23] In précis, the lynching of Majors began a new period in heightened racial violence, as the addition of extreme torture by lynch mobs became the norm, with crowd sizes swelling to numbers well into the thousands as the twentieth century began and continued into its first two decades. On the evening of July 11, 1905, Majors allegedly sexually assaulted Clinnie Robert of Golinda.[24] Mrs. Robert, the eighteen-year-old wife of Capt. Ben Robert, described the assault to local law enforcement officials in graphic detail.[25]

While sitting at the rear of her home in Golinda, she reported that her husband had ventured into town, and Sank Majors, the roughly twenty-year-old son of a woman employed by the Mackey family, walked across her yard. Following this event, Mrs. Robert described being attacked from behind, thrown to the floor, knocked unconscious, and waking to find that she had been sexually assaulted. She advised she never saw the attacker's face but noticed a scar on the hand of the aggressor.

Within hours of the report of the rape, the *Dallas Morning News* reported that five hundred or more men from the surrounding communities went out searching for Majors with intentions of lynching him.[26] Further reports indicated that due to the hysteria and confusion that resulted in the enormous search mob, the vigilante group only hindered the apprehension of Majors and led to erroneous accounts of a lynching. Soon after, Sheriff G.W. Tilley of McLennan County issued reports in major regional newspapers indicating a warrant for Majors' arrest.[27]

Unrest spread throughout Waco and surrounding farming communities as Majors remained at large and women began to fear another attack. A local farmer near the community of Golinda told a local reporter, "With temperatures ranging high up in the 90s at night, our wives and daughters do not dare to sleep with doors and windows open for fear of the entrance of one of those prowlers whose deeds carry terror to all our homes."[28]

Recognizing a need to expedite the arrest of Majors, Sheriff Tilley crafted a petition that would give a monetary reward for the lawful capture of the accused rapist. This petition was received well and endorsed by a citizen committee of McLennan County at a mass meeting. Seizing the opportunity to allow justice to progress as swiftly as feasible, the sheriff presented the petition to Gov. Samuel L.M. Lanham on July 16 as his train momentarily stopped in Waco while en route to Austin from Weatherford. The Governor apprehensively approved a reward of two hundred dollars due to comments made by a citizen reflecting the inflammatory sentiments of vigilantes in the county and an article featured in the *Dallas Morning News* regarding the search for Majors. Assured by the committee and the sheriff that extralegal justice would be avoided and lawful authority would prevail with a fair trial for Majors, the Governor departed to Austin.

After days of numerous newspaper articles describing the manhunt, Sheriff W.T. Jackmon of Hays County and Sheriff J.J. Sanders of Caldwell County captured Majors near Lockhart, Texas, and placed him in the Travis County Jail in Austin on July 21.[29] Upon questioning, Majors sternly declared his innocence to Sheriff Tilley, who traveled to Austin to visit the accused as fear of mob upheaval was prevalent in McLennan County with news of Majors' capture.[30] Majors went on to assert that he left Waco via the Valley Junction or the Lewis Switch in order to assist his brother, Polk Majors, and other relatives with their crops near Lockhart; not because he was guilty of raping Mrs. Robert.[31] A grand jury in Waco quickly convened in special session on July 28 and returned an indictment against Majors, setting a trial date for the following Wednesday, August 2.[32] On the day of the trial, Majors provided an incoherent and illogical alibi of his actions on the day of the assault and then proceeded to admit he only confessed out of duress.[33] Regardless, the confession of the accused was still admitted as evidence in the trial. Mrs. Roberts also gave a passionate testimony against her alleged assailant, identifying the scar on Major's hand as the same as her attacker's. Within seven minutes of deliberation, foreman Pat Vick returned the jury's verdict of guilty and a sentence of death by hanging to

the Nineteenth District Court Clerk. Curiously, the *Dallas Morning News* covered the trial and reported that the reward to be bestowed upon sheriffs Jackmon and Sanders totaled three hundred dollars, not the two hundred originally reported on July 17.

Days after the death sentence, Marshall Surratt, the trial judge who presided over Majors' case, granted the condemned man a new trial on grounds that he as a judge had failed to charge the jury in a correct manner.[34] Concern arose from this technicality as the defense attorney, George Barcus, implied that the conviction would most likely be overturned if appealed. Quickly, Judge Surratt announced a new trial for Majors on Wednesday, August 9, in hopes of expediting the process to prevent mob action. Within a day, the *Waco Times-Herald* ran an editorial in defense of Barcus, as overwhelming criticism and harassment befell him for simply representing a black defendant as effectively as possible.[35] Anger quickly rose from men around the Golinda area, who knew that Mrs. Robert would have to testify again. Before due process could once

again be served in the case of Sank Majors, extralegal justice came in the form of a lynch mob in the early morning hours of August 7, 1905.[36]

Preparation for the lynching began around 10:30 p.m. the previous evening as two hundred men from Golinda and nearby Falls County resolved to take Majors from the McLennan County Jail at roughly 1:30 a.m. As the mob arrived, the jailer and Deputy Sheriffs J. A. Tilley, Harvey B. Ross, and John C. Walton attempted to circumvent the mob action. After being summoned, Sheriff Tilley hastily arrived and tried to subdue the mob by explaining he would resist any invasion. Defiantly, members of the mob brought dynamite to induce law enforcement away from the jail's entrance and began to break down the outer doors with sledgehammers. Reports printed in the *Dallas Morning News* revealed that though neither the vigilantes nor local law enforcement fired any shots, hand-to-hand combat ensued.[37] The Dallas newspaper insinuated that the lynching might have been delayed if members of the McLennan County Sheriff's Office had fired volleys into the air to startle the mob, but declared later in the editorial, "The slaughter of three-fourths of the band of 600 Texas farmers would not have saved the negro."[38]

The extralegal crowd extracted Majors from his jail cell and took him to Austin Avenue and then toward the market square.[39] The angry farmers were first inclined to burn Majors alive, as kindling was apparently available along the route taken on Austin Avenue. After seeing Majors prematurely doused with petroleum and lit with a match, the faction that favored hanging from the suspension bridge overcame those who favored burning, and Majors was extinguished and taken toward the bridge. Majors himself supposedly favored the change in execution style, as he allegedly proclaimed, "I wanted Sheriff Tilley to hang me. I done the crime and ought to be hung, but I don't want to be burnt alive."[40] Reports from the *Dallas Morning News* detailed how Majors attempted to infuriate the mob further by reciting the appalling details of how he sexually assaulted Mrs. Robert a total of three times before the lynch mob reached the suspension bridge.

Historian Patricia Bernstein suggests that any confession that came from Majors en route to his demise was unquestionably coerced by the lynch party.[41] A noose was tied to a crossbeam on the suspension bridge and fitted around Majors' neck while he was being placed on a horse that served the purpose of a makeshift scaffold.[42] Sank Majors died of strangulation ten minutes after members of the mob led the horse away. Shortly after confirming his death, vigilantes began to collect souvenirs of anything remotely related to the night's event, such as pieces of clothing, fingers, and anything else that would serve as a reminder of the incident. They also cut up the rope and passed the pieces out to participants as other mementos. Ironically, former McLennan County Sheriff, Capt. Dan Ford, had used the same rope in two legal hangings. The lynch party left Majors' body hanging until John Fall, McLennan County's undertaker, came to collect it around 2:30 a.m.

The aftermath of the extralegal execution of Sank Majors left little doubt of the assertion of masculine white supremacy upon the black community in McLennan County.[43] While some in the black community hesitantly approved the efforts of the lynch mob as justifiable, others criticized the mob killing. Carrigan contends that the primary issues concerning vigilante violence in Central Texas gravitated around Majors' demise. The insult of a lenient judicial system packed with lawyers who observed minimal civil rights for African-Americans attacked the pride and honor of a breed of men reared in a society that cherished the individual who took the law into his own hands and honored forefathers who were the exemplars of this mentality.[44]

The Trial of Will King

Resistance from the black community also played a key role in the extralegal group that sought to hang Majors. Preceding the work of Majors' defense attorney, George Barcus, was the trial of Will King in McLennan County. Charged with murder, his defense team successfully argued that the grand jury and trial were unconstitutional based on the fact that no African-Americans were present in either jury. After appeals to the Texas State Court of Appeals and the Texas Supreme Court, a new grand jury and trial were announced. African-American educator A.J. Moore sat on the second grand jury. The second trial resulted in a hung jury, and Will King was convicted and sentenced to death after a third trial. King was legally hanged in McLennan County on October 25, 1901.

The effects of the King trial infuriated whites in McLennan County, as it represented a clear attack on the unified front that whites had presented in judicial affairs. Regarding the efforts of the McLennan County Sheriff's Office and other local law enforcement, Carrigan identifies the lack of investigation or indictment of those responsible for Majors' lynching as a major contributing factor propagating the lawlessness of racial violence that ultimately came to a climax in the case of Jesse Washington in 1916.

Jesse Washington (1916)

The discovery of Lucy Fryer's body on May 8, 1916, propelled the Robinson community into rage as Jesse Washington, an illiterate and possibly retarded seventeen-year-old African-American farmhand of George and Lucy Fryer, was implicated as the murder suspect.[45] Shortly before sundown, Mrs. Fryer's daughter, Ruby Fryer, discovered her mother's body in the doorway of the family's seed house showing signs of severe head trauma and possible sexual assault. A blunt object apparently served as the murder weapon, causing at least two of the six visible wounds on her crushed skull. According to the testimony of Dr. J.H. Maynard, blunt-force trauma was the likely cause of death. Initially, Maynard advised the *Waco Times-Herald* that Mrs. Fryer indeed had been sexually assaulted, leading to a rush for local newspapers to publish the details of the crime.

Within hours of the incident an investigation of the Fryer farm yielded incriminating evidence against Jesse Washington, and Deputy Sheriff Lee Jenkins arrested him at his home. Jenkins interviewed Chris Simon, a neighbor of the Fryers, who described Washington planting cottonseed earlier on the morning of May 8, identifying the accused as the closest individual to the scene of the crime. Jenkins also found physical evidence of the crime: Washington's blood-soaked undershirt and pants. For the sake of gaining possible evidence from Washington's family, his mother, father, brother, and a female with the name of "Moore" were detained shortly after Jesse Washington's arrest. Historian Patricia Bernstein contends that the apprehension of Washington's family occurred for the sake of pressuring Jesse Washington to confess to the murder of Mrs. Fryer.

After Washington's arrest, rumors of mob violence swept through Robinson, pressuring Sheriff Fleming to move Washington to an undisclosed location where he could be safely interrogated without fear of mob intervention.[46] In the early hours of May 9, Sheriff Fleming moved Washington to Hillsboro for safekeeping. After initially denying all knowledge of Fryer's murder, Washington confessed to sexually assaulting and murdering Lucy Fryer during a renewed interrogation by Sheriff Fleming and Hill County Sheriff Fred Long. At first, Washington told his interrogators the murder weapon was a piece of iron, but he later recanted and stated the true weapon was a medium-sized blacksmith's hammer. Washington eventually divulged the location of the murder weapon, and after officers discovered the hammer near a hackberry tree off of the main Robinsonville road, as Washington had indicated, this became the most incriminating aspect of his initial confession. The *Waco Times-Herald* reported that the weapon was covered with dried blood, a fact later submitted as evidence in Washington's trial with the addition of bits of cottonseed on the hammer.[47]

Sheriff Fleming realized that news editorials of Washington's confession would ignite the passions of vengeance among the citizens of Robinson, so he transferred Washington to Dallas as a precaution. The illiterate Washington then dictated and signed a formal confession detailing the rape and murder of Mrs. Fryer with an "X" in place of his name under the supervision of Dallas County Attorney Mike T. Lively. Less than twenty-four hours after Mrs. Fryer's murder, Sheriff Fleming and the McLennan County Sheriff's Office had captured their prime suspect, retrieved the murder weapon, and

obtained a signed confession.

On May 10, Waco's three newspapers published Jesse Washington's confession.[48] The confession published in the *Waco Times-Herald* contained edits to appease censorship standards, but it retained elements graphic enough to convey the detestability of the crimes Washington committed:

On yesterday, May 8, 1916, I was planting cotton for Mr. Fryar [sic] near Robinsonville, close to Waco, Tex. and about 3:30 o'clock p.m., I went up to Mr. Fryar's [sic] barn to get some more cotton seed. I called Mrs. Fryar [sic] from the house to get some cotton seed and she came to the barn and unfastened the door and scooped up the cotton seed. I was holding the sack while she was putting the seed in the sack and after she had finished, she was fussing with me about whipping the mules and while she was standing inside of the door of the barn and still talking to me, I hit her on the side of the head with a hammer that I had in my hand. I had taken this hammer from Mr. Fryar's [sic] home to the field that morning and brought it back and put it in the barn at dinner. I had picked up this

hammer and had it in my hand when I called Mrs. Fryar [sic] from the house and had the hammer in my right hand all the time I was holding the sack.

When I hit Mrs. Fryar [sic] on the side of the head with the hammer, she fell over, and then I assaulted her. I then picked up the hammer from where I had laid it down, and hit her twice more with the hammer on top of her head. I saw the blood coming through her bonnet.

I then picked up the sack of cotton seed and carried it and the hammer to the field where I had left the team. I left the sack of cotton seed near the planter and went about forty steps south of the planter and the mules, and put the hammer that I killed Mrs. Fryar [sic] with in some woods under some hackberry brush.

I knew when I went to the barn for the cotton seed that there wasn't anybody at the house except Mrs. Fryar [sic], and when I called her from the house to the barn, I had already made up my mind to knock her in the head with the hammer and then assault her. I had been working for Mr. Fryar [sic] about five months, and first made up my mind to assault Mrs. Fryar [sic] yesterday morning, and took the hammer from the buggy shed to the

*field with me and brought it back and put
it in the barn at dinner time, so that I
could use it to knock Mrs. Fryar [sic] in
the head when I came back for seed during
the afternoon.*

*I planted cotton the rest of the after-
noon, then put up the team and went
home to my daddy's house where I was
arrested.*

*There wasn't anybody else who had
anything to do with the killing or assaulting of Mrs. Fryar [sic] except myself.*

*Signed Jess [sic] Washington, X, his
mark.*[49]

The alleged rape of Lucy Fryer carried more weight than her murder. Similar to the case of Sank Majors, Jesse
Washington's plight began to revolve
around the act that had threatened
white male authority and infuriated the
extralegal mob eleven years earlier.
Patricia Bernstein noted that aside
from the stark violence mingled with
common events, the confession showed
a "strange combination of the grossest
vernacular with rather stilted speech
that probably does not represent the
way Jesse Washington really talked."[50]
Bernstein also noted that Washington's

confession fits into a category of newspaper editorials known as "acceptable
folk pornography," a definition used by
historian Jacquelyn Dowd Hall for the
supposed crimes of typified black male
rapists during the era.[51] Aside from the
possibilities in dialect discrepancy, the
fact remains that Washington was illiterate and probably incapable of the
exact wording of the confession.

Enraged by the published confession,
at least five hundred livid farmers and
citizens from Robinson and the
surrounding communities poured into
Waco in an attempt to find Washington
at the McLennan County Jail.[52] With
Washington in custody in Dallas
County, Sheriff Fleming encouraged the
mob to search the jail for the confessed
murderer, informing the group that
Washington had been transferred out
of McLennan County for safekeeping
until the trial. After an exhaustive
search of the jail, Sheriff Fleming
offered to pay for expenses for the
vigilante group to travel to Hillsboro
and search the Hillsboro jail as well.
However, the group declined the
sheriff's offer and returned to their
homes empty-handed. Shortly after

this preliminary endeavor to bypass due
process, community leaders from
Robinson announced to McLennan
County law enforcement that no
further extralegal action would be taken
under the condition that the judicial
system provided a swift trial and
punishment for Washington.

During the initial attempt to lynch
Washington, Mrs. Fryer's burial went
largely overlooked. After a simple
ceremony at the Fryer farm, Lucy Fryer
was interred at the Lorena Cemetery
in Lorena, Texas, a small community
south of Waco.[53] The cemetery sits near
present-day Interstate 35, a few miles
outside downtown Lorena. Lucy Fryer
was buried relatively near her daughter who had died in early childhood.
Lucy Fryer's grave in Lorena shows a
headstone bearing the surname Fryar in
the same area as the Lucy and George
Fryer headstones. It is unknown if
any connection exists between the
two families, as the aforementioned
Mr. Fryer and Mrs. Fryer were immigrants from the United Kingdom.[54]

The McLennan County judicial system began moving at a rapid pace after
the makeshift vigilante group delivered

their urgent ultimatum regarding the efficiency of the county's legal system in the case.[55] A grand jury indicted Washington of murder after less than thirty minutes of deliberation on May 11. With Washington unable to pay for his legal defense, Fifty-fourth District Court Judge Richard I. Munroe appointed six youthful, inexperienced Waco lawyers to defend Washington in his murder trial set for the upcoming Monday, May 15. Allowed two days to prepare for Washington's trial, the attorneys spent only a short time with the accused late on Sunday, May 14.

Due to the relative lack of experience and the complications of defense attorney George Barcus in Sank Majors' trial of 1905, it can be contended that Washington's young lawyers were appointed simply to let justice play out its course without a great deal of turmoil in the interest of keeping the vigilantes from once again bypassing due process. In an attempt to keep the peace before the trial, Sheriff Fleming made an appearance on Saturday, May 13, at Joe Swayne's store in Robinson to speak with the enraged farmers. Advising the crowd that every possible measure had

been taken to assure the speedy trial of Washington, Robinson leaders received Sheriff Fleming respectfully and advised the community to be patient regarding the trial. Believing that matters regarding mob violence were under control, Sheriff Fleming brought Washington back to Waco on Sunday evening in preparation for the trial.

The Trial and Lynching of Jesse Washington

Sunday and early Monday morning proved vastly different from the calmness that McLennan County saw on Saturday.[56] As predicted by the *Waco Times-Herald*, a great crowd from at least twenty-five miles surrounding Waco came to the city to witness Washington's trial. Though there was a throng of citizens migrating to Waco via train, the McLennan County Sheriff's Office, the Mayor, and Waco Chief of Police Guy McNamara took no action to supply a greater number of officers in anticipation of the large attendance at the trial. Local newspapers advised Waco citizens that Washington would be transferred into Waco on Monday

morning, but Sheriff Fleming brought Washington back late Sunday night so the defense attorneys could meet with him before Monday morning. Advised by his attorneys to spend his last moments of life in prayer, Washington appeared mostly unmoved or unaware of the gravity of his situation.

Presiding over a packed courtroom, Fifty-fourth District Court Judge Richard I. Munroe made no effort to ask men to remove their weapons, and he did not clear the severely overcrowded courthouse.[57] He only routinely asked for silence in the court and frequently requested that all men remove their hats in respect to the court. Twenty-four jurors from Waco and the surrounding communities of Valley Mills, Mart, Moody, McGregor, and West appeared for jury selection. The process moved rapidly, and prominent Waco businessman William B. Brazelton was appointed foreman of the jury with no intervention or questioning regarding jurors from the defense counsel.[58]

Preliminary procedures quickly proceeded as Washington entered a plea of guilty and Judge Munroe explained the penalty of a verdict of guilty to the defendant. The prosecution opened with the medical testimony of Dr. Maynard, who recounted his observations of the head trauma that killed Mrs. Fryer, but made no mention of evidence that would substantiate sexual assault, the apex of local newspapers' attention and the lead motive for previous extralegal attempts at Washington's life. Curiously, records of Washington's case obtained from the McLennan County District Clerk's office have no subpoena information for Dr. Maynard's admission as a witness. After Sheriff Fleming, Deputy Sheriff Lee Jenkins, Dallas County Attorney M.T. Liveley, Hill County Sheriff Fred Long, and investigator W.J. 'Joe' Davis gave their testimonies regarding Washington's apprehension and obtainment of his confession, McLennan County Attorney J.B. McNamara read the confession to the jury and rested his case. The defense's case proved extremely short, as the only witness called was the defendant, Jesse Washington.[59]

After Washington advised he had nothing more to add to his written confession, the defense rested. Further research into the defense's case yielded that numerous entries on the subpoena form indicate both Joe Fee and J.J. Hutcheson, listed as newspapermen, as material witnesses for the defense. No other documentation, however, has substantiated any information regarding those two individuals' testimony.[60] In addition, Henry and Martha Washington, the parents of Jesse Washington, were also subpoenaed along with three other material witnesses with the occupations of baker, architect, and blacksmith, though none of them testified.

After closing arguments by County Attorney McNamara essentially praising the McLennan County judicial system and the defense attorneys for doing their legal obligation, McNamara stated, "The prisoner has been given a fair trial, as fair as any ever given in this courtroom."[61] After loud approval from the courtroom audience, the jury went into deliberation for four minutes. Foreman William B. Brazelton and the jury returned with a guilty verdict and a sentence of punishment by death.

Judge Munroe had only begun transcribing the verdict into the docket book when a white observer yelled for the crowd to seize Washington, and a group of men quickly took custody of the convicted man.[62] Reports of the moment before the seizure of Washington vary. Elizabeth Freeman's report contends that Warren Hunt, the court stenographer, quickly exited the courtroom before the crowd surged forward, and McLennan County Deputy Sheriff Barney Goldberg drew his sidearm for only a moment to realize that other deputies and Sheriff Fleming had already left Washington's side. Other accounts of Deputy Sheriff Goldberg's reaction state that he struck two men in the mob with his revolver, thus inciting threats of violence upon him. The *Waco Times-Herald* article regarding the trial contends that the vigilante crowd surprised the deputies before anyone could interfere.

As the mob carried Washington toward City Hall, Washington was beaten with bricks and shovels and stabbed.[63] By the time the macabre parade reached its destination, Washington was covered in blood. A pyre was lit as members of the mob

A crowd gathers in the old Waco City Square and forces Jesse Washington onto his makeshift gallows and pyre.
Photographs by Fred Gildersleeve, courtesy of the National Association for the Advancement of Colored People.

hoisted him above the fire by a chain around his neck. Other participants castrated Washington and cut off one of his ears. As the fire grew around him, Washington's fingers were severed as he struggled to move away from the flames. After being lowered into the flames several times, Jesse Washington finally died. Shortly after, a member of the mob tied the remnants of Washington's body to his horse and paraded it around the City Hall plaza, later removing it to Robinson. The body was placed in a sack and hung on a telephone pole in front of a black-smith's shop for several hours.

As the gruesome event progressed through the late morning of May 15, 1916, Mayor and former Chief of Police John R. Dollins and current Waco Chief of Police Guy McNamara watched the event unfold from the office of the Mayor in City Hall.[64] The McLennan County Sheriff's Office and the Waco Police Department made no attempt to quell the riotous behavior of the lynch mob after its departure from the courthouse. A crowd of an esti-mated fifteen thousand men, women, and children gathered to watch the

dying pleas of the convicted murderer receiving justice at the hands of extrale-gal vigilantes, not the legal execution sentenced under due process. While the reasons and excuses for attending the lynching of Jesse Washington vary, it is clear that Sheriff Fleming and the city of Waco had been inadequately pre-pared for the insurgency in the court-

room and the brutal lynching that followed.[65]

The day after the incident, the *Waco Times-Herald* published a short article emphasizing the incomplete judgment on the Fifty-fourth District Court's docket, clarifying that no further inquiry would be made regarding the extralegal mob action by the county

attorney's office or the six young law-yers who represented Washington, and identifying the lynching of Jesse Washington as a "closed incident."[66]

Joseph Martin Dawson, pastor of the First Baptist Church of Waco, was pres-ent at City Hall during Washington's lynching.[67] He later introduced numer-ous resolutions at Waco Pastors' Asso-ciation meetings, preached against the lynching, and encouraged law enforce-ment to make more inquiries in the case, but he was met with criticism and lack of support even after news spread that Washington was likely innocent and another individual was arrested. Specifically, Dawson recalls being very disappointed with Dr. Charles T. Caldwell, pastor of the First Presbyte-rian Church, stating that he "refused to say a thing about it, due likely to his intense Southern uprearing."[68] Though Dawson remained one of the few min-isters to publicly denounce the mob's actions, stating "the people who burned the Negro were the lowest order of people in Waco," he concedes support existed among ministers who did not vocally oppose vigilantism.[69] Dawson did not believe the entire lynching was

performed only by Klansmen, but he stated, "I think Klansmen were in it and perhaps induced it."[70] Recalling his shock at the entire episode, Dawson stated, "To my utter surprise, when they discovered they had burned an innocent man. ... the only comment I heard around town, deeply disappointing to me, was, 'Well, it's fine. At last, they got the right Nigger.'"[71]

The Atonement Plaque

In April 2001, Waco attorney and former city council member Lawrence Johnson voiced his opinion to the *Waco Tribune-Herald* that the city needed to acknowledge its complacent behavior in the lynching of Jesse Washington.[72] New dialogue regarding the city of Waco's lack of action in the case of mob violence was revisited a year later by McLennan County Commissioner Lester Gibson. As commissioners were considering restoration of a mural in the McLennan County courthouse, Gibson noted a depiction of the antiquated City Hall, complete with a hanging noose and tree displayed prom-inently. This led to Gibson's association of the depiction to the Washington

lynching and initial wish to paint over the noose. Later, Gibson proposed a resolution to accompany the noose that condemned the actions of the city in 1916, an act he felt would adequately show atonement for the incident. Further dialogue and a vote on the resolution resulted in the denial of the proposed resolution due to lack of sup-port by other county commissioners.[73] Commissioner Gibson accused his col-leagues of taking the same action to his measure as the city did in 1916 to the lynching of Washington and asserted that their silence was the equivalent of support for extralegal violence and racism. For the next three years, the "atonement plaque" became a common staple of Gibson's proposed resolutions.

New dialogue regarding the legacy of Waco's silence in the Washington lynching was brought up in June 2005 as the United States Senate passed a resolution apologizing for the "acts of terrorism against fellow citizens" and described the practice of lynching as the "ultimate expression of racism in the United States following Reconstruc-tion."[74] Once again, editorials were written urging Waco to atone publicly for the Washington lynching in order to begin a process of healing and promote unity within Central Texas. More inquiry was brought in 2006 into the most eloquent method to acknowledge the incident as the Community Race Relation Coalition's Lynching Issue Task Force was set up to present resolutions regarding the matter.[75] Patsy Kilgore, a distant relative of Jesse Washington's victim, Lucy Fryer, was present for one meeting and expressed her sentiment that the proposed resolutions do not take into account Lucy Fryer's death. Her sentiments further alienated racial unity in Waco.

A resolution was passed in June 2006 by the Waco City Council that condemned the multitude of lynchings during the turn of the twentieth century, but did not make specific mention of the Washington lynching.[76] A similar, yet shorter resolution was passed on behalf of McLennan County during June of that same year. Community Race Relations Coalition member Jo Welter praised the city council's resolution and commented, "The goal is to make sure each person in the community feels valued and

The site of Jesse Washington's lynching, 2009 (roughly about where the Waco Convention Center and oak trees meet). *Photograph by Bradley T. Turner.*

loved."[77] Ninety years and a month after the Washington lynching, Waco finally admitted penance and acknowledged a scourge that plagued members of both Caucasian and African-American races with fear, apprehension, and distrust for the greater share of two centuries.

ENDNOTES

1. *Handbook of Texas Online, s.v.*

"Waco, TX," http://www.tshaonline.org/handbook/online/articles/WW/hdw1.html [accessed 21 April, 2009].

2. Patricia Ward Wallace, *Waco: Texas Crossroads* (Woodland Hills: Windsor Publications, 1983), 59.

3. Patricia Ward Wallace, *Our Land, Our Lives: A Pictorial History of McLennan County, Texas* (Norfolk: The Donning Company, 1986), 155.

4. Ken Hammond, "Lynchings in Texas:

The Awful Violence of Frontier 'Justice,'" *The Houston Chronicle*, 1 December, 1985.

5. Patricia Bernstein, *The First Waco Horror: The Lynching of Jesse Washington and the Rise of the NAACP* (College Station, TX: Texas A&M University Press, 2005), 12.

6. William D. Carrigan, *The Making of a Lynching Culture: Violence and Vigilantism in Central Texas, 1836–1916* (Urbana: University of Illinois Press, 2004), 1–3.

7. Ibid., Appendix A–B.

8. Ibid.

9. Ibid., 160–64.

10. Ibid., 165–66, Appendix A.

11. "A White-Cap Horror," *Dallas Morning News*, 21 August, 1896; Carrigan, *The Making of a Lynching Culture*, 164–66.

12. William F. Holmes, "Whitecapping: Agrarian Violence in Mississippi, 1902–1906," *Journal of Southern History* 35, no. 2 (May 1969): 166.

13. Ibid.

14. Ibid.

15. "A White-Cap Horror."

16. Ibid.; "Members of the Waco Bar, 1897," in *The Bench and Bar of Waco and McLennan County, 1849–1976*, ed. Betty Ann McCartney McSwain (Waco: Texian Press, 1976).

17. "Grand Jury Sworn In," *Dallas Morning News*, 8 September, 1896; Carrigan, *The Making of a Lynching Culture*, 164.

18. "The Hillside Whitecapping," *Dallas Morning News*, 23 August, 1896; "Hillside Whitecapping," *Dallas Morning News*, 26 August, 1896; Carrigan, *The Making of a Lynching Culture*, 164–66, Appendix A.

19. Richard Maxwell Brown, *No Duty to Retreat* (New York: Oxford University Press, 1991), 26.

20. *Penal Code of the State of Texas, Adopted at the Regular Session of the Thirty-Second Legislature, 1911* (Austin: Austin Printing Company, 1911), 297.

21. *Penal Code of the State of Texas*, 292.

22. Richard Maxwell Brown, *No Duty to Retreat* (Norman, OK: University of Oklahoma Press, 1994), 28.

23. Carrigan, *The Making of a Lynching Culture*, 163–64.

24. "Wrong Negro Caught," *Dallas Morning News*, 16 July, 1905; "Sank Majors Indicted," *Dallas Morning News*, 29 July, 1905.

25. "Sank Majors on Trial for His Life in the 19th Judicial District Court," *Waco Times Herald*, 2 August, 1905; Bernstein, *The First Waco Horror*, 21–23.

26. "Wrong Negro Caught."

27. "Warrant For Sank Majors," *Dallas Morning News*, 16 July, 1905; "Reward For Capture," *Dallas Morning News*, 17 July, 1905.

28. "Reward For Capture."

29. "Sank Majors Captured," *Dallas Morning News*, 23 July, 1905; "Majors, the Assailant of Mrs. Robert, Captured," *Waco Times-Herald*, 22 July, 1905; Bernstein, *The First Waco Horror*, 22–23.

30. "Sheriff Tilley Sees the Negro," *Waco Times-Herald*, 23 July, 1905; "Negro Placed In Jail," *Dallas Morning News*, 23 July, 1905.

31. Ibid.; Bernstein, *The First Waco Horror*, 22–23.

32. "Sank Majors Indicted," *The Dallas Morning News*, 29 July, 1905; "Sank Majors To Die," *Dallas Morning News*, 3 August, 1905.

33. "Majors Given Death Penalty by the Jury," *Waco Times Herald*, 3 August, 1905; "Sank Majors to Die.;"

Bernstein, *The First Waco Horror*, 22–23.

34. "A New Trial Granted Sank Majors," *Waco Times Herald*, 6 August, 1905; "Sank Majors Gets New Trial," *Dallas Morning News*, 6 August, 1905; Bernstein, *The First Waco Horror*, 23–24.

35. Bernstein, *The First Waco Horror*, 23–24; "Unjust Criticism," *Waco Times-Herald*, 7 August, 1905; Carrigan, *The Making of a Lynching Culture*, 169–70.

36. "Lynching at Waco," *Dallas Morning News*, 9 August, 1905; Bernstein, *The First Waco Horror*, 23–25.

37. "Lynching at Waco."

38. Ibid.

39. Bernstein, *The First Waco Horror*, 24–26; "Lynching At Waco."

40. "Lynching at Waco."

41. Bernstein, *The First Waco Horror*, 25.

42. "Lynching at Waco;" Bernstein, *The First Waco Horror*, 24–25.

43. Carrigan, *The Making of a Lynching Culture*, 168–70; "Lynching at Waco."

44. Carrigan, *The Making of a Lynching Culture*, 167–70.

45. "Negro Confesses to Terrible Crime at Robinsonville," *Waco Times-Herald*, May 9, 1916; SoRelle, James, "The 'Waco Horror': The Lynching of Jesse Washington," *Southern Historical Quarterly* 86 (1983): 520–21; Bernstein, *The First Waco Horror*, 87–90, 104.

46. "Negro Confesses to Terrible Crime at Robinsonville.;" SoRelle, "The 'Waco Horror': The Lynching of Jesse Washington," 520–21; Bernstein, *The First Waco Horror*, 92–94.

47. SoRelle, "The 'Waco Horror': The Lynching of Jesse Washington," 521–22; State of Texas *v.* Jesse Washington, 4141; McLennan County, TX, March, 1916; Bernstein, *The First Waco Horror*, 92–93.

48. "Sworn Confession by Jesse Washington," *Waco Times-Herald*, 10 May, 1916; Bernstein, *The First Waco Horror*, 94–96.

49. "Sworn Confession by Jesse Washington."

50. Bernstein, *The First Waco Horror*, 96.

51. Ibid., 94.

52. SoRelle, "The 'Waco Horror': The Lynching of Jesse Washington," 521–22; Bernstein, *The First Waco Horror*, 94–95.

53. Bernstein, *The First Waco Horror*, 94.

54. Ibid., 88–89.

55. "Grand Jury Indicts Slayer of Mrs. Fryar," *Waco Times-Herald*, 11 May, 1916; SoRelle, "The 'Waco Horror': The Lynching of Jesse Washington," 522; Bernstein, *The First Waco Horror*, 100–101; "Will Permit Law to Take its Course in Negro Boy's Trial," *Waco Times-Herald*, 13 May, 1916.

56. "Everything Ready for Trial Here Tomorrow of Jesse Washington," *Waco Times-Herald*, 14 May, 1916; SoRelle, "The 'Waco Horror': The Lynching of Jesse Washington," 522–23; Bernstein, *The First Waco Horror*, 102–103.

57. "Mob Takes Negro From Court House, Burns Him at Stake," *Waco Times-Herald*, 15 May, 1916; SoRelle, "The 'Waco Horror': The Lynching of Jesse Washington," 523; Texas *v.* Washington, McLennan County, TX; Bernstein, *The First Waco Horror*, 104–105.

58. "Mob Takes Negro From Court House;" SoRelle, "The 'Waco Horror': The Lynching of Jesse Washington," 523, 526; Texas *v.* Washington, McLennan County, TX; Bernstein, *The First Waco Horror*, 104–105.

59. SoRelle, "The 'Waco Horror': The Lynching of Jesse Washington," 523, 526; Texas *v.* Washington, McLennan County, TX.

60. Defense Subpoena Form, Texas *vs.* Washington, McLennan County, TX.

61. SoRelle, "The 'Waco Horror': The Lynching of Jesse Washington," 526; "Mob Takes Negro From Court House."

62. "Mob Takes Negro From Court House." SoRelle, "The 'Waco Horror': The Lynching of Jesse Washington," 526–27; Bernstein, *The First Waco Horror,* 106.

63. William D. Carrigan, "Heritage of Violence: Memory and Race Relations in Twentieth-Century Waco, Texas," in *Making a New South: Race, Leadership, and Community After the Civil War,* eds. Paul A. Cimbala and Barton C. Shaw, (Gainesville: University Press of Florida, 2007), 65; "Mob Takes Negro From Court House."

64. SoRelle, "The 'Waco Horror': The Lynching of Jesse Washington," 527–28; "Mob Takes Negro From Court House." Bernstein, *The First Waco Horror,* 108–109; Roger Norman Conger, *A Pictorial History of Waco* (Waco: Texian Press, 1972), 207.

65. SoRelle, "The 'Waco Horror': The Lynching of Jesse Washington," 527–28; "Mob Takes Negro From Court House." Bernstein, *The First Waco Horror,* 109–10.

66. "Court's Entry Not Finished When Mob Secured Negro," *Waco Times-Herald,* 16 May, 1916.

67. Joseph Martin Dawson, "Oral History," Institute for Oral History, Baylor University, Waco, TX, 53–54.

68. Ibid., 54.

69. Ibid.

70. Ibid., 56.

71. Ibid., 54.

72. "'Waco Horror' recalled: Infamous lynching's anniversary brings 'Night-line' to town," *Waco Tribune-Herald,* 9 April, 2001; "Lester Gibson, Bid to Post Statement of Regret for 1916 Lynching led to Acrimony Among Colleagues; You Can Always Count on McLennan County Commissioner Lester Gibson to Stir the Pot," *Waco Tribune-Herald,* 21 July, 2002.

73. "County rejects expression of 'atonement' for lynching; Gibson proposed plaque by mural that shows noose," *Waco Tribune-Herald,* 8 May, 2002.

74. "Editorial: Atonement," *Waco Tribune-Herald,* 14 June, 2005.

75. Sylvia Moreno, "In Waco, a Push to Atone for the Region's Lynch-Mob Past," *Washington Post,* 26 April, 2006; J.B. Smith, "Waco Council's Resolution Condemns Lynchings," *Waco Tribune-Herald,* 21 June, 2006.

76. Smith, "Waco Council's Resolution Condemns Lynchings."

77. Ibid.

Sending in the Second String:
A Brief History of Camp MacArthur and Rich Field

by Bradley T. Turner

Introduction

In 2009, permanent impressions from thousands of passing vehicles indent the crossing at 19th Street and Park Lake Drive in Waco, Texas. A collection of broken glass and loose gravel gathers as the street curbs envelop a tattered traffic light. McDonald's stands at one of the four street corners, serving fast food to anxious customers impatiently waiting for service. Directly across the street stands a mundane gas station fashioned with thick pinstripes of red, grey, and yellow. On another corner, adjacent to a Dollar General store, lies a quiet, vacated lot where rain puddles collect in the spring and weeds fill neglected cracks with burgeoning greenery. The H-E-B grocery store is the most noticeable structure at the intersection, resting several hundred feet from the road to provide adequate parking facilities for customers. But only a few passers notice one other landmark also at the corner of this intersection—a small black and grey sign with the words "Camp MacArthur" raised in pewter.

On April 6, 1917, the United States of America officially joined World War I when Congress declared war on Germany in a decision that surprised few people. During the following month, the federal government followed the declaration of war with an official military service draft. Along with this military draft emerged the need for new military bases and combat training programs for the immense numbers of volunteers and draftees. Communities across the country competed for the privilege to house these new training camps, primarily because military training camps represented incentives encompassing more than just a patriotic

77

Camp MacArthur historical marker at 19th Street and Park Lake Drive, 2009. *Photograph by Bradley T. Turner.*

service to Uncle Sam; they represented money—lots of money.

Among the nationwide communities bidding for an army camp stood Waco, Texas. After estimating the probable increase in community revenue, Waco officials decided that obtaining an army training center might provide significant economic gains for McLennan County. However, sponsoring a United States Army training ground was no simple feat. Just to bid on quartering a camp required several hundred acres of connected and undeveloped farmland or prairie. Other minimum requirements for a facility included maintaining the common municipal services of water, sewer, roads, trains, and electrical lines to conform with military regulations on the numerous wooden structures that housed officers, mess halls, activities, training locations, hospitals, and a headquarters. Luckily, local resources proved sufficient and in less than one month, Waco secured each basic element required for the training camp. Waco then won a national bid to construct a large army training camp to be named Camp MacArthur in honor of Arthur MacArthur (Douglas MacArthur's father).[1]

The acquisition of Camp MacArthur provided a substantial victory for the local economy, and when the federal government again took bids for U.S. Army air fields, Waco applied and won during the summer of 1917. The area encompassed 690 acres (fifty more than a square mile) including the southern portions of land originally designated for Camp MacArthur and other property from adjacent farms.[2] The government named the base Rich Field, in honor of an officer who died serving in the Philippines. Waco's approval for the Rich Field bid also demanded hefty criteria for government approval—namely, a completely level, large plain free of buildings, ditches, or trees and covered with Bermuda grass. To ensure the airfield's approval, the Waco Chamber of Commerce met during the summer of 1917 and compiled preliminary geographical statements and surveys on the physical conditions of the land designated for the airfield at Waco.[3]

Shortly after the news of Rich Field's approval, a telegram arrived in Waco instructing a city representative, with the power to sign city-lease agreements, to travel immediately to Washington, D.C., to secure a military lease. The telegram

further instructed the Chamber to bring private property owners affiliated with the land proposal and copies of all abstracts, deeds, and titles to Washington, verifying the availability of the land. The federal government required that either the Waco Chamber of Commerce or the City of Waco purchase a minimum of 300 acres for the airway and remove any remaining structures or lone trees on the land parcel.[4]

The two army bases, Rich Field and Camp MacArthur, eventually stood independently of each other with different commanders, lease agreements, and objectives, though both stood in close proximity to Waco and provided the city with large amounts of revenue. By the end of summer 1917, the war had arrived in Waco, and in grand style.

Growing Pains

Concluding statistics reported that the entire Camp MacArthur construction project cost the city of Waco an estimated $700,000 but required only twenty-five days for completion.[5] Other private utility extensions and property investments required estimated additional spending of $5,000,000.[6] A total of 1,284 structures stood in place upon Camp MacArthur's completion. The military established Camp MacArthur's maximum troop capacity at 45,074 with campsites covering 1,377 acres on the 10,699 acres of old farmland and prairie dedicated to combat training.[7] Camp MacArthur officially opened on July 30, 1917 (while still under final construction), but full training exercises did not begin until September 1917.[8] The local Waco newspapers reported on August 1, 1917, that "Troops for Waco camp may begin to arrive soon."[9]

Construction costs proved equally as expensive for Rich Field. The Cotton Belt Railway quickly added a rail line switch to service Rich Field from the main line near present-day New Road and Bosque Boulevard.[10] The city of Waco provided either gravel or paved roads, electric power lines, water mains, telegraph wires, telephone wires, and sewer lines adjacent to the boundary of the base. Other valuable assistance for Rich Field originated from the National Weather Bureau, which contributed immense amounts of environmental information on Waco's climate to the U.S. Army and provided probable weather predictions for flying conditions.[11]

The Jones Construction Company hired 3,500 laborers to build the Rich Field and Camp MacArthur facilities, one-third consisting of Mexican immigrant and migrant workers.[12] William Robert Poage, a future U.S. Congressman from Waco, claimed to be the first man to drive a surveyor's stake into the ground at Rich Field, earning $2.50 per day.[13] Over the next two years, Rich Field evolved into one of the most complete air units in the country.[14] Every aspect of army life looked good for Waco, Texas, but little did the citizens of Waco know that one of the greatest problems associated with Camp MacArthur was soon to occur—the Camp MacArthur Riot.

A year earlier, in May 1916, Waco's nationwide image suffered following the gruesome public lynching of Jesse Washington, a black juvenile male convicted of murder (discussed in Chapter

Camp MacArthur Base hospital and grounds, 1917. *Photograph by F. Mann, courtesy of the Turner Collection.*

4). The horrific spectacle of Washington's charred body remained in the nation's social memory for quite some time—even when the Waco Chamber of Commerce applied for the army camp and airfield in Washington, D.C. The federal government's superior concern largely centered on the U.S. Army's use of the 1st Battalion, 24th Infantry Regiment (an all-black regiment) for guarding camp locations during construction. James Penland, president of the Waco Chamber of Commerce in 1917, promised the federal government that as long as the black soldiers remained devoted to the principles of the uniform, Wacoans would receive the servicemen with a "patriotic spirit."[15]

On July 29, 1917, the *Waco Times-Herald* reported the late arrival of the 1st Battalion, 24th Infantry Regiment at the Katy Depot around midnight. The soldiers remained in the rail car until the following day because of an 11:00 p.m. curfew for all black troops stationed in Waco.[16] The city allowed soldiers to venture into the city, but requested each man return to the camp before the late hours of the night.

On the first full day on duty, several members of the 24th Infantry found themselves in trouble with the law. Early in the evening on July 29, a handful of off-duty troops ventured into town for some rest and relaxation. Once in Waco, the troops became openly hostile for unknown reasons, though race-related problems are speculated. The men forced their way into a bar on Franklin Avenue known as the Waco Club, where they demanded that the bar serve them drinks. The bartender refused the soldiers any service and the troops became unruly, venting their frustrations by, as the newspaper reported, "helping themselves to everything in sight."[17] Waco police soon arrived at the club to break up the soldiers' brawl by punching several of the soldiers and by drawing their police-issued side arms.[18] The soldiers left the club and relocated to another nearby venue. On the south side of Waco's downtown square, the soldiers entered a restaurant that served both whites and blacks. The group spotted a sign designating "For Whites" and became aggravated by the segregationist proclamation. One soldier grabbed the sign, ripped the message into several pieces,

and threw the remnants into the street. The restaurant owner notified the police, who responded immediately to the disturbance. The same police officers who broke up the fight on Franklin Avenue appeared once again and another scuffle followed. On this occasion, a police officer struck one of the soldiers with such might that the officer broke a bone in his finger. After sustaining the injury, the police officer decided instead to respond to the situation by bludgeoning the contentious troop on the head with a pistol.

The troops fled the building, ending up in front of a "negro moving picture show" on Bridge Street.[19] The newspaper later reported that onlookers notified the police of several black men blocking the sidewalk, harassing pedestrians, and inflicting minor injuries on bystanders.[20] Once again, the same police officers arrived, identified the soldiers as the previous aggressors, and proceeded to assault the soldiers. After this last scuffle, the soldiers retreated to Camp MacArthur, though not out of defeat, but to retrieve their rifles.

At 11:45 p.m., Capt. C.F. Andrews, the commanding officer of the 1st

The M.K.&T. (Katy) Depot, about 1915. *Photograph courtesy of the Turner Collection.*

Battalion at Camp MacArthur, ordered all of his men to wake, dress, and prepare for an unscheduled roll call. Each soldier stood present with his rifle as the commanding officer deduced the absent soldiers and accounted for each man's firearm. Andrews notified the Waco police of the situation and the police dispatched a vehicle to retrieve any military men who wished to assist in suppressing the renegade troops.[21]

Several troops assisted the Waco police, including Army Captain Higgins, another officer commanding the black regiment. The combined force patrolled the area intending to detain the rioting soldiers before they reached downtown Waco. The police, assisting soldiers, and Captain Higgins arrived on the outskirts of downtown and shortly thereafter located the armed gang in an alley near 2nd Street. When the soldiers spotted the assisting soldiers with the police, each group immediately opened fire, though it remains unclear who fired first. Participants exchanged an estimated forty to fifty rounds over the next few minutes; luckily, no injuries occurred. After several minutes of skirmishing between Higgins' men and the renegade soldiers, the renegades disbanded and vanished into the night with police only arresting one soldier Higgins captured. As morning approached, the renegade troops slowly meandered into Camp MacArthur one by one and were detained to await a trial by court-martial.[22]

On the morning of July 30, 1917, the Waco newspaper included an official statement from Captain Andrews, the commanding officer of the rebellious troops. In the statement, Andrews scorned the actions of the rioters, but reaffirmed to the people of Waco that "About 95 per cent [sic] of the members of this battalion are men who are proud of the uniform, and realize their position, and want to do the right thing."[23]

Andrews, Penland, and Guy McNamara (Waco's chief of police)

speculated that the public might be planning a lynch mob in response to the lawless actions of the black soldiers, but local citizens appeared to accept a military court-martial as sufficient punishment. After the incident, McNamara instructed the people of Waco to refrain from antagonizing the black soldiers and the public followed the request. In fact, a general apathy toward the entire incident permeated the Waco community shortly after it occurred, something in direct contradiction with the trial of Jesse Washington.[24] The apathy toward the renegade soldiers eased Penland, who feared the federal government might have retracted the bid for the camp had the Wacoans gruesomely lynched a soldier during construction.

On August 21, 1917, Camp MacArthur held its first court-martial and ruled six riot participants receive five years of hard labor with a dishonorable discharge. The accused leader of the group received ten years hard labor (later reduced to five) with a dishonorable discharge for contentious behavior.[25] On August 24, 1917, another battalion of the 24th Infantry provoked a similar riot in Houston, Texas, at

Camp Logan when more than 100 black troops rioted, resulting in seventeen deaths.[26] Tired of the violent fiascos, Texas Sen. Morris Sheppard requested all black troops be removed from Texas and Brig. Gen. James Parker agreed.[27] The 1st Battalion, 24th Infantry left Waco on August 25, five days after the total completion of Camp MacArthur on August 20, 1917.[28]

Penland also arranged for The Reservation, Waco's legalized red-light district, to close on August 11, 1917. The eviction of the prostitutes, Penland claimed, "safeguard[ed] the morals of soldiers and the physical well-being of the men in the Army."[29] The necessity of Camp MacArthur's and Rich Field's financial incentives provided local authorities with the ability to legislate morality—a popular concept during the Progressive era (discussed in Chapter 2).

Basic Training

In late August 1917, 18,000 volunteer troops arrived at the Katy Depot in Waco as part of the 32nd Division; draftees arrived throughout October 1917.[30] Other early trainees had been stationed at the Texas-Mexico border pursuing Pancho Villa and required modified training for modern European warfare.[31] With the first installment of troops, 6,000 soldiers arrived from Wisconsin, 5,600 from Minnesota, numerous from Michigan (exact numbers are not avail-able), and 2,006 from Texas over the span of several months. All units began basic training at Camp MacArthur by the end of September 1917. Several of the first soldiers to arrive at Camp MacArthur greeted other newcomers with a welcome bonfire at 10:30 p.m. on October 1, 1917, using some hay bales from an abandoned farm.[32]

Across town at Rich Field, the first planes arrived on November 14, 1917, and the U.S. Army credited Maj. Arnold K. Krogstad with the first offi-cial flight of the field. Records indicate

A Rich Field pilot, about 1917–1918. *Photograph courtesy of the Red Men Museum and Library.*

that the training expectations of Rich Field were unsurpassed by any other institution in the United States. Rich Field ranked in the top flying schools among the forty others across America, perhaps because Rich Field was also smaller than most other flying schools and housed fewer pilots.[33]

Before becoming an official pilot, soldiers attended flight school to earn their wings. Though a new program, many students found flight education an arduous task in 1917. At Rich Field, only forty cadets of one hundred graduated from flight school and received their wings after waiting several weeks (without pay) for their graduation notice. Before flying, each pilot first attended "Ground School" to learn cartography, signals, basic airplane repair, engineering, and weaponry. Phase two cadets trained on a plane known as a "Jenny." The Jenny was a relatively small plane with a four-cylinder engine capable of remaining in the air for about two and a half hours on twenty-one gallons of gasoline. The plane flew at a top speed of 75 miles per hour, weighed 1,430 pounds, cost $7,500, and required a combination of linen, canvas, and

A crowd gathers around this Jenny, which is likely stuck in the mud. *Photograph courtesy of the Red Men Museum and Library.*

piano string for flight.[34]

Rich Field never housed more than 1,000 soldiers during the war—a dramatic contrast to the tens of thousands at Camp MacArthur. The aviation program represented a new method of warfare that lacked the centuries of combined expertise associated with U.S. Army personnel at Camp MacArthur.

Flight cadets generally enjoyed the base's close proximity to the city of Waco. Rich Field was one mile from the city limits and three and a half miles from downtown and used an assort-

ment of gravel roads, street cars, and rail roads to make transportation easy. A total of eighty-one permanent structures stood on Rich Field and all soldiers (both enlisted men and officers) lived in wood-framed barracks equipped with clean water and electricity. Five steel buildings, four hangars, and a repair shop complemented an additional seventy-six wooden structures that provided other miscellaneous military services. The facility included almost 250,000 square feet in storage space comprised of warehouses, hangars,

The Rich Field YMCA. *Photograph courtesy of the Red Men Museum and Library.*

and unfinished housing. A nearby Hostess House, used for entertainment and social gatherings, and a YMCA, claiming to be the "best in the world," opened for the troops.[35]

Rich Field experienced an overall record of training excellence. During Rich Field's two years, mechanics assembled, tested, and commissioned a total of 982 planes, and built 550 engines varying between four, eight, and twelve cylinders.[36] The modern age produced new weapons previously

unfamiliar to many of the soldiers and Waco, Texas, was one of the few locations in the world to experience the development of these new tactical innovations.

Across town in North Waco, orders required all new recruits to dig the combat training trenches at Camp MacArthur, something the commanding officers considered good practice for combat life in France.[37] Most of the roads inside Camp MacArthur did not exist before summer 1917. Sometimes,

the commanders required the troops to build new roads and structures using the limestone acquired from digging trenches and nearby lumber. In fact, Camp MacArthur work crews used so many surplus limestone rocks from practice trenches and cleared timber that when the road later became 19th Street, the city had to lower the street three feet to pave it for civilian use.[38] Overall, city workers did not face difficulty returning the military base back to public use following the war. The army's high-quality work developing the camp proved a good investment for long-term commercial growth in North Waco.

Camp MacArthur developed a strong reputation for its diverse military schools. The grenade, gas, bayonet, and cooking schools gained favorable regard from many of the troops. On one graphic occasion, the bayonet school tied up a company's mascot, a live goat, and used it as a replacement for a training dummy. Instructors expected the act of butchery to create a zest for "blood on the bayonet," maintaining a sense of barbarism that encouraged troops to use "ughs, groans, growls, gritting teeth flashing from contorted florid faces and ending in a blood-curdling yell, mad as hell."[39]

Soldiers attending the gas school required passing marks before seeing battle. Some soldiers found the odd-looking gas masks surprisingly more comfortable than previously expected. Each mask contained pointed pinchers

A typical scene in Camp MacArthur. *Photograph courtesy of the Turner Collection.*

Camp MacArthur anxiously waits for a meal. *Photograph by F. Mann, courtesy of the Turner Collection.*

A basic street in Camp MacArthur. *Photograph by F. Mann, courtesy of the Turner Collection.*

A company street in Camp MacArthur. *Photograph by F. Mann, courtesy of the Turner Collection.*

that restricted nasal breathing, but troops usually did not find the pinchers unbearable. Instead, many soldiers believed that sharing masks represented the worst aspect of the gas school, especially when large amounts of sweat and mucus collected in each mask after frequent daily usage. Several buildings on the camp grounds housed gas demonstrations that caused blindness and/or uncontrolled vomiting when conducted improperly. While attending the gas exercises, troops remained in each poison-filled room for three full minutes. One soldier stated that he even felt sick walking through the room several minutes after the doors opened and the air cleared out.[40]

The officers school at Camp Mac-Arthur did not officially open until September 15, 1918, though the specialized school had operated before that time without official documentation. The Spanish Influenza outbreak delayed the third set of graduations until the

Tent city at Camp MacArthur. *Photograph courtesy of the Turner Collection.*

A few soldiers moving a building. *Photograph courtesy of the Red Men Museum and Library.*

weekend after the Armistice was signed. Once the Armistice was signed, the need for soldiers recessed and the government provided new officers the option to either remain in the military or return home.[41]

During the training processes provided by Camp MacArthur, both enlisted men and officers commonly lived in temporary structures known as Sibley tents—the complete opposite of the quartering arrangements at Rich Field. Sibley tents were comprised of canvas, wooden floors, stoves, cots, screen doors, and a two-foot tall wood skirt around the base.[42] As time passed, a sturdier, wooden infrastructure usually replaced the single pole in the middle of each tent when soldiers earned enough money to construct a stable permanent frame. Electricity became another soldier-installed bonus accessory inside an upgraded Sibley tent. The tents stood thirty-three to a row and spanned an impressive distance. Oscar Hessdoerfer, a Waco resident during World War I, stated: "It was very interesting to see how they lived."[43]

Historical accounts describe the Camp MacArthur parade ground as huge and multifunctional. Troops learned drills and formations during the day and engaged in various entertainment programs or played sports on the grounds during the evening.[44] The grounds formed a rectangle from present-day 19th Street to 27th Street, and from Park Lake Drive to Edna Avenue. It contained trenches, pillboxes, wire entanglements, basic battlefield patterns, and other features typical of a 1917 French battlefield.[45]

Though soldiers commonly found their quarters and training drills rugged, most Camp MacArthur mess halls contained service waiters who fetched food and drinks for soldiers who requested assistance by raising their hands.[46] On one occasion, German prisoners of war served Camp MacArthur's soldiers in the mess halls during a German POW tour of the area to increase patriotism.[47]

Camp Life

One of the primary reasons why Waco won the bid for a training camp originated from weather records that reported Waco possessed a semi-mild climate of favorable weather that allowed for year-round training exercises. Most of the soldiers agreed that Waco was a pleasant place to train and some officers described Waco as not typical of the "balmy South."[48] The governor of Wisconsin, however, protested his state's soldiers being sent to Waco because he feared the Texas climate would cause a malaria epidemic amongst the Wisconsin soldiers.[49] After some federal reassurance, the governor ended his protest. In fact, there were no great malaria epidemics at Camp MacArthur; the disease to be feared was the Spanish Influenza.

The Spanish Influenza outbreak of 1918 caused increasing absences in the daily rank and file at Camp MacArthur and within several weeks, officers noticed about half of the camp's soldiers absent during daily roll calls with most soldiers being either sick or dead. Disease became so widespread that camp command converted every fourth mess hall into a temporary hospital to compensate for the excessive patient overflow. Nurses placed soldiers on cots with each soldier's head and feet in opposite directions, sending the most critically ill to the general base hospital.[50] During an interview later in his life, R.H. Claypool remembered the graphic scene: "So many soldiers were dying in the base hospital until caskets were sometimes stacked like cordwood."[51]

Several hundred soldiers died at Camp MacArthur from the Spanish Influenza between summer 1917 and early 1919. The military held funeral processions with full honor guards saluting most of the deceased during the short trip between Camp MacArthur and the Katy Depot.[52] One of the first deaths on base created a problem when a soldier in the First Cavalry of Wisconsin died so unexpectedly and suddenly that the deceased did not receive the last rites of the church because a clergyman had not yet arrived at camp (cause of death is undetermined).[53]

The camp faced other problems from the environment between the fall of 1917 and the winter of 1918. On October 25, 1917, a hard sandstorm struck Waco, forcing many of the native Northern soldiers to experience the dusty, natural phenomenon for the first time.[54] Matters worsened three months later in January 1918 when one of the worst snowstorms in Waco's history occurred. One soldier noted the novelty

of "getting up in the morning and washing my face with nice clean snow which I picked up from the floor of my tent."[55] Soldiers found the frigid air difficult, though many of the trainees originated from cold climates. Though previously described by officials as semi-mild, Waco's occasional unstable weather

proved a certain unpredictable oddity during the training days.

On October 23, 1917, the national government officially began the second Liberty Bond Campaign. Troops received verbose speeches from "silver-tongued" Texas bankers over the following weeks, encouraging troops to

These 11,000 Camp MacArthur soldiers bought Fourth Liberty Loan Bonds.
Photograph by Fred Gildersleeve, courtesy of The Texas Collection, Baylor University, Waco, Texas.

The troops lining up for the famous picture on the preceding page. Soldiers can be seen looking up at the plane, originally speculated to have been superimposed in the image. *Photograph by John Davidson, courtesy of the Red Men Museum and Library.*

buy Liberty Bonds with their monthly government salaries.[56] Most of the young men enjoyed the long promotion speeches because the presentations provided valid excuses for refraining from long days drilling on the parade grounds.[57] Other times, the government requested the soldiers volunteer for the bond drive by participating in popular activities. On one occasion, eleven thousand soldiers posed for a photo designed to inspire local bond sales.

During its short tenure, Camp MacArthur brought some unique entertainment to the Waco community. Roger Conger, prominent local historian, politician, and businessman, remembered one night when an artillery crew discovered an abandoned house on base and decided to set the structure on fire. The soldiers then produced a dazzling display by using six-inch guns to extinguish the blaze destroying the house's framework the fire needed to burn. Conger remembered that the shelling did put out the fire (once the house was gone).[58]

Entertainment activities varied at Rich Field, but most cadets deemed the community swimming pool as the

Camp MacArthur soldiers also enjoyed music and occasionally performed publicly. *Photograph courtesy of the Red Men Museum and Library.*

greatest pride of the base, providing the perfect location to waste time during a hot Texas summer. Cadets reported the "boon [of a swimming pool] during the heated season" and that it was "in use day and night."[59] Donations raised by the Rich Field Vaudeville Company funded the majority of the pool. Lt. Ralph W. Barnes organized the vaudeville program to include the Rich Field Orchestra (150th Jazz Band), comical acrobats, magicians, ventriloquists, singers, jugglers, skits, and crayon drawings. The Vaudeville

Company performed all over Texas, ranging from surrounding communities to Corpus Christi and Dallas.[60]

Some of the MacArthur soldiers organized an official football team, playing Baylor University on occasion.[61] Organized Camp MacArthur sporting events commonly occurred on either the Camp MacArthur parade grounds or near the Cotton Palace.[62] Other troops passed the time swimming (some nude) in the nearby Brazos and Bosque Rivers on an old dairy farm beyond the rifle range.[63] Soldiers also retrieved wild pecans from the bottoms near the Brazos and Bosque Rivers. A few soldiers reported picking up hundreds of Waco pecans and mailing them home for only three cents.[64]

Around town, many Wacoans empathized with the loneliness many out-of-state soldiers felt in the alien Texas city.

Wacoans tried to prevent soldier loneliness by introducing special church services, Red Cross dances, welcome parties, and bon voyage parties for the young troops.[65] Baylor students entertained local troops with plays cast with only females once the military draft began in 1917.[66] Despite the abundant popular-

ity of Baylor's theatrical productions, the American Red Cross proved the most active support group in Waco by sponsoring constant social functions and meals. Other local American Red Cross volunteers joined in the war effort by making sandwiches and coffee for soldiers at the Katy Depot. On numerous occa-

Inside the American Red Cross Convalescent House, where many soldiers engaged in recreational activities. *Photograph by Fred Gildersleeve, courtesy of the Red Men Museum and Library.*

Camp MacArthur soldiers march in a parade down Austin Avenue. *Photograph courtesy of the Red Men Museum and Library.*

sions, hundreds of soldiers swarmed the Red Cross table seeking a free lunch. The Red Cross headquarters conducted other programs at Camp MacArthur boosting morale for the troops and providing locals with an opportunity to aid the war.[67] The U.S. Army commonly thanked the people of Waco by organizing parades and public demonstrations.[68]

The Waco community celebrated the annual cotton harvest by organizing a festival each year at the Cotton Palace Complex. In 1917, the Cotton Palace adopted a military theme to promote the two local military establishments. Traditionally, each year during the harvest celebration local elites elected a cotton king, queen, and court who escorted each other around the grounds during the event. But in 1917, Cotton Palace officials allowed military officers to escort female members of the Cotton Court around the grounds instead of their traditional "royal-cotton" escorts. The patriotic exhibition displayed a downed German fighter plane to raise Liberty Bond sales and engage the public's interest in the war effort.[69]

Many Rich Field cadets enjoyed mischief and entertained Wacoans with frequent aerial antics. Before Rich Field's construction, many locals had never seen an airplane before and the flight cadets commonly used this fact to their advantage. On one occasion, several pilots flew over the Cotton Palace Celebration and threw their adult-sized flight dummy (used for counter-balance) out of the plane. The act terrified onlookers who believed the dummy was a pilot falling hundreds of feet to a terrifying death; but, when the dummy hit the ground, most locals found the prank hilarious.[70] Another time, the pilots dropped hundreds of the special "Christmas 1918" edition of the *Rich Field Flyer* (Rich Field's base newspaper) over Waco to show gratitude to local citizens while also requesting donations to the American Red Cross.[71]

Waco experienced another festive event on Christmas 1917 at Camp MacArthur. A Milwaukee pastor named Gustave Stearns decided the camp should organize a large Christmas festival because it might be the last Christmas some men celebrated. Stearns and several troops ventured into the nearby woods to retrieve some decorative foliage and a tree on Christmas Eve. The group placed a tree in the bed of a mule-drawn wagon and returned to camp to decorate the stands with the fresh-cut greenery and tree.[72]

After the greenery harvest, Stearns decided to integrate some northern customs that Camp MacArthur soldiers conducted back home, particularly a popular mural of the Christian Nativity in downtown Milwaukee. The preacher created a makeshift replica on a billboard-sized backdrop using more than twenty different colors and added electricity to illuminate the painting. During the Christmas Eve celebration, the commanding general of Camp MacArthur delivered a "touching" sermon and the troops concluded the service by singing "Silent Night" (a German carol), and "Come Hither, Ye Faithful."[73] Later, Stearns gave his own sermon on Christmas Day.[74]

Throughout the war, downtown Waco boomed every night of the week with Camp MacArthur troops. Men in uniforms with pockets full of spending money filled coffee shops and night spots.[75] Estimates indicate that Camp MacArthur provided Waco's economy with about $2.5 million over eighteen months.[76] One soldier affiliated with payroll reported that he handled between $500 and $1,000 in daily cash exchanges.[77] The combined payroll at Camp MacArthur was about $70,000 every two weeks.[78] Oscar Hessdoerfer, a Waco resident during World War I, remembered that troops filled downtown buildings every night of the week because each soldier had a steady salary and there were few items to buy on base. Some Wacoans discovered a steady secondary income by taxiing soldiers between Camp MacArthur and downtown.[79] Taxiing was a good way to make money off the war, and seeing a civilian car full of soldiers was not uncommon.

A few local businesses attempted to gouge prices when shop owners discovered Camp MacArthur soldiers and Rich Field cadets would buy any item on store shelves at almost any price.

The Waco Chamber of Commerce

Christmas 1917 at Camp MacArthur. *Photograph by Fred Gildersleeve, courtesy of The Texas Collection, Baylor University, Waco, Texas.*

Washday at Camp MacArthur. *Photograph by F. Mann, courtesy of the Turner Collection.*

Advertisements targeting soldiers and patriots alike. *Courtesy of the* Waco Times-Herald, *October 12, 1917.*

intervened, however, and requested that local businesses charge fair prices. Surprisingly, the request worked at most stores in downtown; prices remained relatively low, largely because of the critical role the Chamber of Commerce had served in securing the army bases that provided the excessive revenues.[80]

The End and Effects of the Great War

During late October and early November 1918, news reports flooded local houses with information concerning a possible peace agreement between the Central and Allied Powers. As predicted, both sides agreed to a ceasefire effective on the eleventh hour of the eleventh day of the eleventh month in 1918. On the night of the determined Armistice, many of the Camp MacArthur officers marched to the coliseum on the Cotton Palace grounds to conduct a celebratory ceremony that onlookers remembered as a thing to behold. The soldiers arrived shortly before 11:00 p.m. (when the Armistice took effect) and spectators claimed that the midnight echoes of marching boots and blacked, shadowy silhouettes resembled a ghostly regiment of phantoms. Other locals filled the streets to launch fireworks and sing victory songs. Flags and banners filled the main area of the Cotton Palace and the soldiers placed their weapons on the ground and upright—symbolizing their victory. Mary Sendon described the event by saying, "It was something."[81]

The draft provided replacement troops as needed throughout the war and the last large wave of conscripted men arrived at Camp MacArthur in November 1918, just before the Armistice. Since the camp demobilized soon after the Armistice, many of the late draftees never began basic training.[82] Estimates conclude that more than 30,000 soldiers temporarily lived in Waco—doubling the indigenous population of 32,000.[83] The 32nd "Red Arrow" Division shipped out in January 1918 and, supposedly, was the only division from Waco to experience combat in Europe.[84]

On January 3, 1919, a federal mandate arrived in Waco ordering all the buildings of Camp MacArthur to be scrapped. Workers disassembled each building and relocated some structures to the Mexican border to act as border stations.[85] Local farmers purchased many smaller structures and modified the building fragments into hay sheds and lean-tos.[86] The camp officially closed on March 7, 1919, and the grounds became reintegrated into the city of Waco—Camp MacArthur lived less than two years.[87]

In February 1919, Rich Field Army Flight School also began the agonizing process of decommissioning its inventory. More than $1.5 million in government equipment remained on the grounds before closing with a majority of the 148 planes recording few, if any, hours in the air. Rich Field Army Flight School only suffered eight casualties during its entire training program—a remarkably low number for such new and dangerous technology.[88] Most of the Rich Field cadets taught at other flight schools after graduation. Few of the Rich Field trainees died in combat. The military recommended that other airmen check into possible medical and civilian

pilot licenses.[89] Remaining army pilots in Waco commonly transferred to Love Field in the Dallas-Fort Worth area. The U.S. Postal Service purchased many of the old Rich Field planes and used them for servicing distant mail routes.[90] Rich Field's greatest contribution to Waco's development originated from the establishment of the Waco Regional Airport that eventually moved from Rich Field to a location in the country near present-day China Spring.[91]

Perhaps the longest lasting local contribution from Camp MacArthur originated from something completely unaffiliated with the Army—a bear. In 1914, Baylor University lacked a mascot and for years students and faculty debated the best solution to the problem. Several popular mascot suggestions included: buffalo, antelope, frog, ferret, and bookworm. A group of soldiers from Camp MacArthur heard about the issue and decided the best mascot for Baylor would be a bear. As an incentive for agreement, the soldiers acquired a live bear (though it remains a mystery how the soldiers obtained a live bear) and presented Baylor University's administration with the animal. The MacArthur soldiers believed that Baylor should raise live bears on its campus in the future and, ever since that day, Baylor has kept and raised live bears on its campus.[92]

In 2009, finding physical evidence of Camp MacArthur and Rich Field is difficult for investigators. The land acquired by the city for Camp MacArthur and Rich Field later became multiple neighborhoods. The majority of the artillery range became Lake Waco and nearby public parks in the following decades. Rich Field became the new home for the Heart O' Texas Coliseum and Fair Grounds, while the west side of Rich Field's land serves as home to Waco High School, formerly Richfield High School.

A few remaining vestiges of the World War I Army bases include several locations in North Waco. In 1999, Dave Palacio, a fifty-six-year-old Waco resident, wanted to tear down a small building behind his house to build a carport but was reluctant to destroy the old shed. The shed was five feet by eight feet and had served as a bullet backstop on the old Camp MacArthur rifle range. Palacio's property rested on the edge of

the original Camp MacArthur property line in 1917. Few people showed interest in the old building at the time and most simply desired to run a metal detector over his yard (it remains unknown to this study if Palacio destroyed the structure).[93] In another area, a housing development in North Waco named Chimney Hill marks the location of the old Camp MacArthur Officers' Club. In 2009, the chimney is all that remains of

The Camp MacArthur Officers' Club chimney, 2009. *Photograph by Bradley T. Turner.*

the club, now serving as a centerpiece on a small backyard patio. Hikers and teenagers built fires in the chimney during the early 1980s and carved graffiti into the soft limestone rocks. These structures represent a few of the last known buildings of Camp MacArthur and Rich Field.

The Lions Club dedicated a hallway in its main building, The Lions Den, to Rich Field, calling it "Aviation Hall." Today, the hall is on public display, containing photos and brief discussions of Rich Field's history.[94] The Lions Den and Kiddieland, a small amusement park sponsored by the local Lions Club, sit on a corner of the old airfield.

In 2009, a few remnants of Camp MacArthur and Rich Field can be found when a seeker looks hard enough amidst the modern maze of houses, sewer lines, and paved streets. These ghosts from the First Great War still haunt a backyard on Chimney Hill, a hallway at the Lions Den, the Baylor bear pit, and the corner of North 19th Street and Park Lake Drive. Modern interest in Camp MacArthur and Rich Field generally wanes as most local public schools and colleges do not include

Inside Aviation Hall at the Lions Den, Waco, Texas. *Photograph by Bradley T. Turner.*

the history in any curriculum. Slowly, the story of Camp MacArthur and Rich Field is drifting into a forgotten past, though the lands of Camp MacArthur and Rich Field still act as the foundation for the present-day city of Waco. Waco High School, the Waco Fire Department, part of Lake Waco, part of Cameron Park, the Heart O' Texas Coliseum, the Lions Den, Paul Tyson Football Field, and hundreds of houses are located on the old grounds.

The next time you are at the Heart O' Texas Fair and Rodeo, playing miniature golf at Kiddieland, or simply driving through North Waco, take a moment and reflect on the stories of the thousands of men who used that location to prepare for battle—men who traveled to Europe to make the world safe for democracy, and men who validated Congress' declaration of war when the United States assisted its European allies by "sending in the second string."

ENDNOTES

1. "Modern Homes Cover Section where Thousands Trained for World War I," *Waco Tribune Herald*, 15 October, 1961.

2. *Rich Field Flyer*, The Texas Collection, Baylor University, Waco, TX, 50.

3. Ibid.

4. Ibid.

5. Garna L. Christian, "The Ordeal and the Prize: The 24th Infantry and Camp MacArthur," The Texas Collection, Baylor University, Waco, TX.

6. "Camp Legacy," *Waco Tribune-Herald*, May 29, 2006.

7. Handbook of Texas Online, s.v. "Camp MacArthur," http://www.tsha.utexas.edu/handbook/online/articles/CC/qcc27.html [accessed 20 October, 2006].

8. "Modern Homes Cover Section where Thousands Trained for World War I."

9. "Troops For Waco Camp May Begin To Arrive Soon," *Waco Times-Herald*, 1 August, 1917.

10. "Modern Homes Cover Section where Thousands Trained for World War I;" "Oral Memoirs of Lee Lockwood," The Texas Collection, Baylor University, Waco, TX, 543.

11. Ibid.

12. Ibid. 18, 50.

13. "Oral Memoirs of William Robert 'Bob' Poage," The Texas Collection, Baylor University, Waco, TX, 108–109.

14. *Rich Field Flyer*, 16–17.

15. Christian, "The Ordeal and the Prize."

16. "Guard for Camp MacArthur Arrives At Early Hour," *Waco Times-Herald*, 29 July, 1917; Christian, "The Ordeal and the Prize."

17. "Negro Soldiers Figured, Disturbance In The City Last Night," *Waco Times-Herald*, 30 July, 1917.

18. Ibid.

19. Ibid.

20. Ibid.

21. Ibid.

22. Ibid.

23. Ibid.

24. Ibid.

25. Christian, "The Ordeal and the Prize."

26. "Seventeen Dead in Rioting Negro Soldiers At Houston," *Waco Times-Herald*, 24 August, 1917.

27. Ibid.; "Senator Sheppard Asks War Department To Remove All Negro Troops From Texas," *Waco Times-Herald*, 24 August, 1917.

28. Christian, "The Ordeal and the Prize;" "Construction Work On Camp MacArthur Will Be Finally Complete On Time Tomorrow," *Waco Times-Herald*, 19 August, 1917.

29. "When Waco Went to War," *Waco Tribune-Herald*, 11 November, 1993.

30. "Modern Homes Cover Section where Thousands Trained for World War I."

31. "World War I Comes to Texas," *Waco Heritage & History*, 16, no. 3 (Summer 1986): 2.

32. Harold E. Woehl, "Memories of Service: World War I," Camp MacArthur

Vertical File, The Texas Collection, Baylor University, Waco, TX.

33. *Rich Field Flyer*, 16, 18.

34. "Waco Was a Military Center in World War I," *Waco Citizen*, 5 July, 1973.

35. *Rich Field Flyer*, 16.

36. Ibid., 16.

37. Ibid.

38. "Modern Homes Cover Section where thousands trained for World War I."

39. Woehl, "Memories of Service: World War I;" Patricia Ward Wallace, *Our Land Our Lives: A Pictorial History of McLennan County, Texas* (Waco, TX: Donning Co., 1986), 107.

40. "A Milwaukee Pastor looks at Waco," *Waco Heritage & History*, 16, no. 3. (Summer 1986): 29.

41. *Farewell Book: C.I.O.T.S. 1918, Camp MacArthur*, The Texas Collection, Baylor University, Waco, TX.

42. "When Waco Went to War."

43. Oscar Hessdoerfer, "The Oral Memoirs of Oscar Emil Hessdoerfer," The Texas Collection, Baylor University, Waco, TX, 39.

44. Woehl, "Memories of Service: World War I."

45. "Army's Camp MacArthur Boomed for Two Years," *Waco Tribune-Herald*, 26

October, 1975.

46. "When Waco Went to War."

47. Mary Sendon, "Oral Memoirs of Mary Kemendo Sendon," The Texas Collection, Baylor University, Waco, TX, 183.

48. *Farewell Book*.

49. "War Reminder-Little Remains of Short-Lived Troop Camp," *Waco Tribune-Herald*, 22 May, 1980;" "When Waco Went to War."

50. "When Waco Went to War."

51. Ibid.

52. "World War I Comes to Waco."

53. Woehl, "Memories of Service: World War I."

54. Ibid.

55. "A Milwaukee Pastor looks at Waco," 30.

56. Woehl, "Memories of Service: World War I."

57. Ibid.

58. "When Waco Went to War."

59. *Rich Field Flyer*, 18.

60. Ibid., 44.

61. Woehl, "Memories of Service: World War I."

62. Sendon, "Oral Memoirs," 201–202.

63. Woehl, "Memories of Service: World War I."

64. Ibid.

65. "World War I Comes to Texas."

66. "Oral Memoirs of Cornelia Marshall Smith," The Texas Collection, Baylor University, Waco, TX, 93.

67. "Oral Memoirs of Adrienne Wilkes Olenbush," The Texas Collection, Baylor University, Waco, TX, 131.

68. Woehl, "Memories of Service: World War I."

69. "Oral Memoirs of John Morris Hawes, Sr.," The Texas Collection, Baylor University, Waco, TX, 50-3.

70. Sendon, "Oral Memoirs," 282.

71. *Rich Field Flyer*, 24.

72. "A Milwaukee Pastor looks at Waco," 25–27.

73. Ibid.

74. Ibid.

75. "Modern Homes Cover Section where thousands trained for World War I."

76. Christian, "The Ordeal and the Prize."

77. "A Milwaukee Pastor looks at Waco," 24.

78. "Army's Camp MacArthur Boomed for Two Years."

79. Hessdoerfer, "The Oral Memoirs," 39.

80. Ibid.; "Waco's Newest Name, 'The Young Soldier's Home,'" *Waco Times Herald*, 30 April, 1919.

81. Sendon, "Oral Memoirs" 202.

82. "War Reminder-Little Remains of Short-Lived Troop Camp."

83. "Modern Homes Cover Section where thousands trained for World War I."

84. "Camp Legacy."

85. Ibid.

86. "When Waco Went to War."

87. "Camp Legacy."

88. *Rich Field Flyer*, 18.

89. Ibid., 44.

90. Ibid., 24.

91. "Modern Homes Cover Section where thousands trained for World War I."

92. "Freshmen discover Baylor's heritage in campus symbols," *Baylor Lariat*, 6 November, 1998.

93. "Man Wants to Shed Historic Shed," *Waco Tribune-Herald*, 22 November, 1999.

94. "Rich Field Foyer open to public," *Waco Tribune-Herald*, 1 February, 2001.

The Approaching Storm:
The 1942 World War II Home Front in Waco

by Bradley T. Turner

The Approaching Storm of War

*"We cannot whip the Germans
with a forty-hour work week.
The Nazis are five years ahead
of America on the production front.
If the Germans conquer America,
you juniors and seniors had just as well
cut your throats, for life will
have been ended for you!"*

—Guy B. Harrison, history professor at Baylor University, addressing the Junior-Senior Banquet audience at Crawford High School in Crawford, Texas, March 21, 1942.[1]

In 2010, at any of the Walmart stores in Waco, local shoppers venture through an organized maze of products promising immediate gratification to the consumer. Shelves upon shelves contain prepackaged foods as haphazard explorers elect and claim their finds. Each shopping cart slowly accumulates assorted combinations of food, commonly consisting of cuts of beef, spicy sausage links, vacuum-sealed Colombian coffee, and sweets containing several pounds of sugar. Meat, coffee, and sugar help create some of the most-noted edibles in

contemporary American culture, lining ribs daily with muscle and fat while concurrently filling patrons' veins with caffeine. Modern grocers supply local stores with the essential ingredients for home-cooked hamburgers, grilled hotlinks, Grandma's Christmas cake, and an instant cappuccino; each fulfilling culinary desires in a modern American repast. But, during an era when European fascism was strong and bombs unexpectedly fell from clear Pacific skies, the grocery store shelves did not always provide a plethora of ingredients for local shoppers. Instead, the shelves emptied to provide one of many means needed for delivering a global victory.

In 1940, Texas stood as a rural location focused on private agriculture, oil, and ranching. When the Second World War began, the country's demand for war materials and agricultural efficiency increased exponentially and created new pressures on Texas' economy and industry.[2] Some historians around the world regard Americans as complacent about the war since the continental United States never experienced desolate battlegrounds laden with human carnage and skeletal building structures. Perhaps some areas in the United States initially seemed tranquil; but McLennan County was not a sleepy, complacent environment during the Second World War—neither at the beginning of the battles nor the conclusion of the conflict.[3] Wacoans immedi-ately responded to the public call for unification by participating in an assortment of activities securing an American victory.

Wacoans fought the global war at home by donating essential items to scrap drives, buying war bonds, and participating in war rationing. Scrap drives collected unused varieties of common household items, especially rubber and metal. War bonds provided a temporary increase in federal revenue and served as a propaganda tool to sell (literally) the war to the American public. War rationing provided the greatest impact on local life when the federal government limited the consumption of various products by allotting predetermined portions to each citizen, guaranteeing a fair share of the basic commodities to all Americans.

Each domestic maneuver (drives, bonds, and rationing) shared the same objective—global victory. Shortly after the Americans joined the war in 1941, the Allies were losing on numerous fronts and little seemed to stall the advancing Axis powers. The Soviet Union, France, and Great Britain engaged Ger-

Walmart's plentiful grocery aisles, 2009. *Photograph by Bradley T. Turner.*

man and Italian armies several years before the U.S. joined the European crusade in December 1941, but neither Britain and France nor the Soviets had delivered a significant victory over their European fascist foes. Meanwhile, in the Pacific Ocean during the late 1930s, the Japanese organized multiple invasions of numerous countries and islands, attempting to create the Greater East Asia Co-Prosperity Sphere—a colonial synthesis of smaller nations and stolen territories under Japanese control. In 1941, the United States responded to Japanese aggression with economic and oil sanctions that limited Japan's ability to expand. Japan responded to the sanctions by attacking Pearl Harbor, which provided the U.S. with legitimate justifications for joining the global conflict. Following an official declaration of war from Congress, the government faced its next dilemma—preparing the U.S. Army for the largest war in history.

The global war introduced numerous challenges to the American economy and the government faced those trials by staging a variety of programs. American soldiers required pay, food, muni-

tions, clothing, and other basic supplies while serving in war, so the government countered these expenses with war bonds. War bonds paid soldiers' salaries and provided excess money for defense jobs like building bombs. Other federal policies limited the civilian clothing markets during the war, providing resources to meet excessive demands for uniforms, camouflage, parachutes, tents, and other provisions. Rationing domestic products guaranteed that Americans, both at home and in the field, received a fair supply of food. The American government monitored domestic production because an Allied victory required a steady control of market goods.

The fear of an unknown future gripped McLennan County on December 8, 1941, the day after the Japanese attack on Pearl Harbor. Local officials responded to the national turmoil by updating safety procedures to conform to new wartime civil defense requirements. Waco City Manager William C. Torrence instructed local citizens to prepare for a series of blackouts and air raid drills during the remainder of December 1941.[4] Just as before in 1917, a world war was coming to Waco—and

in grand style.

Initially, the legal justification for rationing resided in one vague clause in the Emergency Price Control Act of 1942 as part of the Second War Powers Act. The passage granted the President of the United States proper authority to ration any item the government classified as "scarce material" or any product whose shortage hindered the war effort.[5] Even though the legitimacy, power, and authority of the nation's rationing boards in 1941 only rested in one passage, December 1941 witnessed the organization of a federal rationing program for safeguarding public supplies and preventing a volatile economy. Programs began slowly in January 1942 and the federal government decided to implement additional restricting policies when needed or if product shortages inflated the market.[6]

Across Texas, factories called for new workers and technical education programs to quickly mobilize production forces and modify curriculum for war work. Public school attendance declined by several hundred students across McLennan County during the winter break between 1941 and 1942 when teenagers left school for service and war work. Baylor University answered the call for change and implemented new curriculums designed to assist the war effort and industrial productivity.[7] In other realms, some Americans believed the war represented a catalyst of new social and economic opportunities for women and racial minorities; but, in reality, the American government was not prepared to embrace immigrants, blacks, and women as the solution to the shortage of workers—that idea remained largely un-American at the start of the war.[8]

Modern research indicates that the federal government reviewed few plans for executing a rationing policy before 1941, and the early struggles of local rationing boards confirm the notion. The journey between no plan in December 1941 and a successful program in January 1943 proved no simple feat for society, especially in McLennan County. The tremendous size of the nationwide home front programs proved a harsh challenge for bureaucrats. Allocating compensation for local war workers presented the first large issue for federal rationing; but luck-

ily, patriots across the country agreed to conduct local rationing programs without pay.[9] At the conclusion of the war, each member of the various rationing boards only received a certificate of appreciation from the Office of Price Administration and the President of the United States for compensation.

Riding the Storm Out: Tires and Rubber

On the first day of 1942, Coke Stevenson, governor of Texas, issued a proclamation requiring district judges and county governments to nominate prominent citizens to serve on local tire rationing boards.[10] On January 2, 1942, local officials responded and established W.V. Dunnam of Waco as chairman, with Stanton Brown of Waco and John Gorham of Bosqueville as the official members of the McLennan County Tire Rationing Board.[11] Each of these men knew little of what they actually agreed to establish in McLennan County— pilot programs for implementing wartime federal authority.

Soon after the local Tire Rationing Board's creation, Wacoans discovered the complications associated with

acquiring a new tire. Purchasing a new tire required a special clearance voucher from the Tire Rationing Board. Following a self-examination and long application form, applicants visited the rationing board during scheduled hearings at the Liberty Building in downtown Waco to request a new tire before the board. Once authorized, the recipient purchased a new tire from an authorized dealer for exactly $14.75.[12] Several professions in McLennan County automatically qualified applicants for a new tire, specifically any activities associated with public services and healthcare (doctor for house calls, ambulance, police, fire truck, freight truck, or construction equipment).[13] Farmers received specialized treatment from local rationing boards. The board automatically authorized new tires on implements and trailers, but not for implement/trailer-pulling vehicles such as trucks. Federal law prohibited unauthorized use of implement/trailer tires on a car or truck, threatening to fine and remove the violator from future rationing considerations.[14]

Time passed and Wacoans discovered clever alternatives to new tires. The

Tire Rationing Board provided needy civilians with a retreaded tire when a new tire was not available. Introduced on February 19, 1942, and implemented during the first week of March, tire retreading fused new tread on bald tires providing old tires with an opportunity for longevity. A retreaded tire did not retain the same rugged durability as a new tire, but the government considered the substitute safe at slow speeds.[15]

As summer 1942 approached, policies on tire rationing slowly changed for applicants. Truck drivers, once immune to rationing, failed to receive a new tire if the truck experienced a blowout caused by excessive weight. All recipients of replacement tires, new tubes, or retreaded tires signed a receipt verifying their identity. Other problems resulted when the local tire market inflated and produced a sixteen percent cost increase on new tires, despite federal ceilings.[16] With the economic strain associated with rationing, sixteen percent does not appear to be as high as the unique war situation could have caused.

In several unexpected results, tire and gasoline rationing (gasoline rationing is discussed later in this chapter) forced the

This Firestone advertisement includes options for retreading and repairing old tires. *Courtesy of the* Waco News-Tribune*, October 1, 1942.*

cancelation of numerous public schools' and colleges' graduation ceremonies because of the new difficulties in long-range travel for families. Local schools canceled distant extracurricular activities because of limited tire availability for schools.[17] On other occasions, Wacoans left their cars parked downtown for longer periods to avoid driving, providing the city with record parking meter revenue during April 1942.[18]

In June 1942, the quest for conserving rubber expanded from tires to include all forms of rubber, and a massive search for scrap rubber became a large, nationwide campaign sponsored by President Franklin Roosevelt. McLennan

County began participating in the national scrap drive several days after the primary announcement. Local air raid wardens worked diligently in their neighborhoods venturing door-to-door to ask residents for rubber scraps.[19] One hundred trucks traveled across the county to collect random piles of community scrap rubber.[20] Local newspapers rallied around the topic and informed the public that no item was insignificant or too small for donation—even pencil erasers and shoe soles.[21] In a display of patriotism, one child donated her rubber toys and rubber shoe heels to the national scrap drive, commenting that the troops needed the rubber for fighting more than she did for playing.[22] The citizens of McLennan County ultimately contributed a total of 500,000 pounds in scrap rubber to the war effort and the federal government determined that nationwide response to the program proved a complete success, even though no government information circulated explaining the basic alchemy of converting pencil erasers into jeep tires.[23]

By the final quarter of 1942, new rationing laws placed both new and

county rationing boards.[24] The official prices of used tires varied from $1.50 for a bald tire to $11.15 for a slightly used tire.[25] Each local tire dealer was required to conduct an inventory of used tires by October 15, 1942, to give the local rationing board an itemized list of all available used tires in the county.[26] In the following weeks, the McLennan County Tire Rationing Board members publically asked local people either to sell or donate any remaining used tires to the county rationing board to prevent shortages, and local Wacoans responded by selling or donating 137 used tires to the board.[27]

The motivation of county residents to donate or sell their extra tires possibly originated from a combination of patriotism and an "honesty" form that tire applicants signed before receiving a new tire. On the form, each applicant reaffirmed that he or she did not hoard tires by possessing more than one spare tire per vehicle. By the end of 1942, the Tire Rationing Board punished convicted rationing abusers by denying violators new gas rationing cards.[28] By the end of September 1942, the Texas Legislation banned private tire transactions, establishing the Tire

Rationing Board as the only venue for buying and selling used tires.[29]

In another attempt to conserve rubber, the Texas Congress lowered the state-wide speed limit to a sluggish thirty-five miles per hour in October 1942 to prevent accelerated tire erosion.[30] Enforcing the new mandate during the following week, police arrested one Waco man for driving seventy miles per hour, fined him ten dollars, and prohibited him from acquiring a new tire and from obtaining a gas rationing card in 1943.[31] Local authorities did not tolerate violations of rationing laws.

Gasoline

Gasoline and oil, the lifeblood of war, became a gigantic industry in Texas during World War II. Oil provided one of Texas' primary exports and sixty-two new oil fields opened in 1942 designated specifically for military and aviation fuel.[32] Gasoline was a significant American commodity, and by mid-February 1942, gasoline shortages occurred across the nation. The federal government decided to ration gasoline and issued a federal mandate freezing oil and gasoline costs at March 1942

prices.[33]

Though the nation suffered from shortages, gasoline remained abundant in most Texas locations during 1942. Texas served as the primary American oil producer during the early twentieth century and Texas oil rigs produced more than enough gasoline for each Texan. Unfortunately, the federal government believed an abundance of gasoline encouraged more driving and provided civilians opportunities to increase tire erosion. Despite Texas' sufficient production levels, the federal government decided to issue gasoline rationing to keep tire usage low—not conserve gasoline.[34]

Nationwide gas rationing efforts began during mid-October 1942 and authorities established the McLennan County Gasoline Rationing Board to organize local efforts, naming W.E. Terrell chairman.[35] In preparation for gas rationing, community service workers modified the traffic lights' timing on Austin Avenue to follow a quicker sequence, providing cars an opportunity to avoid wasting gas by idling engines for long periods of time.[36] The new members of the McLennan County

Gasoline Rationing Board traveled to Fort Worth to learn the rules and regulations associated with gas rationing according to the Texas Office of Price Administration (OPA).[37] The OPA scheduled registration for gasoline rationing for November 12–14, 1942, and issued rationing cards at local schools by closing campuses and using teachers/educational staff for the distribution process, similar to sugar rationing (discussed later in this chapter).[38] Farmers instead registered for gasoline rations at the Waco Chamber of Commerce.[39] Each applicant (city resident or farmer) required a vehicle ownership certificate, tire serial numbers, and a completed application to receive a gas ration book.[40]

The Gasoline Rationing Board issued stamps and tokens that commonly represented between two and a half to five gallons of fuel. By controlling the number of stamps and tokens issued to citizens, the board controlled the gasoline each citizen purchased, though "crucial" war workers received slightly more gasoline allowances.[41] Gasoline rationing books, tokens, and cards contained numbered items representing predetermined portions of gasoline.[42]

The OPA divided the gas rationing books into categories based on the needs of the applicant and the relevance of the applicant's job to the war effort. Ration Book A contained thirty-two coupons, which approved drivers with gas for 240 miles per month and provided the most common program for non-war work applicants. Ration Book B contained sixteen coupons and provided drivers 320 miles per month. Next, Ration Book C contained ninety-six coupons and authorized civilians with more than 470 miles per month, with additional coupons available from the Gasoline Rationing Board upon the applicant's request. Ration Book D, designed for motorcycles, contained forty-eight coupons and allocated motorists with 240 miles per month. Ration Book T represented the greatest amount of gasoline availability. The OPA issued Ration Book T1 (ninety-six coupons) and T2 (384 coupons) to trucks, buses, taxis, hearses, and tractors.[43] Any tardy applicants (regardless of vocation) automatically received Ration Book A.[44]

After only a few weeks, many local Wacoans found dissatisfaction with the limitations of Ration Book A, which provided an average of four gallons of gasoline per car each week. Most McLennan County residents believed that they were entitled to more gasoline than four weekly gallons. Ration Book A provided an opportunity for civilians to request additional rations, and the McLennan County Gasoline Rationing Board expected 95 percent of all Ration Book A holders to file for an increase in gasoline amounts during the first few weeks.[45]

Other Texans joined Waco's gasoline crusade. Gov. Coke Stevenson protested gas rationing to the OPA, claiming that Texans did not need gas rationing.[46] U.S. Sen. W. Lee (Pappy) O'Daniel agreed, proclaiming that rationing gasoline in Texas was like "rationing sand in the Sahara."[47] Hoarders bought tremendous levels of gasoline the day before federal rationing took effect and local news reports included stories of people flooding local gasoline stations. On one occasion, news reporters saw a woman filling half-gallon mason jars (commonly used for preserving foods) with gasoline. The Waco newspapers responded to hoarding by reporting that any house containing an excess of five gallons of gasoline became a fire hazard and voided the protections of home insurance.[48] Gasoline continued to serve locals as a controversial commodity in McLennan County and throughout Texas. Texas held massive levels of fuel, and the rationing of gasoline remained a hot topic throughout the war.[49]

Law enforcement officers acted tough on gas rationing violators. Anyone caught buying gasoline without a stamp stood subject to jail time and a $10,000 fine.[50] People wishing to conserve their stamps commonly called on private transportation services, and taxis reported a forty percent increase in business despite increased waiting times.[51]

Baylor University felt the weight of the war when administrators changed the traditional Homecoming Parade to accommodate the war effort in 1942. Instead of an automobile, the Baylor homecoming queen rode in a horse-drawn carriage, and the parade floats could not use gasoline engines or rubber tires.[52] Baylor University President Pat Neff hoped the temporary change in the parade encouraged the public to embrace alternative solutions and war rationing.[53]

Gas rationing officially took effect in McLennan County on December 1, 1942, and many local residents responded by conducting Christmas shopping during late November.[54] Downtown Waco retailers reported no negative impacts from gas rationing during the Christmas season largely because the early November splurge in shopping filled expected sales quotas for 1942.[55]

War Bonds

War bonds and stamps proved two of the most effective weapons for war participation in 1942 McLennan County, achieving immense goals throughout the year. An average war stamp cost ten cents and physically appeared similar to a postage stamp in size and design. Purchasers filled small, postcard-sized books with war stamps and exchanged a completed book for a series-type war bond. The government distributed war bonds in three basic forms: Series E, Series F, and Series G. Each bond series provided differing options for repayment to the investor. A Series E war bond accrued 2.9 percent interest over a period of ten years. A Series F war bonds accrued 2.53 percent interest over a dozen years, pro-

viding a seventy-four dollar investment in 1942 with a $100 return in 1953. Series G war bonds grew at 2.5 percent interest for every year they were held over a dozen years. Walter Lacy, Jr., president of the Waco Banking Systems and member of the McLennan County Bond Board, advised financial clients that a Series G war bond provided the best investment for McLennan County residents in 1942.[56] Local Merrill Lynch investor Chester A. Johnston introduced a new investment plan for his McLennan County clients during the third week of January 1942, heavily emphasizing war bonds. Each financial consultant justified the change from peacetime strategies by saying that the government provided a stable and secure investment during the chaotic times of war.[57]

In January 1942, local grocers and retailers organized defense-stamp sales booths during all hours of operation, with special promotions on the weekends, when most county-wide shopping occurred.[58] The Bond Board established the 1942 McLennan County annual bond sales quota at an ambitious $5,722,500. After creating a salary deduction plan for large companies of ten

President Roosevelt's message. *Courtesy of the* Waco News-Tribune, *October 4, 1942.*

additional stamps in reserve in case of a rapid increase in sales; third, participating businesses placed signs proclaiming, "WE SELL STAMPS!" in a clear and visible location of the store or front window; fourth, the retailer sold both series-type bonds and less-expensive war stamps; and finally, the retailer encouraged sales by participating in national

An advertisement for the 10% Club. *Courtesy of the* Waco News-Tribune, *October 4, 1942.*

Local newspapers encouraged readers to purchase stamps and bonds from carriers. *Courtesy of the* Waco News-Tribune, *October 2, 1942.*

or more employees, the McLennan County Bond Board approached the management division at numerous local factories and retail stores, hoping to obtain a large increase in sales by providing locals with calculated bond purchases for convenience war investing.[59]

Retail businesses participating in bond sales completed a "stamp pledge" to ensure ethical sales in McLennan County. The pledge included five provisions: first, a retailer voluntarily sold stamps; second, the retailer always held

sales drives.[60]

National promotions used unique methods and themes for fund-raising designed to shock and awe observers. In February 1942, one campaign provided Waco with a large bomb replica to inspire bond sales. Lacy, chairman of the County Bond Board, wanted the bomb placed in the intersection of 6th Street and Austin Avenue, one of the busiest locations in Waco, to inspire local interest in the national bond drive. Lacy formally requested permission for the publicity maneuver, but Waco police denied the request believing the bomb increased the probability of an automobile accident.[61] National campaigns ensured that bond sales remained high during the first quarter of 1942, but bond revenues slumped between March and April because of federal income taxes.[62] Between taxes and bond sales, if a man, woman, or child owned a dime, the government wanted that money exchanged for a war stamp.

War bond sales quotas and goals across Central Texas encouraged a continuous boom in the area. Local Waco club members selling bonds adopted slogans to rally interest. Two memorable slogans include: "Plant Your Dimes And Grow Defense Stamps!" and "Give Generously For Gallant People!"[63] The local Bond Board established a new monthly quota during the spring of 1942 that varied between

$250,000 and $500,000. The bond drives generally lulled mid-month, but bond sellers usually reached their goals at the end of each month when potential purchasers commonly received their paychecks.[64] On Mother's Day 1942, local war officials encouraged children to purchase their mothers a "War Stamp Bouquet" that would grow over the next decade instead of dying the following week like a traditional bouquet.[65]

Wacoans continued to aid the war effort with money, food, scrap materials, and gasoline. During October 1942, the McLennan County war effort established the Community War Chest to provide a unified organization of wartime funds and donations that met both local and global needs.[66] Initially, many locals viewed the new program as just another war machine for generating revenue, but this drive provided each donor with the opportunity to tell the Community War Chest which organizations merited patriotic donations— the Community War Chest became an entity that served as a one-stop shop for local war donations.[67] This project emerged a complete success by the first week of November 1942, collecting more

than $120,000 and achieving its county-wide goal early in December 1942.[68] Bond sellers encouraged employers to use war bonds in lieu of a Christmas bonus in 1942, and the local Bond Board recommended civilians give each other bonds as gifts.[69]

Sugar

When asked today about life in the war, those who lived in McLennan County during 1942 almost always begin by discussing their memories about sugar rationing. Sugar represents one of the most-remembered ration items because of its numerous impacts on fond dessert delicacies. In a coupon system, similar to the gasoline rationing system, the federal government issued postcard-sized books filled with numbered stamps (similar to a non-self-adhesive postage stamp) and each stamp represented a specific portion of a rationed item. For example, Stamp 7 in War Ration Book One might allow a stamp holder the opportunity to purchase two pounds of sugar between month A and month B. This system provided a fair distribution system among rich and poor, black and white. When the book ran low on stamps, the government issued a new book (War Ration Book Two) filled with more stamps and the entire process repeated. War Ration Book One contained twenty-eight stamps and lasted about six months between 1942 and early 1943. Each person (man, woman, or child) qualified for one book of stamps, with parents/guardians registering for dependents. Officials organized the ration books so applicants received a book for each person living at their address.

The government called on volunteers to distribute war rationing books and used local public schools and teachers to distribute War Ration Book One, providing children holidays over March 18–21, 1942, to prevent teacher scheduling conflicts. Officials projected issuing more than 140,000 rationing books in McLennan County alone.[70] Before registration, teachers took an oath, similar to county rationing board members, promising honesty and integrity while issuing ration books.[71] The government required applicants to state the amount of sugar in their possession during the application for War Ration Book One

and the government temporarily refused to issue a ration book to individuals who confessed hoarding large supplies of sugar. The inability to receive War Ration Book One cost each applicant about one pound of sugar per week.[72] Sugar rationing did not take effect until May 1942, after being nationally postponed because of insufficient books and decreased sugar supplies from excessive hoarding.[73] Jackie Lavender, a student in 1942, remembered one woman who never ran out of sugar during the entire war. Lavender recalled, "It was as if she had a hundred-pound bag of sugar hanging in her attic."[74]

The remainder of McLennan County residents who either had excessive sugar in March 1942 or did not obtain a book because of printing shortages received War Ration Book One during an event known as "R-Day," scheduled May 4–7, 1942. The Waco Chamber of Commerce used the delay between March and May 1942 to request the federal government provide an increase in sugar levels to mimic consumption rates of 1941, but federal officials rejected the proposal.[75] The newspaper encouraged locals with excessive supplies either to

bake a cake or give the surplus sugar to a neighbor.[76]

Local authorities estimated that several thousand McLennan County residents failed to register for War Ration Book One during spring 1942.[77] Those applicants who did not receive ration books on R-Day obtained War Ration Book One from the county rationing board (in a method similar to obtaining a tire voucher). Each late applicant required "a valid excuse" for non-participation in R-Day.[78] The government initially provided each citizen eight ounces of sugar per week on a trial basis, while some other locals qualified for an extra five pounds of sugar for canning fruits and vegetables for winter.[79]

Throughout the war, the *Waco Times-Herald* reported numerous occasions when people violated rationing laws. Ration books represented an important factor in daily war life that required special attention and responsibility. Luther L. Lavender, an employee at a local grocery store during the war, remembered one instance when a customer left a ration book at the store and some employees snatched up the active sugar stamps for that month to purchase some cakes and sweets for an afternoon snack. This instance might sound unique, but questionable instances involving rationed items became more commonplace as the war continued.[80]

Throughout the war, sugar remained a valuable item that required strict regulation. During the final month of 1942, War Ration Book One Stamp 10 allowed civilians three pounds of sugar between December 16, 1942, and January 31, 1943.[81] Industrial sugar users such as bakeries and bottling plants acquired clearance for sugar increases in McLennan County near Christmas time. The temporary increase in sugar guaranteed local industries experienced profits until February 1943.[82]

War Work and Housing

In McLennan County, a noticeable change occurred when the federal government began construction in 1942 on the Bluebonnet Ordnance Plant (BOP) to build bombs in McGregor, Texas. Almost overnight, McGregor began booming, with hundreds of people applying for defense jobs to fill an estimated 8,000 vacancies.[83] In most cases, the federal government encouraged plant managers to hire non-traditional employees to remove the labor strains created by the vacated enlisted men.

Initially, some women did not know how to interpret the idea of working full-time for a defense company.[84] Prevailing social norms in 1942 frowned on full-time women workers outside of nursing, teaching, and secretarial positions and many people in McLennan County appeared reluctant to challenge traditional feminine roles, despite the drastic labor shortages. The hesitancy proved short-lived and local women joined thousands of other non-traditional American workers in defense plants when the high wages offered by government contracts proved too tempting.

Before hiring women, the government required each facility to install separately designated bathrooms. Second, employers had to provide women with specially designed industrial clothing that adjusted to basic male/female anatomical differences. Third, employers installed new machinery that eliminated heavy lifting and prevented injuries. Last, the government required more complex hygienic measures to prevent women from contracting lead poisoning, which could harm their ability to reproduce.[85] In other adjustments, BOP required special clothes for both men and women to protect them from the harsh chemicals used in developing explosives. To compensate for the needed special attire, each worker at BOP received additional rationing privileges for clothes and shoes.[86]

The Great Depression hurt Waco's economy, and pre-war wages never

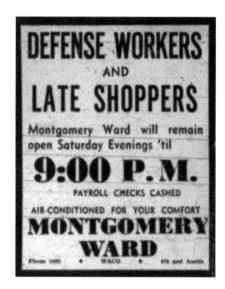

Businesses offered special hours to cater to new demands for goods.
Courtesy of the Waco News-Tribune, *October 2, 1942.*

returned to the high averages of the prosperous 1920s. BOP provided wages and benefits to most white females—wages many women had previously never experienced. Dixie Dick Pringle worked for BOP during the war, but moved to Waco after the war when postwar work and salaries returned to the low wages experienced in McLennan County before the war.[87]

The Owens-Illinois Glass Company arrived in Waco about 1942 and proclaimed itself the largest factory of its kind in the entire world.[88] Owens-Illinois proved extremely profitable during the war and specialized in creating glass containers used to seal and transport a variety of military goods. Glass production became a lucrative business during the year and even the head basketball coach for Baylor University resigned his coaching position to become a manager for the Owens-Illinois Glass Company.[89]

Despite the great industrial developments occurring in McLennan County, housing proved an irritating problem for many new workers. The federal government responded to the shortage by providing funds and supplies to erect housing structures in McLennan County for defense-worker families.[90] Local programs provided funding to transform old homes into duplexes in cooperation with the reconditioning part of the War Housing Program.[91]

Scrap Metal

Waco officials and volunteers sponsored a scrap metal drive throughout McLennan County during early May that proved one of the most popular salvage drives of the year.[92] The salvaging event began when the McLennan County Defense Council discussed the concept of collecting scrap iron from local neighborhoods. Once the scrap drive was approved, Judge Douthit Y. McDaniel appointed a county salvage committee to centralize local scrap iron collections.[93] Locals welcomed the effort and two days after the creation of the salvage committee, volunteers collected 10,000 pounds of scrap metal throughout McLennan County.[94] The Waco newspapers proclaimed, "Backyards and Cow Pastures of Central Texas will Feed Hungry Munitions Factories."[95]

The scrap metal collections gained momentum and many local organizations joined the scrap metal drive by the middle of June 1942. The Waco Chamber of Commerce located sponsors for assisting in scrap metal drives and the Working Boys Club organized a scrap drive in East Waco.[96] Officials deposited most of the acquired scrap metal on a vacant lot at the corner of 6th Street and Mary Avenue during the summer of 1942.[97] The American Legion scrapped its flagpole as a token of patriotism and other local clubs sponsored a variety of differing themes for a scrap drive.[98] The Jaycees sponsored a public dance during mid-October 1942 that required one dozen tin cans for admittance.[99] The Waco Lion's Club ransomed its club bell by setting a goal and promising to toss the bell into the scrap pile if the goal fell short.[100] Luckily, in October 1942, the Lions Club exceeded its required ransom and acquired about twenty tons of scrap metal.[101]

During September 1942, most county scrap trucks averaged collecting between one and two tons of metal each day. Local school children continually roamed the community looking for scrap metal for the war effort. Throughout 1942, children proved such effective scrap metal sleuths that the state of

Scrap drives targeted school children for assistance by using a variety of methods. *Courtesy of the* Waco News-Tribune*, October 2, 1942.*

Texas designated October as an official month to bring scrap metal to school.[102] Other programs challenged children to find their weight in scrap iron for the school drive, and children received an early dismissal on October 12, 1942, to locate scrap.[103]

During October 1942 the *Waco News-Tribune* encouraged parents to "bring in scrap so your boy can have weapons for battle."[104] A chart in the newspaper informed locals that one pressing iron (for ironing clothes) allegedly equaled three hand grenades, an ice box equaled twelve Thompson sub-machine guns, a water pail equaled three bayonets, a trash can equaled two M1 rifles, and a stove or electric range equaled ten artillery shells.[105] Nationally, scrap metal drives represented the beginning of a new campaign to keep the American home front united by supporting the war in every realm of domestic life.

Scrap iron collections in Waco reached their peak for 1942 during the final quarter of the year with the culmination of several unique strategies for scrap campaigns. Vacant lots opened around town, each requesting a specific type of metal—tin, iron, steel, aluminum, etc. The Jaycees lot collected tin while the Lions Club lot on Austin Avenue collected non-specified scrap metal. The Lions Club tried to collect more than one million pounds of scrap metal, but struggled to fill the lot during the remainder of the 1942 because previous collections had already obtained a large portion of existing scrap metal.[106] Meanwhile, Army trucks helped gather scrap iron from local, country, and suburban neighborhoods by canvassing each small community during October 1942.[107]

In one of the most public endeavors to acquire scrap metal during the war, the city of Waco removed abandoned steel rails from the streets and trestles around town that had supported a trolley car several decades earlier.[108] City workers removed a massive 260 tons of old rails by October 18, 1942.[109] In 2009, the only remaining vestige of the trolley rails can be seen at 28th Street and Maple Avenue.

Public advertisements used emotional slogans to encourage continual donations of scrap metal. Some examples of the emotional advertisements included: "Your scrap will save some brave boy's life!" and "Mountains of Scrap will Save Thousands of Lives!" as well as the pointed slogan, "Whose Boy Will Die Because You Failed?"[110]

Across the country, scrap metal salvage totals broke all-time records

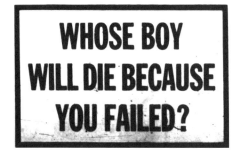

Typical Waco wartime propaganda. *Courtesy of the* Waco News-Tribune*, October 5, 1942.*

and provided smelting plants with plenty of raw material.[111] Local officials transported twenty-three tons of tin cans to the scrap metal collection center in Dallas during 1942. Even though the donations were high, Waco City Manager W.C. Torrence speculated Waco contributed only half of all its available tin cans to the scrap piles.[112]

A Few Unique Items

The federal government required all retail and grocery stores to remove varying items from the store shelves throughout early 1942 to coordinate with military needs. In January, the government instigated a program to salvage wasted paper and encourage product recycling. Other miscellaneous products such as burlap bags (imported from India), nylon hosiery, flashlights, washing machines, jukeboxes, typewriters, vacuum cleaners, pinball machines, and radios became difficult, if not impossible, for a civilian to obtain during the war. The OPA never established a local rationing board to control product distribution for these items because most manufacturers temporarily ceased assembling domestic goods and modified production lines to generate war

The war truly affected everything.
Courtesy of the Waco News-Tribune, *October 1, 1942.*

items.[113]

By summer 1942, some unexpected national mandates arrived in McLennan County. Any buyer purchasing a new tube of toothpaste or can of shaving cream needed to exchange an old tube of toothpaste or empty can of shaving cream at the checkout counter before making the purchase.[114] Golf clubs, sewing machines, electric ranges, and even

baseballs fell under short supply. As the year concluded, lingerie represented the most obscure item regulated by the OPA, allowing the attire to maintain all basic functions but not include any "unnecessary frills."[115]

Coffee Rationing

For most of 1942, grocery stores held plentiful supplies of coffee; then a series of national shortages during the final months created a panic. The OPA decided to counter the shortages by implementing a rationing policy in December 1942.[116] New regulations dictated that sugar rationing boards become responsible for coffee rationing as well, guaranteeing fair shares of coffee for local people.[117] Coffee production levels remained high throughout the Americas (North, Central, and South) in 1942, but limited shipping options caused coffee exports from Colombia to reach the U.S. at slower paces. The OPA speculated that a need for strict coffee rationing should abate once federal officials determined an alternative means for importing coffee.[118]

The third week of November was the last week civilians purchased unrationed portions of coffee.[119] Rationing took effect during the first week of December 1942 and the price for coffee in 1943 froze at the December 1942 rate.[120] Coffee rationing programs used stamps issued from War Ration Book One and local grocers handled all coffee transactions with the same precautions and rules used in distributing sugar. The OPA prohibited coffee sales to hoarders and people with surplus coffee supplies.[121] In War Ration Book One, Stamp 27 guaranteed one pound of coffee for each registered citizen before January 4, 1943.[122] Once coffee disappeared from the local shelves, tea and cocoa emerged as the replacements for most coffee drinkers in McLennan County.[123]

Farm Life

Across the country, farmers experienced tremendous problems when they lost the ability to obtain tires, implements, and good labor freely. Local agricultural advisors recommended pooling neighboring farm implements together to provide local farmers with some form of support.[124] Of all the difficulties, acquiring young farm labor represented the biggest hurdle in McLennan County during 1942. Other rural areas also experienced labor shortages and the federal government responded by providing draft deferments to any worker whose skill increased local agricultural production levels. Texas farmworker populations remained low, however, despite the draft deferment.[125] In an attempt to figure out why workers preferred war over farm life, the state government conducted a survey and discovered that a combination of money, anxiety, and extreme boredom were the primary reasons young men and women left the family farm.[126]

Livestock provided another large government interest in agriculture. Federal officials urged farmers and ranchers to breed every available sow and cow to provide sufficient meat during the approaching months.[127] During late 1942, Texas' hog production quota grew to 2,672,694 and Chicago markets reported record-high prices on pork. Fearing overproduction and inflation, the federal government imposed a ceiling on pork at early 1942 rates.[128]

In late 1942, meat rationing emerged as a controversial subject when popular meats, such as pork and beef, became limited because of the government's necessity to feed soldiers. Families who owned hogs and cattle held more options for acquiring meat since they could slaughter an animal when the family needed food. Nell Lavender lived on a farm in 1942 and still remembers that farmers typically butchered a pig on the first frigid day of the fall season.[129] During and before the war, farmers commonly butchered a pig during the fall and dried or smoked the meat to provide multiple people with a steady meat supply during the unstable winter season. Communal livestock slaughters commonly occurred between neighboring families.[130] A standard slaughter included a pig or cow, which fed a small family of four or five for almost six months. Once the family completely consumed the meat, the farmer either slaughtered another large livestock animal, or the family lived on chickens and vegetables, depending on the season.[131]

Meat Rationing

During the first week of September 1942, the federal government announced that meat rationing would take effect sometime between January and February 1943 and would follow the pattern of the coupon system.[132] The federal government braced for the new policy by implementing a price ceiling on beef that would not exceed regional market prices for October 1942.[133] In mid-November, the government approved each American for meat rations of two and a half pounds per person, per session.[134] The federal government only rationed select cuts of beef, however, and allowed all Americans unlimited access to the liver, heart, kidneys, sweetbreads, brains, and pigs feet.[135]

During early October 1942, McLennan County also experienced a shortage of pork products, though the OPA announced that nationwide meat production broke all previous records during the year.[136] Other cities around the nation experienced similar problems in obtaining meat and the OPA requested a twenty percent cut in all domestic meat deliveries to even the supply lines.[137]

Texas lawmakers claimed hunting and fishing as important methods for assisting in the emergency meat shortage.[138] Gov. Coke Stevenson prepared for meat rationing by shooting a deer on the first day of the season.[139]

Meat remained a difficult item to find

in stores during November 1942 and the Waco meat shortage grew more severe.[140] County commissioners responded to the problem by suspending beef meals at the county jail until further notice.[141] By mid-December, even Christmas turkeys (a non-rationed meat) became expensive and scarce in Waco.[142] The OPA warned Americans at the end of 1942 to expect further decreases in meat production during January 1943. Clearly, McLennan County residents faced another troublesome year in 1943.

Once meat rationing began in the United States, civilians sought other tasty sources for meals. Poultry and fish provided popular alternatives to traditional red meats and local businesses profited by selling alternative meats in lieu of the standard beef and pork.[143] Substitutions of lamb, goat, chicken, fish, turkey, rabbit, and even horse appeared on the menus of several local restaurants, though most Wacoans had trouble adjusting to the new selections and preferred to do without beef or pork. Wallace Lavender, a local school student in 1942, remembered one occasion when a rumor circulated that a local meat processing plant in downtown Waco once

served horse meat in place of beef. Lavender elaborated and said that the secret substitution temporarily ruined sales for the company and angered several local customers who mistakenly consumed the horse meat.[144] Local meat rationing stirred mixed responses but did provide locals with the opportunity to develop new recipes for unrationed poultry and fish. By 1944, local markets responded to the meat rationing program by joining with national campaigns that prohibited meat sales on Tuesdays and Fridays, inspiring the terms: "Meatless Tuesdays" and "Meatless Fridays."[145]

Holding On

One year after Pearl Harbor, the national debt reached a staggering $100 billion and the total American dead numbered nearly 60,000; but the American people remained more unified than ever in history.[146] The federal government openly stated that industry fell short of 1942 wartime goals, and the government decided to increase the number of soldiers and defense workers to sixty-five million by the end of 1943.[147] The numbers were astounding, considering that the economy already

A military recruitment form. *Courtesy of the* Waco News-Tribune, *October 4, 1942.*

stood dangerously close to runaway inflation and suffered from chronic labor shortages.

In one of the most unique aspects of the war, local newspapers reported daily updates about Santa Claus' Christmas workshop and the dilemmas of making toys during the war. In early November 1942, the *Waco News-Tribune* informed children St. Nicholas was substituting tin and metal toys with wood, because Santa knew the war required any extra metals.[148] A week later another update informed children that Santa also found difficulty in obtaining sugar candy and chocolate during the war, and that he would provide other types of sweets in lieu of traditional candy.[149] As December 1942 concluded, the situation intensified when Santa Claus reported placing war stamps and war bonds at the top of his gift lists—the clear choice for any pre-adolescent on Christmas morning.[150]

No matter the location (even the North Pole), the war clenched a fierce stranglehold on each American during 1942.

Over the duration of one year, Waco witnessed the successful acceptance, development, and implementation of numerous federally mandated rationing programs regulated by local leaders. The home front kept local people involved in the war effort through scrapping toys, smelting electric ranges, and modifying cookie recipes. The war encompassed every aspect of American life; like the great leviathan, it consumed all items, big and small, foolish enough to encounter the beast.

The Storm

Gruesome hurricanes devastate American coastlines several times a year, tossing aside the many toils of man as they smash into the continent. Before each torrential ocean storm, beach dwellers remaining at home prepare for the threatening event by hoarding food, fuel, and freshwater in the case of an emergency; during times of desperation, even the smallest item can suddenly become worth its weight in gold. Grocery store shelves empty all along the shoreline as people hurriedly grab items they believe will grant a chance at survival both during the storm and throughout the grueling recovery process.

In Waco, a similar sociological phenomenon occurs once or twice a year when local news stations report the strong likelihood of severe snow and ice with several days of sub-freezing temperatures. Many panic about the advancing storm, worried their houses will fall void of electricity and supplies will run out when the reported Arctic apocalypse strikes the heart of Texas.

Storm hysteria and war rationing hysteria share many things in common: panic, hoarding, and chaotic uncertainty. The short duration of a hurricane or an ice storm and the extended length of World War II represent the greatest contrast between the hoarding examples. Even the largest storm will pass in a matter of days, whereas a global conflict commonly requires years before dissipation. Regardless of the season or the type of storm, closely watch the horizon as there is no way to know absolutely when something troublesome may fall from the sky and announce the abrupt arrival of an approaching storm.

ENDNOTES

1. "Juniors, Seniors Hold Banquet at Crawford School," *Waco Sunday Tribune-Herald*, 22 March, 1942.

2. Clay Reynolds, "Gearing Up for Total War," in *1941: Texas Goes to War*, eds. Carolyn N. Barnes, Kent A. Bowman, Laura Crow, and James Ward Lee (Denton, TX: University of North Texas Press, 1991), 23.

3. Michael C.C. Adams, *The Best War Ever: America and World War II* (Baltimore: Johns Hopkins University Press, 1994), 73.

4. Patricia Ward Wallace, *Waco: A Sesquicentennial History* (Virginia Beach, VA: The Donning Company, 1999), 111.

5. Ibid., 150, 245.

6. Seymour E. Harris, *The Economics of American Defense* (New York: W.W. Norton & Co., Inc., 1941), 155.

7. Kevin Brady, "Baylor at War" (M.A. thesis, Baylor University, 2002), 48.

8. Robert C. Weaver, "Defense Industries and the Negro," *The Annals*, 223 (September 1942): 61; Alice Kessler-Harris, *Out to Work: A History of Wage-Earning Women in the United States* (New York: Oxford University Press, 1982), 225.

9. Harvey C. Mansfield, *A Short History of the O.P.A.* (Washington, D.C.: Government Printing Office, 1947), 143.

10. "McLennan to Get 219 Passenger Car Tires in January," *Waco News-Tribune*, 2 January, 1942.

11. "McLennan's Tire Rationing Board Named by Mayors," *Waco News-Tribune*, 2 January, 1942.

12. "How to Get a New Tire—if You are Eligible—Told by Board, Ready for Work," *Waco News-Tribune*, 9 January, 1942.

13. "McLennan's Tire Board gets First Data on Rations," *Waco News-Tribune*, 7 January, 1942.

14. "Farmers to Get Tires," *Waco News-Tribune*, 22 January, 1942; "Farmers Can't Get Tires for Autos, Local Board Told," *Waco News-Tribune*, 3 February, 1942.

15. "Retread Ration Opens this Week," *Waco Sunday Tribune-Herald*, 1 March, 1942; "Retread Rationing to Start Feb. 19," *Waco News-Tribune*, 12 February, 1942.

16. "No Tires Will Be Given to Overloaded Trucks in County," *Waco News-Tribune*, 29 April, 1942; "16% Hike in Retail Prices on New Tires Set," *Waco*

17. "War to Postpone Mass Graduation of County Units," *Waco Sunday Tribune-Herald*, 10 May, 1942; "Restrictions on School Bus Tires," *Waco Sunday Tribune-Herald*, 10 May, 1942.

18. "Waco Parking Meters Take in More Cash in Spite of Rationing," *Waco Sunday Tribune-Herald*, 3 May, 1942.

19. "Instructions for Rubber Salvaging Sent to McDaniel," *Waco Sunday Tribune-Herald*, 14 June, 1942; "100 Trucks Asked to Help Collect Rubber Thursday," *Waco News-Tribune*, 16 June, 1942.

20. "100 Trucks Asked to Help Collect Rubber Thursday."

21. "Whirlwind Scrap Rubber and Iron Collection Today," *Waco News-Tribune*, 18 June, 1942.

22. "Waco Tot Gives up Rubber Toys and Shoe Heels," *Waco News-Tribune*, 18 June, 1942.

23. "Wacoans Build Huge Scrap Pile," *Waco News-Tribune*, 19 June, 1942.

24. "Used Tired to be Rationed: Stocks now Held Frozen," *Waco News-Tribune*, 1 October, 1942.

25. "Prices Range from $1.50 to $11.15 for Tires," *Waco News-Tribune*, 15 October, 1942.

26. "Tire Dealers must turn in Inventory Report by Oct. 15." *Waco News-Tribune*, 1 October, 1942.

27. "137 Extra Tires Are Surrendered," *Waco News-Tribune*, 22 October, 1942.

28. Ibid.

29. "Sale or Gift of Used Tires since Oct 1 Is Illegal," *Waco News-Tribune*, 29 October, 1942.

30. "35 MPH Limit on All Highways in Texas is Ordered," *Waco News-Tribune*, 7 October, 1942.

31. "It Happened Yesterday…" *Waco News-Tribune*, 8 October, 1942.

32. "62 Oil Fields in Texas Set Aside for Military Fuel," *Waco News-Tribune*, 7 January, 1942.

33. "Plan Studied to Ration Gasoline," *Waco News-Tribune*, 18 February, 1942; "Gasoline Prices Frozen at March Levels All Over U.S.," *Waco News-Tribune*, 29 April, 1942.

34. "Gasoline Rations Elicit Outcry in Senatorial Ranks," *Waco News-Tribune*, 25 May, 1942.

35. "W.E. Terrell to Head Gas Ration Board in County," *Waco News-*

Tribune, 16 October, 1942; "Registration for Gas Rationing to Start on Nov. 9," *Waco News-Tribune*, 14 October, 1942.

36. "Signal Lights on Quicker Time Experiment Here," *Waco News-Tribune*, 7 October, 1942.

37. "County Boards to Learn Gas Ration Details from OPA," *Waco News-Tribune*, 26 October, 1942.

38. "Texas Car Owners Register for Gas Cards Nov. 12–14," *Waco News-Tribune*, 24 October, 1942; "Schools Will Close 3 Days Next Week for Gas Sign-Up," *Waco News-Tribune*, 5 November, 1942.

39. "Farmers Rush to Get Help on Gas Application," *Waco News-Tribune*, 10 November, 1942.

40. "Necessary Papers of Obtaining Gas Cards Are Listed," *Waco News-Tribune*, 6 November, 1942.

41. "Three Gallons of Gas a Week is the Official Rule," *Waco Sunday Tribune-Herald*, 10 May, 1942.

42. "Gas Ration," *Waco News-Tribune*, 23 April, 1942; "Ickes Denies Gas Rations to Be as Short as Reported," *Waco News-Tribune*, 24 April, 1942.

43. "A, B, C's of Mileage Rationing," *Waco Sunday Tribune-Herald*, 8 November, 1942.

44. "Tardy Motorists Can Get A Cards Starting Friday," *Waco News-Tribune*, 24 November, 1942.

45. "Extra Gas Is Big Headache Now to Rationing Board," *Waco Sunday Tribune-Herald*, 22 November, 1942.

46. "Officials of Texas Watch Progress of Gas Ration Fight," *Waco Sunday Tribune-Herald*, 22 November, 1942.

47. "O'Daniel Declares Gas Rationing Is 'Bureaucratic Edict,'" *Waco News-Tribune*, 25 November, 1942.

48. "Motorist Crams Fruit Jars with Precious Liquid," *Waco News-Tribune*, 1 December, 1942.

49. "O'Daniel Declares Gas Rationing," *Waco News-Tribune*, 25 November, 1942.

50. "Gas Coupons Must Be Removed When Hoarded Gas Used," *Waco News-Tribune*, 4 December, 1942.

51. "40 Per Cent Hike in Taxi Business since Gas Ration," *Waco News-Tribune*, 14 December, 1942.

52. "No Tires, No Gas Will Be Used in Baylor's Parade," *Waco Sunday Tribune-Herald*, 11 October, 1942; "Baylor's Parade for Homecoming Queen Due Today," *Waco News-Tribune*, 24 October, 1942.

53. Brady, "Baylor at War," 60.

54. "Start of Gasoline Rations Delayed until December 1," *Waco News-Tribune*, 11 November, 1942; "Shop Now before Gas Is Rationed, Wacoans Advised," *Waco News-Tribune*, 10 November, 1942.

55. "Gasoline Curbs Fail to Hinder Yule Customers," *Waco Sunday Tribune-Herald*, 13 December, 1942.

56. "County Purchase of War Bonds to Aid War Bounds High," *Waco News-Tribune*, 5 January, 1942.

57. "Investment Firm Backs Defense Bond Campaign," *Waco News-Tribune*, 21 January, 1942.

58. "Retail Merchants Organize to Sell Defense Stamps," *Waco News-Tribune*, 9 January, 1942.

59. "McLennan Leaders Preparing to Push Bonds and Stamps," *Waco Sunday Tribune-Herald*, 11 January, 1942.

60. "Merchants Speed Efforts to Raise Sales of Stamps," *Waco News-Tribune*, 1 January, 1942.

61. "Wacoans Get an Idea of What Japs Have Coming by Viewing a Bomb in

the Square; $300 in Bonds Will Buy One," *Waco News-Tribune*, 25 February, 1942.

62. "Texans Dig Deep into Pockets to Pay Income Levy," *Waco News-Tribune*, 9 March, 1942.

63. "Plant Your Dimes and Grow Stamps, Waco Women Urge," *Waco News-Tribune*, 5 April, 1942; "Downtown Booths Set Up as China Drive is Boosted," *Waco News-Tribune*, 14 April, 1942.

64. "$50,000 Per Day Needed," *Waco News-Tribune*, 27 April, 1942.

65. "Bouquet of War Stamps Mother's Day Offer Here," *Waco News-Tribune*, 9 May, 1942.

66. "Advantages of a 2-Purpose Chest Drive Are Shown," *Waco News-Tribune*, 21 October, 1942.

67. "Chest Committee Meetings Slated," *Waco Sunday Tribune-Herald*, 18 October, 1942.

68. "$65,554 Given for War Chest," *Waco News-Tribune*, 5 November, 1942; "War Chest Total Passes $120,676," *Waco News-Tribune*, 14 November, 1942.

69. "Change Bonus to War Bonds, Urges County Chairman." *Waco Sunday Tribune-Herald*, 20 December, 1942; "Christmas Gifts of War Bonds to help Hike Total," *Waco Sunday Tribune-Herald*, 13 December, 1942.

70. "Sugar Rationing Rules," *Waco News-Tribune*, 7 February, 1942; "Citizens will Get 28 Stamps with Ration Booklets," *Waco News-Tribune*, 5 March, 1942.

71. "Dates Postponed, But Same People Will Work Later," *Waco Sunday Tribune-Herald*, 8 March, 1942.

72. "Sugar Rationing Rules Disclosed," *Waco News-Tribune*, 7 February, 1942; "Sugar Rationing Delayed," *Waco News-Tribune*, 5 February, 1942.

73. "Sugar Rationing Delayed as Stamp Booklets Printed," *Waco News-Tribune*, 5 February, 1942; J.H. Kultgen, Oral History, Institute for Oral History, Baylor University, Waco, TX, 59.

74. Jackie Lavender, interview by author, 29 June, 2005, Hewitt, TX; tape recording.

75. "Increased Sugar Quota for Waco Section Is Asked," *Waco News-Tribune*, 11 April, 1942.

76. "Give It Away or Eat It, Is Advice on Excess Sugar," *Waco News-Tribune*, 1 May, 1942.

77. "Several Thousand in McLennan Fail to Obtain Cards," *Waco News-Tribune*, 8 May, 1942.

78. "May 21 Day Set for Sugar Books by Tardy Signers," *Waco Sunday Tribune-Herald*, 17 May, 1942.

79. "Ration," *Waco News-Tribune*, 5 May, 1942; "Sugar Saved if Drying Process Used on Fruits," *Waco Sunday Tribune-Herald*, 17 May, 1942.

80. Luther Lavender, interview by author, 1 July, 2005, Waco, TX; tape recording.

81. "Sugar Stamp 10 Worth 3 Pounds Dec. 16 to Jan. 31," *Waco Sunday Tribune-Herald*, 13 December, 1942.

82. "More Sugar for Industrial Users in this County," *Waco Sunday Tribune-Herald*, 20 December, 1942.

83. "McGregor Beehive of Activity with Job Offices Open," *Waco Sunday Tribune-Herald*, 12 April, 1942; "Peak Construction Due for McGregor Plant in 2 Weeks," *Waco News-Tribune*, 25 June, 1942.

84. "Wacoans Shirking their War Duties in Civilian Work," *Waco Sunday Tribune-Herald*, 26 April, 1942.

85. Frances Perkins, "Labor Standards and War Production," *The Annals*, 224

(September 1942): 54.

86. Luther Lavender interview.

87. Nell Lavender interview by Brad Turner, 1 July, 2005, Waco, TX; tape recording.

88. "Glass Containers to Be Made Here by Owens-Illinois," *Waco Sunday Tribune-Herald*, 28 June, 1942.

89. "Glass Factory is Gearing Machines for War Material," *Waco Sunday Tribune-Herald*, 3 May, 1942; Brady, "Baylor at War," 53.

90. "Duration Houses for War Workers Washington Plan," *Waco News-Tribune*, 25 May, 1942.

91. "Wacoans Urged to Remodel and Help Housing Shortage," *Waco Sunday Tribune-Herald*, 31 May, 1942.

92. "Waco Pledges to Salvage Material for Use in Fight," *Waco Sunday Tribune-Herald*, 3 May, 1942.

93. "Defense Council to Talk Plan of Collecting Scrap," *Waco Sunday Tribune-Herald*, 10 May, 1942; "Salvage Group in County Set Up to Push Scrap Drive," *Waco Sunday Tribune-Herald*, 17 May, 1942.

94. "Salvaging Scrap Is Important as War Plants Push," *Waco Sunday Tribune-Herald*, 24 May, 1942.

95. "Tons of Scrap to Help Whip Hitler Will Be Gathered," *Waco News-Tribune*, 27 May, 1942.

96. "Scrap Collection Committee of C-C Hears WPB Man," *Waco News-Tribune*, 18 June, 1942; "Working Boys to Help Scrap Drive," *Waco News-Tribune*, 10 June, 1942.

97. "Dump Tin Cans at 6th and Mary for War Salvage Pile," *Waco Sunday Tribune-Herald*, 2 August, 1942.

98. "Scrap Metal Is Club's Flagpole for Local Boys," *Waco Sunday Tribune-Herald*, 23 August, 1942.

99. "Jaycees to Lead Collection of Tin Cans in County," *Waco News-Tribune*, 9 October, 1942; "Dozen Tin Cans Is Admission Fee to Jaycee Dance," *Waco News-Tribune*, 16 October, 1942.

100. "Trucks Will Pick Up Metal; Bell to Be Ransomed Out," *Waco Sunday Tribune-Herald*, 20 September, 1942.

101. "20 Tons of Scrap Brought by Lions to 'Ransom' Bell," *Waco News-Tribune*, 1 October, 1942.

102. "School Children Will Help Gather Vital Scrap Iron," *Waco News-Tribune*, 24 September, 1942.

103. "Waco School Kids Will Seek Their Weight in Scrap," *Waco News-Tri-bune*, 2 October, 1942; "School Kids Quit Classes at 1:30 to Rake in Scrap," *Waco News-Tribune*, 12 October, 1942.

104. "Bring in Scrap so Your Boy Can Have Weapons for Battle," *Waco Sunday Tribune-Herald*, 27 September, 1942.

105. "Here's what Your Scrap Metal Can Do," *Waco News-Tribune*, 30 September, 1942.

106. "Lions will Assort Scrap Offered in Industrial Drive." *Waco News-Tribune*, 5 October, 1942.

107. "Army Trucks will Help Gather Scrap Metal Here Today," *Waco News-Tribune*, 7 October, 1942.

108. "Removal of Rails Is Slowing Down," *Waco News-Tribune*, 1 October, 1942.

109. "260 Tons of Iron Rails Taken Out of Waco Streets," *Waco Sunday Tribune-Herald*, 18 October, 1942.

110. "Your Scrap Will Save some Brave Boy's Life!" *Waco News-Tribune*, 26 October, 1942; "Mountains of Scrap will Save Thousands of Lives!" *Waco Sunday Tribune-Herald*, 4 October, 1942; "Whose Boy Will Die Because You Failed?" *Waco News-Tribune*, 4 October, 1942.

111. "October Salvage Collection Sets New High Mark," *Waco Sunday Tribune-Herald*, 1 November, 1942.

112. "23 Tons of Cans Sent to Dallas from Waco Area," *Waco Sunday Tribune-Herald*, 29 November, 1942; "Test Shows Waco Gives Only Half its Old Tin Cans," *Waco News-Tribune*, 15 December, 1942.

113. "Salvaged Paper Protects Most Lend-Lease Goods," *Waco News-Tribune*, 22 January, 1942; "Asked to Save Materials," *Waco News-Tribune*, 22 January, 1942; "Bottles and Coat Hangers to Help National Defense," *Waco Sunday Tribune-Herald*, 1 February, 1942; "Maximum Prices on Tea and Nylon Hosiery Set," *Waco News-Tribune*, 5 February, 1942; "Price Ceiling on Washing Machines," *Waco News-Tribune*, 3 February, 1942; Price Ceilings on Radios Fixed," *Waco News-Tribune*, 30 January, 1942; "Three Industries Ordered to Turn to Work for War," *Waco News-Tribune*, 13 March, 1942.

114. "Purchasers Must Bring Empty Tube to Get Toothpaste," *Waco News-Tribune*, 1 April, 1942.

115. Ibid.; "Production of All Gold Clubs Ended Effective May 1," *Waco News-Tribune*, 10 April, 1942; "Sewing Machine Production Will End on June 15," *Waco Sunday Tribune-Herald*, 26 April, 1942; "WPB Halts Sales of All Domestic Electric Ranges," *Waco Sunday Tribune-Herald*, 3 May, 1942; "Texas Loop Must Hoard Baseballs Due to Shortage," *Waco News-Tribune*, 14 May, 1942; "Lingerie Lengths Are Fixed by WPB to Save Material," *Waco News-Tribune*, 11 May, 1942.

116. "Coffee Rationing Foreseen by OPA," *Waco Sunday Tribune-Herald*, 4 October, 1942.

117. "Sugar Panel Will Take over Job of Coffee Rationing," *Waco News-Tribune*, 27 October, 1942.

118. "Coffee Ration to Be Increased if Shipping Better," *Waco News-Tribune*, 6 November, 1942.

119. "2nd Cuppa Coffee for Breakfast is out Next Sunday," *Waco Sunday Tribune-Herald*, 22 November, 1942.

120. "All Retail Sales of Coffee End as Ration Prepared," *Waco Sunday Tribune-Herald*, 22 November, 1942.

121. "Figure Coffee Supply," *Waco News-Tribune*, 27 November, 1942.

122. "Pound of Coffee per Ration Book May Now Be Sold," *Waco Sunday Tribune-Herald*, 29 November, 1942; "Coffee Deadline Near," *Waco News-Tribune*, 31 December, 1942.

123. "It Happened Yesterday," *Waco News-Tribune*, 4 December, 1942.

124. "Farm Tools Pooled for War Effort," *Waco News-Tribune*, January 9, 1942.

125. "Farm Deferments with Local Board," *Waco News-Tribune*, 11 February, 1942.

126. "Why do Farm Boys Leave Home? State Seeks Answer in Texas Survey," *Waco News-Tribune*, 13 February, 1942.

127. "Pig Outlook for Year Is Called Good," *Waco News-Tribune*, 6 January, 1942.

128. "Texans Quick To Answer Call For Country's Needs," *Waco News-Tribune*, 20 March, 1942; "Hog Prices Soar to 16-Year High," *Waco News-Tribune*, 5 March, 1942; "Wholesale Price Ceilings are Set on Pork Products," *Waco News-Tribune*, 11 March, 1942.

129. Nell Lavender interview.

130. Margie Stuth, interview by Brad Turner, 30 June, 2005, Crawford, TX, tape recording.

131. Nell Lavender interview.

132. "Coupon System on Beef, Pork, Etc., in 4 Months Ordered," *Waco News-Tribune,* 1 September, 1942.

133. "Meat Rationing Seen in 20 Days," *Waco News-Tribune,* 24 September, 1942.

134. "Meat Ration May Be Set under Two and Half Pounds," *Waco News-Tribune,* 19 November, 1942.

135. "Several Kinds of Meat not Subject to Quota Rules," *Waco News-Tribune,* 15 October, 1942.

136. "Bacon, Ham Hard to Find in Waco; other Foods Low," *Waco News-Tribune,* 9 October, 1942; "Meat Production Reaches All-Time High Past Month," *Waco News-Tribune,* 2 October, 1942.

137. "San Diego without Meat; Washington Urged to Give Aid," *Waco News-Tribune,* 14 October, 1942; "20 Per Cent Cut in Meat Delivery to Civilians Set," *Waco News-Tribune,* 2 October, 1942.

138. "Hunting, Fishing Are Important to War Emergency," *Waco News-Tribune,* 23 November, 1942.

139. "The Austin Viewpoint," *Waco News-Tribune,* 24 November, 1942.

140. "Meat Shortage in Waco Is Growing," *Waco News-Tribune,* 11 December, 1942.

141. "It Happened Yesterday," *Waco News-Tribune,* 9 December, 1942.

142. "Turkeys Are High and Getting Hard to Find in Waco," *Waco Sunday Tribune-Herald,* 20 December, 1942.

143. Tom Harper, "Poultry Raisers Planning Bigger 1942 Production," *Waco Sunday Tribune-Herald,* 22 March, 1942.

144. Wallace Lavender, interview by Brad Turner, 29 June, 2005, Hewitt, TX, tape recording.

145. "Increase in Meat Rations To Take Effect on Sunday," *Waco Times-Herald,* 1 March, 1944.

146. "U.S. Public Debt Now Past 100 Billion Mark," *Waco News-Tribune,* 3 December, 1942; "U.S. Casualties Total 58,307 in First War Year," *Waco News-Tribune,* 9 December, 1942.

147. "U.S. War Output in 1942 Short of Mammoth Goal," *Waco Sunday Tribune-Herald,* 6 December, 1942; "65 Million People Needed in Armed Service, War Work in 1943," *Waco News-Tribune,* 30 December, 1942.

148. "Santa Claus Goes in for Wood Toys; War Takes Metal," *Waco News-Tribune,* 11 November, 1942.

149. "Santa Claus is Threatened with Candy Shortage," *Waco Sunday Tribune-Herald,* 22 November, 1942.

150. "Santa Claus to Put War Stamps on Gift Roster," *Waco News-Tribune,* 24 November, 1942.

"Lord Have Mercy": The Horrific Tornado of 1953

by Bradley T. and Andrea R. Turner

Introduction

"You snatch me up and drive me before the wind; you toss me about in the storm."
—Job 30:22[1]

"The clouds poured down water, the skies resounded with thunder; your arrows flashed back and forth."
—Psalm 78:17[2]

On the corner of 5th Street and Austin Avenue stands Waco's epic monument to early twentieth-century progress—the Alico Building. At present, the archaic colossus of steel and mortared brick stands as the defining characteristic of Waco's skyline to travelers on Interstate 35. Directly across the street from the main entrance to the building sits a parking lot landscaped with young trees and a beige wall, standing about waist high. Behind the short wall, cars fill empty spaces as commuters take advantage of the optimum parking location under Waco's Goliath and near bustling daytime businesses. But, few people visiting the downtown area stop and wonder why such a pristine piece of land only houses a vacant lot. The answer lies on the corner of 5th Street and Austin Avenue, on a little sign with the words "The Waco Tornado" raised in grey letters.

In the years following the monumental Allied victory of the Second Great War, Waco experienced a steady series of economic developments and recessions common to post-wartime economics. War, an entity unconcerned with the value of human life, is a perfect opportunity for economic development because wars require immense production and labor demands in an effort to provide soldiers, allies, and political agendas with the proper equipment for obtaining

The view at 5th Street and Austin Avenue in 2009, facing City Hall. *Photograph by Bradley T. Turner.*

victory. Following a war, however, many capitalist economies experience an unavoidable state of decline when the countless people paid by government dollars suddenly face unemployment and salary cuts when the war no longer requires specialized services from citizens.

In Waco, people survived the economic ripples created as World War II ended, and local businesses commonly survived the economic changes relatively well because of the limited war work in the area. But economic times remained turbulent as local businesses fought to maintain what little economic stability existed on Austin Avenue, Elm Street, Washington Avenue, Bridge Street, Waco Drive, and Franklin Avenue. On any given day, local Wacoans ventured through Sachs' racks on Austin Avenue and inspected potential furniture purchases a block or so down the street at the R.T. Dennis Company, a massive structure known for its flashy show-windows, checkered tile floor, and furniture sales.[3] Most every day, Waco experienced meager commercial exchanges beneficial to the wavering post-war economics as the 1950s

arrived. Teenagers, working adults, retired grandparents, young house-wives, and visitors of all races commonly ventured into downtown Waco and nearby commercial zones to exchange folding money and loose change for goods and entertainment.

Commercial developers, over a century, constructed various types of buildings along Bridge and Elm Streets, and Franklin, Austin Avenue, and Washington Avenues. Most of the buildings' frames and support structures used technologies popular in the late nineteenth and early twentieth centuries that did not include unique designs for combating foundation collapses and structural strain, most likely because local architects did not know much about the new forms of architectural design involving steel structures during the buildings' constructions. The mostly square buildings of brick, wood, and glass did not possess architectural designs ready to combat the most furious tornado ever to assault the black Texas prairie—an F5 tornado that hovered twenty feet over downtown Waco with winds topping 260 miles per hour, produc-

ing enough torque to levitate cars and explode buildings in seconds. Between 4:10 and 4:45 p.m. on May 11, 1953, a horrific, swirling cloud pillaged the earth and damaged more than 1,000 structures and 2,000 vehicles—claiming more than 100 human lives in only a matter of minutes.[4] Today, few young Wacoans understand the despair of witnessing such devastation and many other Wacoans have become jaded to the story of the old tornado, commonly depicted in semi-blurred photographs of black and white antiquity. These innocent Wacoans need a reminder that enumerates the devastation caused by the storm and the true impact of the horrific weather phenomenon that pillaged the Waco community. Other local myths and urban legends surrounding the tornado require special attention and explanation to weigh the truth and determine the factual impact of history and an emerging social memory.

Birth of the Assailing Cloud: The Front

On May 9, 1953, an immense squall line entered the Midwest and spurred a series of violent storms that wreaked havoc on several cities and families. In one morose twist, a migrant family from Waco working on an asparagus farm in Hollandale, Minnesota, died from injuries sustained from a tornado that lifted people an estimated seventy-five feet in the air and tossed their bodies to earth while ripping "their tarpaper and cardboard house … to bits."[5]

The weather front continued south the following days and produced two small tornadoes in West Texas, but the National Weather Bureau assured Wacoans in frequent news reports that there was "No Cause For Alarm Here."[6] The official weather forecasts from the National Weather Bureau predicted that most of Central Texas would only experience thunderstorms on Monday (May 11) and that the severe storms would strike between Oklahoma and the Gulf Coast.[7] Around 3:00 p.m. that Monday afternoon, the predictions held true as rain washed Waco's streets clear of mud.

Across town, life continued on May 11, 1953, just as on any other mundane Monday. Theatres eagerly welcomed patrons, and the Joy Theatre proclaimed Monday the last opportunity to see *The Lusty Men*.[8] The Baylor Theater department prepared a special performance of *The Hasty Heart*, set to begin at 6:00 p.m. with unreserved seats costing between forty-five and sixty cents, while the Waco Pirates prepared for a Monday-night game at Katy Park.[9] At the R.T. Dennis Company in downtown, salesmen marked baby furniture half-price for a big sale. Across town, some schools and downtown businesses released their employees early because of the severe thunderstorm warnings, but the precaution bothered few.[10] Wacoans found most plans going according to schedule that morning and early afternoon with no possible way of knowing of the forthcoming disaster on the horizon.

Hewitt and Lorena

The day's rain continued and flash floods began to flow across rural McLennan County as the clouds grew an ominous pitch-black. At 1:30 p.m., the U.S. Weather Bureau's Waco chief, C.A. Anderson, reported that any developing tornadoes would remain west of Waco.[11] But throughout the day, conditions worsened and at about 4:10 p.m., a black funnel touched the ground between present-day Lorena and Hewitt. Witnesses described the tornado as small, following what the *Waco News-Tribune* described as "a hit-and-miss path" springing into the air and extending to the ground in unpredictable patterns.[12] Three miles from Lorena, Mr. and Mrs. Wilson B. Stanford's home shredded into debris as the infant twister scattered their possessions across their yard and launched their refrigerator about fifty yards from their residence; somehow the couple suffered no injuries. Several local Samaritans arrived soon after the storm and moved all of the family's belongings to Lorena before night fell and the rains grew stronger.[13]

The black twister gained velocity as it tore across the open farm land and the storm officially reached the outskirts of Hewitt, Texas, at about 4:15 p.m.[14] Mr. and Mrs. Oscar Evans sustained the only two injuries from the tornado in Hewitt. A local dairyman, Homer Warren, conducted a brief survey of the area, determining that the Evans' home represented the only house damaged by the storm in Hewitt, though numerous electric poles and buildings suffered other wind damage. Floyd Dennard, a Hewitt local, exchanged the confines of his truck for a drainage ditch, where he watched his truck lift off the ground and land in a field several hundred yards from his muddy sanctuary.[15] From Hewitt, the tornado barreled straight toward South Waco, stopping first at about 4:30 p.m. to harass a traffic circle on South 23rd Street, then traveling north at thirty miles per hour.[16] At 4:32 p.m., the infamous tornado entered the city limits, reaching Bell's Hill at about 4:34 p.m. with baseball-sized hail.[17]

South Waco and Bell's Hill

At the Cotton Palace Grounds' Sun Pool, people ran for cover on the bottom floor of the manager's office and in the brick dressing room when the tornado appeared on the horizon. Suddenly, the winds increased and the top floor of the manager's office collapsed, killing a lifeguard taking shelter in the bottom of the structure. Across the pool, the wall of the boys' dressing room collapsed, killing some who sought shelter behind the brick walls.[18]

Down near Katy Park and across South Waco, the tornado continued to gain power and inflict damage. At a

Sun Pool after the tornado. *Photograph courtesy of the Withrow family archive.*

shopping center at 11th Street and Jackson Avenue, the Dixie Appliance Company, Yarbrough's Grocery, Sinclair Mattress Company, Select Beer Distributing, and the old Cotton Palace coliseum stage each faced either serious damages or full destruction by the tornado.[19] Also nearby, at 19th Street and Gurley Avenue, the roof of Emmanuel Baptist Church collapsed into its sanctuary.[20]

Behrens Drug Company

The tornado reached the intersection of Clay Avenue and South 9th Street at 4:35 p.m.[21] At 221 South 4th Street, Behrens Drug Company suffered an estimated $400,000 in damage when a 30,000-gallon steel water tank crashed through the center of the building, killing one employee and ripping a thirty-foot hole through four stories in the center of the structure that flooded the basement in five feet of water.[22] David Turner, an employee of the drug company, heard the roar of the winds near his office and ventured to the loading dock to investigate the noise where winds blew and debris intermittently filled the sky. Turner, remembering a promised favor in the front office, left the scene and walked

The interior of Behrens Drug Company, as seen through the hole that was torn from the basement to the roof. *Photograph by Osa David Turner, courtesy of the Turner Collection.*

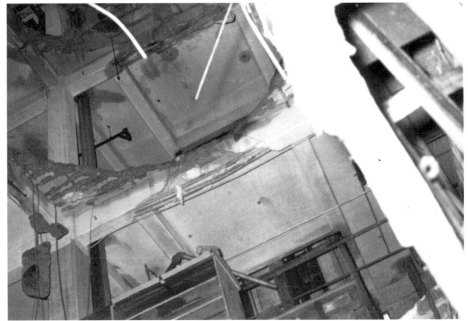

The Behrens Drug Company basement after being drained. *Photograph by Osa David Turner, courtesy of the Turner Collection.*

through the warehouse into the front offices seconds before hearing the water tower begin its doomed ascent. In a split second, the very spot where he had stood in the warehouse filled with the mixed elements that once served as the building's floors. During cleanup, workers discovered the body of a worker missing an arm, apparently severed when the tower collapsed. Loved ones buried the man without his arm a few days after his death, only to discover that workers located his arm after crews drained the basement. In the following decades, whenever a storm struck downtown Waco, the top floors of Behrens Drug Company emitted unknown pops and creaks (sounds common in old buildings), and employees said the noise was caused by the armless man looking for his arm.[23] In 2009, locals know the building that housed the Behrens Drug Company as The Lofts, a popular living quarter downtown.

As the storm arrived downtown at about 4:36 p.m., the twister's width grew to two blocks.

Downtown: The Dennis Building

"I dug myself out with my bare hands. I knew it was dig or else. I was covered completely with bricks. Another 10 or 15 bricks and I wouldn't have made it … I don't see how it kept from killing me."[24]
—Gus Levy, manager
of Central Produce Company

The corner of 5th Street and Austin Avenue represented some of Waco's prize real estate in 1953.[25] When the tornado struck downtown, the destruction of the R.T. Dennis Building was the greatest catastrophe of the storm—killing twenty-two people inside and around the perimeter of the structure. Debris from the collapsing Dennis building killed Baylor philosophy teacher Keith James and his wife at the corner of 5th Street and Austin Avenue, where they had waited for the storm to pass, crushing and burying their car to a height of two feet.[26] When the Dennis building collapsed onto Austin Avenue, the debris field caused

Products lay scattered across the Behrens Drug Company warehouse floor after the disaster. *Photograph by Osa David Turner, courtesy of the Turner Collection.*

by the multi-story building obtained the nickname "Rubble Mountain" from volunteer rescuers who began work immediately as the tornado moved into East Waco.[27]

Among those retrieved from the R.T. Dennis Building were the bodies of a father and son, Rush and Edward Berry. Rush Berry, the father, had worked for the Dennis Company since 1911 and eventually earned promotions to vice president of the company, a position he held on the day of the tor-

nado. Berry also loved music and had organized the first orchestra at Columbus Avenue Baptist Church and the World War I Liberty Bond Drive by using Camp MacArthur's musical band to entice local bond sales. Ed Berry, the son, served on the Waco School Board and had served as an officer in the U.S. Navy during World War II.[28] A Baylor student located the body of Ed Berry, who had died in his office surrounded by typewriters and facing Austin Avenue.[29] With the death of the Berrys, a

piece of local history died, too.

The Professional Building

Eugene Field received an aerial view of the storm from his windows on the 9th Floor of the Professional Building at 5th Street and Franklin Avenue, where he witnessed the destruction of downtown. Field watched a black mass spark power lines in Bell's Hill and destroy buildings in downtown. When the windows shattered in Field's office, he retreated into the hallway for a few moments, and then reentered his office only to notice the Tom Padgitt Building had vanished. Throughout the entire storm, the Professional Building only suffered the damage of broken windows and downed utilities.[30]

Jack Diddie worked at a dental lab downtown on Franklin Avenue. When the tornado struck, Diddie and his co-workers sought shelter on the floor behind their sturdy work benches, where the room grew blacker than night. The tornado passed and Diddie immediately began to sprint home, neglecting the status of his car, to check on the safety of his family. As Diddie ran, a stranger offered him a ride, which Did-

The wreckage of the R.T. Dennis Building. *Photograph by Tillman "Bill" Caldwell, courtesy of The Texas Collection, Baylor University, Waco, Texas.*

The west side of the Waco square. *Photograph by Fred Gildersleeve, courtesy of The Texas Collection, Baylor University, Waco, Texas.*

and broken glass, barber Benny Frank Smith prayed, "Lord ... have mercy."[32]

Also on the square, tornado debris blocked the entrance to the Western Hatcheries' incubators at 200 South 3rd Street. Throughout the following days, many of the 21,600 eggs housed in the incubators hatched, causing passers to hear cheeps outside the store. But the hatchery's owner, H.L. Eide, believed city inspectors condemned his building, and he refused to enter the structure to rescue the baby birds (and his $14,000 investment). Each

die eagerly accepted. Once home, Diddie found everyone safe and immediately changed clothes to return to downtown and assist in the rescue crisis.[31]

The Square

The First National Bank clock on 5th Street and Austin Avenue stopped at 4:39 p.m. as the tornado pressed forward into the square. On the east side of the city square, men took cover under a stairway as glass windows and mirrors shattered. Terrified by the roar of the wind and the sounds of twisted metal

The view at 2nd Street and Bridge Street after the tornado. *Photograph by Fred Gildersleeve, courtesy of The Texas Collection, Baylor University, Waco, Texas.*

Two young men clean up debris near the Brazos River. *Photograph courtesy of the Withrow family archive.*

bird in the basement incubators died.[33]

Bridge Street and East Waco

The tornado touched down again near Preston and East Live Oak at 4:41 p.m.—the first time the twister touched the ground since being in the Hewitt/Lorena area. On Bridge Street, an observer noted the buildings shattered and crumbled "like tissue paper."[34] City Fire Chief Lee Harrington ruled every structure on either side of Bridge Street unsafe for tenants. Store fronts and roofs littered the streets and ground.[35] In East Waco, the area along Elm Street to Old Dallas Road suffered heavy damage.[36] Witnesses last saw the fiendish twister within the city limits, on the far side of East Waco, at 4:45 p.m.[37]

The morning after the tornado, a large crane finished demolishing a remaining portion of the Mecca Drug Company, and another crane retired the debris to a dump truck. Fort Hood rescue workers found a shattered barber's pole and a dismembered corpse. Reports described the Gaiety Hotel at 100 Bridge Street as "a skeleton" and Sgt. Robert Adsit of Fort Hood claimed to have never seen anything quite like the destruction he saw in Waco.[38] The Joy Hotel Building at 118 South 2nd Street, described by the papers as a "walk-up hotel [and] popular gathering place for Negroes visiting Waco," completely collapsed into a pile of rubble. For days, Fort Hood soldiers continuously worked at the site, combing the wreckage for any sign of life crying to be rescued.[39]

The Tornado: Descriptions and Statistics

Witnesses across the county described the tornado as black and extremely wide, bouncing between the ground and the sky. In fact, expert weathermen who viewed the damage caused by the twister speculate that the funnel hovered between fifteen and twenty feet above the ground as it ripped through the city.[40] Other witnesses later told the Waco newspapers that they witnessed two tornado funnels extend from the sky, one about one-third of a mile wide and a second that lacked the size of the primary funnel, appearing "serpentine, twisted [and extending] down to the Amicable Building."[41] Other reports described the secondary funnel as "thin like a snake, and curled and twisted about the sky."[42] One woman described

A wrecked house, likely in East Waco. *Photograph by Tillman "Bill" Caldwell, courtesy of The Texas Collection, Baylor University, Waco, Texas.*

the tornado as a low, dark cloud that "looked like smoke curling from a pipe."[43] The funnels moved at an estimated thirty-six miles per hour while inflicting unparalleled carnage throughout Waco. The largest funnel spanned a distance varying between a quarter- and a half-mile, damaging an estimated four to five blocks at one time. The storm only spent three minutes in downtown—no more than a few seconds at each location it destroyed.[44]

Staff Sgt. David Fetherlin, on home leave from Korea, told a news reporter that areas damaged by bombs in Seoul, Korea, looked better than Waco's downtown. In fact, Fetherlin stated, "I don't believe a bomb could have done to that furniture store what the wind did."[45] Another man who survived a terrible hurricane told locals that though the damaged area was smaller, the area contained worse damages than experienced in Miami.[46] An engineer from San Antonio believed the scenes of Waco's damage reminded him of wartime-London after raids from V2 rockets.[47]

Tornadoes often gain reputations as being finicky and odd. In Waco, the tornado removed the façade of a building on the square, but left its restaurant's dishes neatly stacked in a cabinet; removed a large portion of a grocer's ceiling, but caused no damage to the fragile soda cans under the damaged roof; and removed the exterior walls of a leather store in the city square, but left a row of mirrors undamaged on the wall.[48] In one of the strangest occurrences, a rescue soldier found one body lying directly next to an unbroken egg.[49]

Experiences of the Storm

"It all happened so fast, you didn't have time to get excited."
—Q.Z. Valentine[50]

Jack Diddie's daughter, Sharyn (now Sharyn Nourse), recalled her fifth birthday had just passed the day the tornado struck. Sharyn Nourse remembered her grandmother constantly kept standing at the front door looking out the little window—not saying a word, just watching the weather. Nourse explained: "She didn't tell us until after she knew we were all safe that she had seen the tornado."[51]

***

Dr. Hannibal Jaworski stood in the Amicable Building when the tornado hit, looking out his office window at 5th Street and Austin Avenue (across from the R.T. Dennis building). Jaworski noted the extreme darkness of an approaching black cloud and walked to another window to catch a better view of it. He recalled that, "Suddenly it felt like the air had been cut off, like inside a vacuum. The next thing I knew, the buildings in front of me were gone."[52]

***

Beatrice Ramirez, a nineteen-year-old employee at the R.T. Dennis Company, stood near the middle of the store on the ground level. At about 4:40 p.m., the lights flickered once and permanently extinguished with lightning providing the only means for Ramirez to see.

Carrie Patton, Ramirez's coworker, ran toward Ramirez and the two embraced in fear. Another flash of lightning revealed Rush Berry (killed in the storm) bolting toward the 5th Street entrance.[53] Patton later recalled, "There was the most awful bumping, tearing, crumbling noise. I woke up in a pool of blood and found my arm almost torn off. It hung by only little fragments, cut to pieces with jagged pottery."[54] Patton screamed out in pain to Ramirez, asking her to identify Patton's snare. Ramirez later remembered, "I ran my hand on down her right arm and felt that it [Patton's arm] was hanging just by a thread, while her hand was pinned under something. I couldn't see a thing." Ramirez tried to free Mrs. Patton's hand in vain. After some persuasion, Ramirez crawled and climbed through tunnels of debris, then ventured through an elevator shaft to find help for Patton and others trapped inside the rubble.[55] Once freed of the debris, Patton remembered: "I almost gave out. I guess it was an hour before we got out. When they pulled away debris enough for us to get out, I walked to a stretcher carrying my arm in my left hand so it wouldn't drop to the ground."[56] Doctors later amputated Patton's arm, torn to shreds by the china dishes sold in the Dennis gift shop that Patton had managed for more than thirty years. Patton did not seem too angry over the loss of her right arm, however. Still in bed following her surgery, Patton remarked, "It's wonderful to be alive."[57] A year later, Ramirez became a news reporter after impressing the editor with her account in the paper.[58]

***

A little past 4:30 p.m., Max Halve, an independent electrician, finished repairing some fans on the top floor of the R.T. Dennis building when the storm hit. Halve approached the stairway on the east wall of the building (a joint wall with the Joy Theatre) when the lights went out, and the building began to collapse. Halve reported:

I saw I couldn't make it. I didn't know any other way down so I figured I'd just ride it out. The top of the building was shaking like a sailboat in the wind and it sounded like sledge hammers were popping away on the building below. Then all of a sudden everything went out from under me. It seemed as if I was floating on top of the building with a ringside seat on the tornado.[59]

A piece of debris pinned Halve in a standing position as he rode the top floor of the Dennis building to the ground like a surfer riding waves in the ocean. Halve continued:

"Suddenly everything stopped and I found myself standing hip deep in debris next to the Joy Theater wall, facing toward Austin Avenue. Right there I stopped and thanked the Lord. It was time to … When it stopped everything stopped. There wasn't a stick that moved afterwards."[60]

Halve stood twenty feet above the street and proceeded to dig himself out of the debris. Halve's tools remained in his pockets, glasses on his nose, and his clothes did not receive a single tear—only his hat was missing. Halve walked away with a cracked rib and leg bruises, saying: "I guess I was just close enough to Heaven."[61]

***

Gloria Mae Dobrovolney, age seventeen, had dropped her father off at the Texas Seed Company to buy food for her pet parakeet. W.J. Dobrovolney ran into the store while Gloria circled the block twice with her friend Barbara Johnson riding in the passenger seat. All at once, the wind grew violent and Gloria stopped the car in front of the store. Dobrovolney's father motioned for the girls to come inside the store and seek shelter. Barbara ran for the door first. As Gloria slid across the driver's seat to the passenger-side door, the entire building crumbled, pinning Gloria in the car and crushing and killing her father and friend. After rescuers freed Gloria from the car, she immediately ran to the crumbled building and began digging out the rubble with her bare hands at the location where she last witnessed her father standing. Rescuers took the frantic teen home.[62]

***

Mrs. Jack Parnell and her four-year-old daughter, Jeanette, sat in the Joy Theater as the tornado struck. The walls suddenly fell and other viewers screamed. Parnell later stated, "I thought the end had come … I just closed my eyes and prayed. I don't think the atom bomb could be any worse."[63] Miraculously, every person in the Joy Theatre survived, unlike the tragedy of the R.T. Dennis building next door. The roof failed but, for some unknown reason, stopped several feet above the floor and provided the audience with a narrow escape to the safety of the street.[64]

***

Patsy Coates, a twenty-three-year-old mother, received a phone call from her husband John, age twenty-six, checking on the family because of a tornado warning. Patsy responded positively, informing John that all was fine, but she was warming a bottle for their two-week-old daughter and needed to return his call in a few moments. John agreed and waited. John Coates worked for Patsy's parents, Mr. and Mrs. John Neely, at a paint store in downtown Waco. Patsy Coates returned John's phone call at 4:36 p.m. When John answered the phone, he said: "Oh my God! The building's falling in!"[65] Instantly following the horrific message, the line went dead. Hours and days passed, and Patsy Coates waited nervously at the front window of a neighbor's house, but her husband never returned home—nor did her parents. A car pulled into the driveway and Patsy Coates ran to the car, believing the visitor to be her husband—but it was not John Coates. Workers located John Coates' body in the wreckage of the paint store on Wednesday and the bodies of Mr. and Mrs. Neely huddled together (Mr. Neely had his arm around Mrs. Neely) under wreckage in the basement on Thursday.[66] Patsy Coates collapsed in the rain and was hospitalized for shock.[67]

***

Monday morning, Mrs. Cecil Parten awoke from a nightmare in which a large black cloud separated her from her husband. "I seldom dream," Parten stated, "but I called so loud when I was hunting him in the dream, it woke us both up."[68] Parten said her husband returned home almost every day at 5:40 p.m., but had not arrived by 6:15 p.m. on the day of her nightmare. A neighbor informed Mrs. Parten about the horrific tornado and, upon learning the news, Parten headed straight for the R.T. Dennis building where her husband worked as a bookkeeper. Once in downtown, guards stopped her near the post office and did not allow her to pass. Parten spent her next sleepless days and nights at either the Red Cross headquarters or Compton's Funeral home—waiting for news. On Thursday morning, workers discovered Parten's body in the wreckage. Mrs. Parten, whose husband preached at Lone Star Baptist Church near Lott, took the news without weeping: "My husband knew the Lord. If he hadn't, I would have been terribly sorry and terribly disturbed."[69]

***

While working as the switchboard operator at the R.T. Dennis Company, as she had done for thirty-three years, Miss Lillie Matkin heard an unidentified voice cry, "Here it comes!" and the building collapsed.[70] "And oh, such a crash of glass I never heard. The next thing I knew I was on my left side with my legs up against me. I could just wiggle my feet a little," Matkin said. She cried for help but heard no response, so she prayed. "I asked the Lord if I couldn't get out to take me then, I was ready."[71] Time passed and rescuers found her delicately balanced in the debris—still alive.[72] Soldiers from the James Connally Air Force Base attempted to reach her by tunneling underneath the former 5th Street entrance to the building but the troops could not remove Matkin. "At first we could get to her from under two layers of floors, but the building kept sinking," reported Sgt. Robert Spotts, rescue worker on the site. At about that time, another crew rummaged through fifteen feet of bricks, flooring, and heavy beams above Matkin, working her free one piece at a time.[73] James Connally Sgt. J. D. Smith and FlyTAF Airmen Second Class Dennis Schotlz took turns giving the elderly Matkin oxygen and coffee through a small opening in the rubble. Matkin remained calm throughout the ordeal as the soldiers conversed with her to evaluate her oxygen levels—even asking Matkin for a date to help keep her spirits high to which Matkin played along with the gag. Smith said an hour before Matkin's rescue she told the men to be sure to grab her shoes because she wanted a steak dinner right away.[74] But, new problems appeared when, as Smith

later recalled, "We could hear the porcelain crack on the appliances and we knew it was sinking." At 2:30 a.m., rescuers on the Dennis building asked bulldozers working on the Austin Avenue side of the building to cease excavation to prevent the beam holding Matkin from shifting and crushing her body. Officials did not allow newsmen and spectators near the area because rescue officials feared the shifting weight would displace the "delicately balanced beam." Workers called on the skills of a carpenter to assist cutting the debris and preventing problems.[75] When Matkin finally emerged from the wreckage at 6:55 a.m. (after fourteen hours and ten minutes of rescue), ten to twelve police, fire deputy sheriffs, highway patrolmen, a *Life* photographer, and her rescuers surrounded her in victory.[76] Matkin's shoes, which rescuers were sure to retrieve, were left on the ambulance.[77] She escaped serious injury.[78]

***

T.M. Hickman, a bus driver, was caught on Austin Avenue about half a block from the R.T. Dennis building in the middle of the tornado. Hickman

described his experience as follows:

The wind started blowing awful hard, and I looked up and saw a yellow pickup truck flying through the air at me. It wasn't even touching the street—four or five feet in the air. I slammed the brakes and stopped the bus, and the truck landed near me. The fellow got out and ran into a building. The front of the bus reared up like a horse, and I kept my foot on the brake. My windshield busted, and I saw something blow out of a store into the street, I thought, "My God, I'm going to have to get out of here somehow and help that poor woman," I looked up again, and it was a dummy. Boy, I was glad! I couldn't see out of the bus too good, I could see some things blown-down. I drove on up the street, I didn't pick up any passengers. Up at Twelfth Street I stopped and got out to get a drink of water. I told the fellows around there that there had been a "pretty good wind up town" and got back in the bus and went on out on the route.[79]

***

Dr. Milton Spark was sitting in his car outside of his office when the storm approached. His car suddenly began to shake under the strain of the violent winds. Spark also noticed the eerie darkness of the clouds and the sudden appearance of hailstones. Instantly, a huge pecan tree uprooted and a nearby concrete sidewalk began levitating in the sky, only to fall parallel to the building it serviced.[80]

***

The anxious employees at the Douglas Company stood in a line waiting for the time clock to strike quitting time at 4:45 p.m. when suddenly, winds scalped the building's roof, front to back. Once the roof disappeared, the building's brick facade fell onto Webster Street, pinning a passing car. The dismissed workers helped the plant superintendent for an hour to free the car's passengers. Had the storm struck one minute later, the same wall that pinned the car would have crushed the seventy-five to eighty employees on the sidewalk headed home.[81]

***

The tornado also crushed a local landmark, Chris's Café, located on Austin Avenue.[82] *Waco Times-Herald* reporter Woody Barron found Chris

Stermas (manager/owner) standing silently in front of the café's debris on Tuesday, watching as hundreds of rescue workers waded through the rubble of his fifty-year-old restaurant looking for Chris's brothers Vic and Angelo. "I have lost both of them. They are both in there," Chris said, with tears streaming down his face. Twenty minutes later, rescue workers located both of his brothers—they were dead.[83]

***

Following the tornado, Paul Vass, a Baylor student, emerged from a pool hall and stumbled into an alien world of dust and debris piled twenty feet into the air. Vass explained, "You went out and looked and wondered which way do you go? The thing I remember the most was the car horns. It seemed like 100 of them were jammed. I came toward the Square. I could see the beginnings of police arriving."[84]

***

The wreckage of Chris's Café. *Photograph by Tillman "Bill" Caldwell, courtesy of The Texas Collection, Baylor University, Waco, Texas.*

Woody Zachry, an attorney, stood in the Roosevelt Hotel and noticed a man lying in the gutter across a flooded Austin Avenue. Seeing several people standing near the unresponsive figure, Zachry screamed for the adjacent people to assist the man lying face down, but Zachry received no response from the idle group. Zachry decided the entire fate of the man rested in immediate action and rushed across Austin Avenue during the storm to save the man. When he arrived amidst the wind at the fallen man's side, Zachry discovered the body was not a man—but a mannequin dressed in a full suit and hat. Zachry told the newspaper, "About the time I dropped the dummy and looked around, I saw the buildings falling apart. Something, I don't know what, took my breath away. They tell me it was suction from the wind. Anyway, it didn't knock me down. Things started flying around me and I ran."[85]

Intense Flooding

Local agricultural agents for the state and county predicted that the intense rainfall would damage the cotton harvest in the upcoming year—particularly between Gatesville and Bosqueville. Many of the farmers from western McLennan County (McGregor, Crawford, Moody) complained of receiving an excess of six inches of rain for two days after the tornado and later reports indicated even higher amounts.[86] During the week of the tornado, a record-breaking 8.55 inches of rain fell on downtown Waco, with more than seven inches of the rain falling within one day following the tornado's strike, breaking a sixty-one-year-old record for the most rainfall in a twenty-four-hour period.[87] On Thursday, May 14, 1953, the Brazos River's depth reached 25.09 feet, only three feet away from obtaining flood stage and submerging portions of East Waco. The gates of the old Lake Waco Dam closed to prevent the Bosque River from intensifying the flood problem in downtown Waco, though the locked gates slowed gutter/runoff water drainage from the city and storm drains, stalling cars in deep water around town.[88] On 22nd Street and Austin Avenue, and 24th Street and Bernard Avenue, intense rainfall caused police to radio for boats to participate in a rescue mission for people in flooded homes.[89] Other portions of central McLennan County flooded, and one young boy in Bellmead disappeared in the flood waters (this study could not determine if the boy drowned).[90] In McLennan County, twenty-five families evacuated their homes in response to the floodwaters that filled some houses with up to five feet of water.[91] A few days later, the sewer lines of Bellmead remained jammed from all of the flooding and runoff water.[92]

Aftermath

Waco Times-Herald reporter Betty Dollins climbed on top of the two-story-high mountain that once framed the R.T. Dennis Furniture Company. Dollins noted the heavy gas fumes emitted near the wreckage and how workers repeatedly reminded each other not to light matches or spark cigarette lighters near the debris. Dollins reported that, looking down from the top of the wreckage, the streets were not visible, but were instead covered with water, bricks, planks, sand, heavy construction equipment, emergency power plants, ambulances, and fire trucks.[93]

Every building in downtown suffered

damage between 9th Street and the Brazos River, and Franklin Avenue and Washington Avenue.[94] Only the Amicable Building on the corner of 5th Street and Austin Avenue remained standing. Harelik's Man's Shop was the first store to break the domino effect caused by the Dennis Building.[95] One reason why the Amicable (Alico) Building and the Roosevelt Hotel (now the Regis Retirement Center) survived the storm with minor damage probably originated from their strong and forgiving steel frames.[96]

On Tuesday, the *Waco Times-Herald* reported, "Although salvage operations centered mostly on the former five-story R.T. Dennis Building and the corner of 5th Street and Franklin, that scene of disaster was only a fly speck when compared to the total picture."[97] The tornado almost destroyed every part of Waco's City Square and Bridge Street with City Hall remaining upright (City Hall has a steel frame), though losing most of its glass.[98]

During the continuous rains, many people worked in Bell's Hill to remove fallen trees and debris with axes, saws, and shovels.[99] Homes in South Waco suffered extensive damage as roofs and

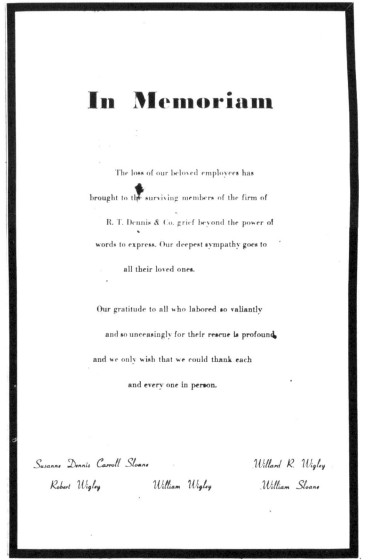

A statement issued by the R.T. Dennis Company. *Courtesy of the* Waco Times-Herald, *May 14, 1953.*

walls scattered around the neighborhoods near Katy Park, with zones between South 3rd and 8th Streets suffering the worst damage.[100]

Hospitals

Ambulance crews from all parts of Central Texas ran victims to Providence Hospital, Hillcrest Hospital, James Connally Air Force Base (hospital), and the Veterans Hospital during the night.[101] On May 11, 1953, many of the Hillcrest Hospital administrators were attending a conference in Galveston, leaving a Hillcrest evening house supervisor, Ms. Wetona Mayfield, age twenty-two, in charge of the entire hospital. All seemed well on her shift, until a flustered doctor entered the hospital about 5:00 p.m. and frantically informed Mayfield, "Young lady, prepare yourself, prepare the hospital, downtown Waco has been blown away."[102] Dr. Hannibal Jaworski began running triage on the ground floor of Hillcrest, where workers tagged patients after they received an evaluation and morphine. Throughout the night, the X-ray machine ran continually.[103]

Providence Hospital experienced a similar influx of injured, with so many patients that attendants placed adhesive tape on the victims' foreheads, recording names and addresses on the tape to keep the hurt identified. Providence kitchen supervisor Eugenia Franklin estimated she served twenty-five gallons of hot coffee by 9:00 p.m. Monday.[104] Nurses and doctors reported for work at both hospitals without being called; nursing students, private duty nurses, and doctor's office nurses also arrived to help work.[105] Hillcrest received assistance from approximately 100 volunteer nurses throughout the night, and Baylor pre-med students also helped in emergency rooms or when needed.[106] Members of the McLennan County Medical Society voted unanimously to offer services free of charge to tornado victims.[107] The Waco Chiropractic Society learned of the decision and also decided to provide free professional services to those who suffered injuries in the tornado or while conducting rescue work.[108]

Cost

Two days after the tornado struck, the *Waco News-Tribune* reported that the storm caused between $10 and $25 million of damage. Walter Lacy, Jr.,

Courtesy of the Waco Times-Herald, *May 13, 1953.*

Courtesy of the Waco Times-Herald, *May 14, 1953.*

An informative article soon after the tornado. *Courtesy of the* Waco Times-Herald, *May 13, 1953.*

president of Citizens National Bank, responded to the estimate, "There is not [a] reason to try to estimate the damage to the Waco business district. It is almost beyond comprehension."[109] Later estimates guess the damage at more than $50 million.[110] Across town, insurance adjusters raided the streets, and the papers placed basic claim information in daily reports.[111]

Public Reaction

The local veterans of World War I who trained at Rich Field recalled earlier times when U.S. soldiers stationed in Waco saved people stranded during a 1918 flood in East Waco. William E. Bengel, president of the Richfield Veterans' Association, issued a public proclamation on behalf of the World War I cadets, saying:

The hearts of Richfield veterans over the United States are stunned to learn about the destruction, loss of life, and suffering that has befallen the fine citizens of a grand community and the city we love. We send our sympathy to those whose loved ones have been taken. We join in your fervent prayers for an early and complete recovery of those injured and lend an encouraging word to all in your challenging hour.[112]

Central Texas blood banks boomed with those responding to the need for blood. Donors trailed into the Red Cross to donate blood until 1:00 a.m. Tuesday morning and Red Cross workers processed blood work until 2:30 a.m., serving an estimated 200 donors.[113] Two days after the tornado, Dallas sent

fifty pints of blood to add to an already 200 pints of local donations, and by Thursday, May 14, 1953, the Waco blood center possessed enough blood to compensate for the situation and prepare for another emergency.[114] Numerous Texas cities donated immense amounts of food, blankets, canteens, and cots, though money proved the easiest and most popular type of donation.[115] Throughout the weeks following the disaster, local newspapers published the names and amounts that each person donated to the relief effort—ranging from a penny to thousands of dollars. Local authorities encouraged all donors to give their funds to established agencies like the American Red Cross, Waco Disaster Fund, Salvation Army, or Waco Chamber of Commerce instead of any illegitimate organizations or solicitors.[116]

Around the county, other local people opened their homes to homeless victims of the tornado. In an act of kindness, Community State Bank established a distribution center for tornado victims utilizing specialized substations and thirty volunteer workers to provide survivors with the donated food, clothing, and blankets that continuously poured into Waco.[117]

Numerous locals brought food for the workers. On one occasion, a local woman brought in 600 dozen cookies for the relief group to use in the best way needed, promising to return with more in the morning, while the women of St. Mary's Parish baked 2,000 rolls as a donation to the relief effort.[118] Mrs. Truett Grant and her class made 900 sandwiches, while Ridgewood Country Club supplied an additional 1,000 sandwiches for the workers.[119] Any workers still hungry could receive free sandwiches and coffee at the Purple Cow (a diner).[120] Other random donations, like bubble gum and cigarettes, also found their way to the rescue workers digging in the rubble around the city.[121]

Helping Hands

"You can't get away from the smell of death. And you can't sleep for thinking about those poor people. So you just keep working."
—Anonymous worker

Volunteer work crews continued tirelessly through the night, hoping to find life amidst the wreckage. The newspapers gave "hope" credit for the fervor of the workers—a hope "that somewhere in the mess even a single spark of life still might be left."[122] Local firemen caught a break from alternative duties when no fires began in Waco (the intense rainfall dampened the debris) and the community's employees joined rescue efforts downtown.[123] James Connally Air Force Base dispatched more than 7,000 soldiers and 200 pieces of industrial machinery to assist in the search for the living in the downtown debris.[124] Wolters Air Force Base in Mineral Wells and Fort Hood in Killeen contributed by sending either machinery or troops for rescue efforts. Fort Hood hurried a convoy of 200 soldiers to assist in rescue efforts, largely concentrated on and near the Waco Square.[125] The local Connally soldiers primarily worked in the worst-wrecked locations, along the 4th and 5th Street disaster areas, all day and night.[126] A construction crew from Fort Worth, scheduled for a building project, served as the first rescuers with heavy machinery downtown, the boss remarking, "Our job can wait. There's a big job right here."[127] Capt. Sam Gardner, highway police disaster relief chairman, started some of the first rescue attempts on Austin Avenue. The *Waco Times-Herald* reported, "Veteran disaster people marveled at the speed at which the teams worked in what appeared to be utter confusion."[128]

Funeral Homes

The morgues continued to be overcrowded with corpses.[129] By May 14, twenty-four embalmers arrived in Waco from out of town to assist preparing the dead for burial—five (some from as far away as Florida) to prepare black victims, eleven assisting Connally Funeral Home, three assisting Compton Funeral Home, and four assisting Wilkerson and Hatch Funeral Home. At one point, morticians had to use the parking garage to store some of the dead until there was space in the preparation room.[130]

On Thursday, John Ledbetter and a co-worker from Bird-Kultgen Ford went to the railroad station to pick up automobile glass from Dallas. Once there, the man at the station asked a favor of the two car workers: "He wanted us to drop off five gallons of embalming fluid. It was kind of an eerie feeling. We dropped it off at Compton Funeral Home."[131]

Communication and Utilities

All across the city of Waco, phone circuits overloaded with news of the disaster and long-distance calls experienced a wait of several hours on the switchboards that could only support 100 calls each. In downtown, an estimated eight percent of local lines and forty percent of long distance lines experienced damage during the tornado. On Wednesday, Southwestern Bell Telephone Co. reported the greatest long distance phone jam in Texas history. R. A. Acker, Bell Division Manager, estimated that 4,000 lines were out of commission in Waco.[132] Additional service crews from areas between Austin and Dallas piled into town on Monday night, using an estimated 50,000 feet of cable (weighing nearly three tons) to reconnect Waco to the national grid. R.C. Seton, the Waco district commercial superintendent, sent an urgent message to the National Broadcasting Company in New York, requesting a broadcast to tell people across the country to limit their calls into Waco to emergency-only.[133] Maj.

Thanks!
for Your Understanding . . .

We of Texas Power & Light Company extend our deepest sympathy to our neighbors in Waco among whom we have lived and worked for 40 years, and we pledge our resources and the co-operation of our organization to restore normal conditions within the city at the earliest possible moment.

Immediately after the tornado struck, the Company activated an emergency program of rehabilitation. Portable generator units were placed in service in the stricken area as fast as possible; and, on Tuesday, 24 of these were in service here. Also, repair crews were sent to Waco during the night from other areas. Employees from other areas began arriving early Monday evening and now 400 TP&L workers are assisting in the job of restoring service.

Waco has always been a city of great courage and resourcefulness. In these uncertain hours those traditions have been exemplified time and again. We join hands with you in building a finer and greater Waco than any of us have ever known.

Texas Power & Light Co.

A public statement issued from Texas Power & Light Company. *Courtesy of the* Waco Times-Herald, *May 13, 1953.*

Don E. Kelley, stationed in Brussels, Belgium, during the tornado, waited twelve hours before connecting a call to Waco and learning the status of his parents, Mr. and Mrs. John T. Kelley.[134] Another call from Paris, France, involved Sgt. J.W. Dudley inquiring about the status of his parents at 2205 Webster Avenue.[135]

Western Union opened three branch offices in Waco on Wednesday and brought thirty-four extra employees from all over Texas to serve the needs of locals. With a total of fifty-nine employees and ten extra circuits, District Superintendent F.H. Austin reported only one-hour delays in sending messages. On Tuesday, the office handled 15,000 messages—ten times the number on a normal day.[136]

The post office continued to function during and after the storm, sustaining damages of broken windows, a partially missing roof, and no electricity. Using candles and kerosene lamps immediately following the storm, and then a portable power unit from Texas Power and Light Company, postal workers continued to sort and ship mail in the bare-bones basement. During the week of the tor-

nado, Waco's post office received the biggest rush of special delivery letters in its history. On Tuesday, Wednesday, and Thursday, mail carriers delivered an estimated 10,000 letters to Wacoans, most of the letters likely inquiring about safety. The largest rush amount before the tornado was 2,000 special deliveries on the weekend of Mother's Day 1952.[137]

Power lines experienced massive setbacks and throughout the days following the tornado, the Texas Power and Light Company (later TXU) sent an additional 125 men to restore power to a sixty-square-block area of downtown Waco, followed by an additional eighty workers when the company learned the extent of the problem. A total crew of 320 experts worked diligently, and by slightly after midnight, 80 percent of downtown Waco had power restored (about fifty blocks).[138] By the weekend, Bell's Hill, East Waco, and South Waco regained electricity and the local papers urged any people still without power to contact the Texas Power and Light Company to file a new outage report.[139]

Structures

Throughout the days and weeks immedi-

Courtesy of the Waco Times-Herald, *May 13, 1953.*

ately following the tornado, city engineers and building inspectors flooded the downtown area, surveying the safety of standing structures. During the inspection time, a rumor developed in Waco that the city was condemning buildings capable of repair and razing the buildings before consulting the owners.[140] The rumor, later proven false, instigated a panic and caused some business owners to remain closed while inspectors double-checked the safety of their facility. In one example, the city of Waco cleared Goldstein-Migel Department Store to reopen for business, but A.M. Goldstein refused to open his doors "until I [Goldstein] am certain that the building and area is perfectly safe for our customers."[141]

Bridges

The tornado crossed the Brazos River between the Washington Avenue Iron Bridge and the Suspension Bridge as it continued its path into East Waco. The Iron Bridge remained structurally unaltered by the storm but gained an excessive number of paint nicks from debris. A few of the support cables along the tops and sides snapped as tin scraps twisted tightly around makeshift snares. Gas and water lines ran underneath the bridge, but suffered no leaks—only a cracked brace. The iconic Suspension Bridge also held strong in defiance of the twister, "swaying like a cradle." The bridge experienced some minor damage, but nothing to impact the long-term usage of the structure.[142] The converted Interurban Bridge (used as an observation platform in 2009) suffered a downed power line that threatened

Advertisement for the First Methodist Church's services for the Sunday after the tornado. *Courtesy of the* Waco Times-Herald, *May 15, 1953.*

FIRST METHODIST CHURCH
FIFTH AND JACKSON

WORSHIP SERVICES WILL BE HELD MAY 17TH

The Army Corps of Engineers, as well as private engineers have asured us that our church is safe for continual use. Walls and structural part of church are all right.

Roof repairs and cleaning have made the church ready for worship this Sunday.

Sunday School, 9:30 A. M.
Morning Worship, 10:45 A. M.
Evening Worship, 7:30 P. M.
Fellowship Groups, 6:00 P. M.

HEAR MAGGART B. HOWELL, PASTOR
10:45 A. M.
"THANK THEE, FATHER"

7:30 P. M.
"THE TORNADO AND GOD"

Let every member of First Methodist Church attend church Sunday, May 17th, and express gratitude to God for salvation from the storm and pray for the distressed.

electrocution to any person who crossed, but also suffered no permanent damage. At one point, the tornado picked up a Waco transit bus crossing the Interurban Bridge and slammed the vehicle into the side of the Homer Martin Feed Store at 1st and Bridge Street. Following the storm, wreckage appeared scattered in a metallic medley along the Brazos' banks. As a safety precaution, each bridge closed for public use directly following the tornado, until city inspectors and engineers could make necessary improvements.[143] Before long, the bridges reopened for public and long-distance transportation to and from Waco, while Greyhound, Central Texas Bus lines, and the MKT (Katy) Railroad (which used a different bridge) each reported a safe passage along the various means in and out of Waco.[144] By May 20, 1953, less than ten days after the tornado, public buses began servicing every section of Waco and providing routine public transportation across the river.[145]

Churches

The First Methodist Church at 5th Street and Jackson Avenue lost its stee-

ple in the tornado and held Sunday services with standing room only. Nicknamed by some locals "The Mother of Methodism," the church held services without its steeple, as it had crashed into the ground near a railroad track along 5th Street, where it destroyed four cars. The First Methodist Church also lost most of its roof and its organ.[146] Across the city at Emmanuel Baptist Church, a collapsed roof prompted the raising of a tent on the grounds to provide for services. The Christians at Emmanuel read Romans 8:38-39 as a tribute to the storm, a passage that only reiterated their resolve to serve God in the midst of disaster.[147]

Schools

On Thursday, the *Waco Times-Herald* reported Waco public schools would not open again until Monday, May 18. Superintendent E.N. Dennard commented on Wednesday that constant rainfall delayed efforts to clear debris. With the exception of the damaged East Waco School, officers of the U.S. Corps of Engineers determined the schools safe for returning students and Dennard informed parents that the East

Waco building would not be used that year because the storm removed most of the top floor. Officials also roped off one room of Bell's Hill School because of the damage. Dennard received good news from the State Associate Commissioner of Education I.P. Sturgeon who said Waco would not be bound by the law requiring 175 days for a school year.[148]

Baylor University closed for only one day for the tornado because it received just minor damage: uprooted trees, broken windows, damaged cars, and loss of basic utilities—which forced staff to serve dorm meals by candlelight.[149] Paul Quinn College resumed classes on Thursday after closing for two days.[150] The tornado did not damage the classroom buildings, but did tear at the George B. Young Auditorium and the gymnasium.[151] The auditorium suffered damage to its roof on one side with portions of its walls destroyed on the front and rear sides of the building. A school organ and concert piano also experienced damage from the storm and the front of the gym's roof blew away, damaging the remaining windows.[152] After only two weeks, workers mended the damages to the satisfaction of city inspectors, who declared the auditorium safe just in time to house spring graduation.[153]

Waco High's Municipal Stadium and football grounds experienced little harm, though its adjoining baseball diamond, Kiwanis Field, lost its fences. Baylor Field, separated from Municipal Stadium by a narrow road, also received minor damage. Light poles and the electric scoreboard survived though the wiring tore loose. Seats from the bleachers broke free on the east side along with the tin siding of the scout box, the roof of the press box, and the concession stands.[154]

Katy Park

Katy Park, Waco's center for baseball and other sports for more than fifty years, experienced the damaging winds of the tornado.[155] The storm removed portions of a large wooden fence and blew the stands behind the first base line onto the railroad tracks, blocking rail traffic for several hours. The chicken-wire screen that protected fans from wild balls fell onto the stands, making the task of clearing the rail lines even more difficult.

Other miscellaneous damages included the third base line and a toppled scoreboard.[156] General Manager Buster Chatham and Business Manager Jack Berger, Jr., fled the grandstand offices when the tornado struck, hiding under a locomotive that Chatham had previously described as a nuisance. The hiding place saved their lives. Katy Park was rebuilt during the following months.[157]

Relocating Debris

As the weeks passed, several locations around town emerged as dump sites for the tornado debris. The most popular sites included an old gravel pit at 4th Street and Colcord Avenue, the old city dump at 1st Street and Jones Avenue, another old city dump off Dripping Springs Road, a large depression on the east bank of the Brazos River south of Waco Drive, a site off the Marlin highway, and near the mouth of Waco Creek (presently located under the Baylor Athletic Center).[158] Community trash collectors worked double shifts

Katy Park after the tornado. *Photograph by Tillman "Bill" Caldwell, courtesy of The Texas Collection, Baylor University, Waco, Texas.*

transporting debris around the area and sorting specific debris types (bricks, paper, lumber, etc.) in separate piles at the dump.[159] Charles D. Turner, a Waco native, recalled his grandfather, Osa Turner, worked for the City of Waco. Charles speculated his grandfather used the debris to extend the depth of his backyard, which backed into a ravine near Cameron Park.[160] This study took no core samples to test Turner's assumption, but did note a distinct length difference of Turner's old yard in comparison to his neighbors'.

Reclaiming Property

Mayor Ralph Wolf announced on Wednesday, May 13, from disaster headquarters (located in the First National Bank building) that a forty-block section of downtown was temporarily closed to the general public.[161] Once workers relocated the debris, local police guarded the grounds until owners could claim the displaced property.[162] When the rescue mission ended and the recovery mission began, many of the soldiers returned to their bases, with a few National Guardsmen staying to prevent looting. At noon on Friday, May 15, 1953, local business-

men who had not already begun working in their stores obtained special passes that provided clearance into the restricted downtown areas and returned to their businesses to begin salvaging inventory in the rubble.[163] After a few days rummaging through the debris, many downtown shops announced a full preparation to begin business transactions starting Wednesday, May 20, 1953.[164] Other stores opened when their districts reopened to the public or when

Waco Transit began servicing adjacent areas of downtown.

Across downtown, between 1,500 and 2,000 cars were smashed or damaged in some way. Of the thousands, approximately 800 likely suffered substantial damages, while the remaining 500 to 1,000 suffered only minor damages (bent steel and broken glass). Workers moved and stacked cars at various places around downtown, waiting for their owners to come and claim their property.[165]

Service Mutual Ins. Co.
Emergency Claim Office
Community State Bank Building
18th & Washington Ave.

If you have a claim, come to the Community State Bank at 18th & Washington and—
BRING YOUR POLICY

PROTECT YOUR SALVAGE

Courtesy of the Waco Times-Herald, *May 14, 1953.*

The Highway Patrol spent time painstakingly cataloging hundreds of cars recovered in the rubble according to license number and, later, providing a phone number informing citizens how to locate their car.[166]

A Second Chance

In the days following the disaster, the Waco Chamber of Commerce began a program requesting businesses on the

Square to commit to rebuilding and updating their area by not selling their land, but instead rebuilding new stores together and purchasing new construction materials at bulk costs.[167] The plan received mixed reactions from owners who felt that their businesses had already been nearing financial problems before the tornado and "uncertainty" became the word of choice for reporters describing the episode.[168]

Operation Cleanup

Many local people assisting in the cleanup faced the discouraging task of shifting the operation from a rescue operation to a recovery. Excitement dwindled as civilian workers continued removing debris, but by Friday nobody expected to find anyone still alive in the rubble. In an effort to keep the free-labor cleanups progressing, the city of Waco called for volunteers on an official Cleanup Day on May 26, 1953—results varied.[169] "Operation Cleanup" only impacted the neighborhoods hardest hit by the storm.[170] Two hundred volunteers showed for "Operation

Courtesy of the Waco Times-Herald, *May 14, 1953.*

Cleanup," a fraction of the number present during the initial rescue crews. As an additional inspiration, the owner of Leed's Clothiers at 408 Austin Avenue promised to pay $1 per hour for two men to help with the cleanup—an obvious disappointment on the larger city-wide scale.[171] But, the city still called the "Operation" a "huge success."[172] Perhaps Operation Cleanup proved successful because all of the free labor from the volunteers saved the city an estimated $850,000, though the cost in overtime for city employees totaled $10,641.[173]

The National Guard continued to patrol the area, some with bayonets attached to the end of their rifles, as they walked through the mud and crumbled bricks along downtown sidewalks.[174] Approximately thirty-eight percent of Texas' State Patrolmen were assigned to Waco during this time to ensure no chaotic episodes followed the disaster.[175] The square was the last area to be cleared.[176]

The city crews experienced a shortage of tools when volunteers did not return the borrowed tools to the city of Waco. No records existed to track the tools because time was of the essence when the city distributed the equipment. Several days throughout the following month, advertisements appeared in the Waco papers requesting that equipment be returned.[177]

One week after the tornado struck, downtown police and guards experienced problems when a small mob of civilians approached the area in hopes of seeing the remaining vestiges of downtown. Radio stations WACO and KWTX broadcast several requests for people to leave, but to no avail. One anonymous man suggested that in order to clear the traffic, news stations broadcast reports that another tornado was coming—authorities ignored his idea.[178]

On the first Sunday following the tornado, May 17, 1953, Waco Mayor Ralph Wolf expressed thanks to all of the people who assisted in the tornado disaster recovery project, but the true recovery was not even close to finished.[179] That same morning at 9:30 a.m., Bishop Joseph Gomez of the African Methodist Episcopal Church spoke on the radio station WACO concerning the tornado and its impacts.[180] Other ministers praised Mayor Ralph Wolf

and his staff for their excellent leadership skills and guidance during the disaster's aftermath.[181]

Tornado Abroad

"I wonder if I will ever sleep again."
—Howard Wilkerson, on a cigarette break after pulling the mangled bodies of a man and woman from a car crushed by a falling wall[182]

On Monday morning, May 11, 1953, the *New York Times* reported the story of the Martinez family killed in Minnesota amongst "the twisted rubble of their small home."[183] The following day, May 12, 1953, news of Waco's horrific tornado appeared on the front page under the headline "Tornadoes Kill 34 In Two Texas Cities."[184] Many newspaper articles tended to over-emphasize the destruction along the bridges crossing the Brazos, stating: "The steel sides of a bridge over the Brazos River were sliced open as if by a can opener." These articles are contradictory to the evidence found for this study that stated the bridges fared the storm well.[185]

On May 13, 1953, rescue efforts

involving floods and tornado clean-ups once again graced the front page of the *New York Times* as the paper summarized the scene with a vivid description: "Hard rain that had been falling here for hours slackened but water ran ankle-deep in streets patrolled by men with carbines and revolvers."[186] Other descriptions listed Waco as being at a stage that almost required martial law under the control of troops and volunteer officers to prevent looting in the streets following the disaster.[187]

In Washington, D.C., the top headline of the morning read: "Tornado Fells 6-Story Building: Two Texas Cities Hit By Twister; Three Dead."[188] The *Washington Post* included a detailed account of early tornado reports of collapsing buildings and crushed cars in Waco, Texas. Aubrey Graves, a reporter for the *Washington Post*, composed a story in the nationally-read newspaper discussing the impact of the tornado and the Indian legend of the Huaco Indians. In one report, a man buying a watch for his fiancée he was to marry in a few days was sucked out the window of the store and later revived only to find himself still holding the watch. He then discovered his car 200 yards away from his parking spot, with a 2×4 board and a shattered 108-piece fine china wedding gift inside.[189]

Two weeks after the devastating event, *Time* magazine included an emotional description of sifting through the ruins in hopes of locating "the thin sound of human voices."[190] *Time* included a popular Jimmie Willis photograph of the tornado and several statistics describing the damage. The magazine also included a story describing a time when all of the machines stopped running so workers could listen for cries of help in the debris with hopes of rescuing a scared victim.[191]

The *Christian Science Monitor*, based in Boston, Massachusetts, reported a story on the Red Cross' mobilization of a disaster relief effort in Waco. News correspondents told of local people demonstrating initiative but that "nobody seemed to have a 'master plan' of rescue. It was just dig, dig, dig."[192] The following day, the *Christian Science Monitor* included a description of the downtown scene, mentioning a few tales of troops using sleeping bags and a concrete floor at Baylor University for shelter from the storm.[193] Waco reporters interviewed the news correspondent from the Boston newspaper, Bicknell Eubanks, about his experiences in the storm and in other tornadoes. Eubanks described other storms he had reported on in comparison to Waco's.[194]

In the May 25, 1953, edition of *Life*, featuring a cover with Jane Russell and Marilyn Monroe dancing in *Gentlemen Prefer Blondes*, the story of Lillie Matkin's rescue and basic descriptions of the tornado provided the first entry in *The Week's Events* for the magazine.[195] Details surrounding the extent of the tornado's devastating impacts and the fourteen-hour rescue of Lillie Matkin filled the pages, along with detailed photographs taken by the *Life* photographer (mentioned previously in this study).

European news also covered the tragedy of the Waco tornado. On Wednesday, May 13, 1953, the *London Times* included a story similar to that of the *New York Times*, detailing the events surrounding the stories of the known dead and tales of martial law. The British newspaper also included a small side note that Baylor University was home to a large collection of the works by the Brownings, famous English authors.[196] The following day, Thursday, May 14, 1953, the London newspaper included a brief update, changing the known dead to ninety-seven and informing readers of the abating flood waters.[197]

Conclusion

"Not since the Indians left the Brazos springs to the white man did the area experience such a terrific blow. The extent and effect of it continued to increase with inspection of buildings."
—Waco News-Tribune,
May 14, 1953[198]

"The old Indian saying, quoted so many times in the past few terrible days, is responsible for this comparatively small [insurance] coverage. People just didn't believe we would ever have a tornado here; they didn't insure against it."
—Waco Times-Herald,
May 14, 1953[199]

*"The path of the tornado leads but to the grave.
Over Waco, the tornado ended at the closing of a grave,*

time and time again.
Away from the urgency
of the downtown disaster relief work, away
from the town buildings,
scenes like the one above
[the triple funeral of Mr. & Mrs. Neely
and Mr. Coates] *will be repeated*
113 [sic] *times."*
—Waco Times-Herald,
May 17, 1953[200]

"The Waco tornado is the nearest thing
to an atomic bomb disaster area nature has
planted in these United States
since the world became infested
with atomic jitters."
—Sam Wood, Waco News-Tribune,
May 21, 1953[201]

"Be more active for the Lord,
and be at your very best all the time.
You have no idea how soon
your own summons may come …"
—Dr. Forrest C. Feezor,
Pastor of the First Baptist Church
of Waco, May 18, 1953[202]

Twenty-two people died in the Dennis building on May 11, 1953.[203] Sixty-one people died on the block between

Courtesy of the Waco Times-Herald, *May 13, 1953.*

Franklin and Austin Avenues. Thirty-eight died on the Waco City Square. Twenty-two died when windows or walls blew out. Seventeen of the dead were young boys or teenagers.[204] In the months following the Waco catastrophe, the U.S. Army Corps of Engineers determined that ninety percent of the deaths could have been prevented through strict building codes—placing the burden of progress on the people who now, once again, verified the safety of existing structures.[205]

In the four days following the tornado, the city of Waco recorded no natural causes of death.[206] On May 20, 1953, C.J. Eschenburg, a sixty-two-year-old man from Waco, died from complications caused by an injury he acquired during the tornado—marking 114 dead from the Waco tornado, tying the Goliad tornado of 1902 for the most deaths in Texas from a single tornado.[207] The amount of property damage debris, however, made the tornado in Waco the deadliest in Texas history, remaining so as of 2009.

On May 13, 1953, a report arrived in Waco via the United Press, that stated since January 1, 1953, the United States had experienced twice as many tornadoes as normal. The predicted number of tornadoes had already occurred for the entire month of May by May 11, 1953.[208] Few people across the country knew how to explain the sudden increase in tornadoes, but some civilians believed they knew its origin—the atomic bomb. Rumors circulated in the American public that atomic energy entered the atmosphere and caused disruptions, but authorities reassured

people that though atomic blasts have a local impact on ecosystems, the bombs do not bear any impact on global climate systems—a subject that remains debatable in 2009.[209]

In a federal mandate, the House of Representatives cut the staff of the local Waco Weather Bureau to only five people beginning June 1, 1953. Only three weeks after the worst tornado in Texas history, the federal government reduced the weather staff needed to predict inclement weather.[210] On June 23, 1953, however, participants at the Texas Tornado Conference, including public safety agencies, the military, and electric companies, "agreed to link Texas Department of Public Safety and Weather Bureau offices with a direct phone line and developed procedures to warn the public."[211] The group also started plans that led to the country's first radar network that soon expanded nationwide.[212]

Other lasting impressions from the tornado appeared when storms entered the Waco area. Kathryn Diddie, an elementary school teacher in East Waco, later recalled that for several years following the tornado, parents would pick up their children from school any time

the sky grew dark, fearing another tornado.[213] The horrific storm left a lasting impression on the social memory of local people that resulted in a weather phobia for several decades.

Sometime during the late twentieth century, a rumor began about the Waco Tornado of 1953—a rumor of vengeance. For some time, the black community circulated an urban legend that the horrific tornado of 1953 followed the same path up Austin Avenue as Jesse Washington's charred corpse had on a hot May afternoon in 1916. Because the tornado destroyed the traditionally segregated portions of town and the old town square next to the location that hosted the gruesome lynching in 1916, numerous people believed that the tornado acted as tangible proof that God stood with the cause of the discriminated and acted in accordance with a feeling of injustice. This urban myth, however, holds more than a few inaccuracies.[214] In fact, the myth of Washington's Revenge only represents a common misunderstanding of a natural tragedy that killed both whites and blacks together—a catastrophe that wrecked generations of both black and white businesses and locations, damaged both black and white schools, and left a lasting impression on all members of the community. In fact, the tornado did not follow the path of Jesse Washington's charred corpse that was dragged around the square and up Austin Avenue. The tornado began in Hewitt (not Robinson, the site of Washington's arrest), entered through Bell's Hill into downtown (not Washington Avenue, from a side door to the courthouse) and caused irreparable damage to Bridge Street and East Waco (a place unaffiliated with Washington's corpse).

In June 1953, the Karem Shrine Temple invited renowned Christian evangelist Billy Graham to speak in Waco in memorial of the 114 dead.[215] On Sunday, June 14, 1953, Graham spoke at the Heart O' Texas complex to an audience of 5,000 people. Graham praised the local people for a lesson in unity and their ability to work beyond ethnic and economic boundaries to pick up the city—but also encouraged local people to continue their process of working beyond racial lines. In reality, the racial bridge needed a few more years to cross.[216]

In conclusion, the tornado caused more than 1,000 injuries and countless structural damages in the Waco area.[217] More than 6,000 donors, both individuals and organizations all over the country, gave $419,542 to help victims of the tornado and an estimated 8,000 people received care from the American Red Cross.[218] When Benny Frank Smith cried out for mercy as he prayed for his life under a wooden stairway on the city square, he likely meant mercy from the unimaginable winds that launched the humblest of items with the velocity of a bullet.[219] But, in the end, Waco did receive mercy—in the form of donations of money, clothes, and other goods from thousands of people around the world and in the form of numerous volunteers who sacrificed countless hours in hard labor for rescue and clean-up. The desperation experienced by Waco's people following the tornado merited a cry for help—a cry for mercy. Waco's mercy did not originate from the weather, however, but from the people around the world who loudly heard Waco's cry, "Lord, have mercy …"

ENDNOTES

1. Job 30:22, *NIV*.
2. Psalm 78:17, *NIV*.
3. *A Pictorial History of Waco, Volume II* (Waco: Texian Press, 2000), 120–21.
4. Terri Jo Ryan, "Texas' deadliest twisters," *Waco Tribune-Herald*, 15 March, 2009.
5. The National Weather Bureau believed that this same front later produced the Waco tornado. "Funnel Blasts House, Tosses Bodies 75 Feet," *Waco Times-Herald*, 11 May, 1953; Betty Dollins, "Six Wacoans Among Dead In Midwestern Tornadoes: Tornado Victims' Kin Torn by Grief," *Waco Times-Herald*, 11 May, 1953.
6. "Storms Hit West Texas; 'No Cause For Alarm' Here," *Waco Times-Herald*, 11 May, 1953.
7. "Weather Fotocast," *Waco News-Tribune*, 11 May, 1953.
8. Movie Advertisement for Joy Theatre, *Waco News-Tribune*, 11 May, 1953.
9. Production Advertisement for Baylor Theater, *Waco News-Tribune*, 11 May, 1953; "Katy Park Blown Away," *Waco News-Tribune*, 12 May, 1953.
10. J.B. Smith, "Winds of Change," *Waco Tribune-Herald*, 11 May, 2003.
11. Ibid.

12. "Hewitt, Lorena Also Hit By Tornado; 2 Injured," *Waco News-Tribune*, 12 May, 1953.

13. Ibid.

14. Smith, "Winds of Change."

15. "Hewitt, Lorena Also Hit By Tornado."

16. Smith, "Winds of Change."

17. Ibid.

18. John Chopelas and Jim Cox, "One Body in Debris at Sun Pool; Second Feared Dead," *Waco News-Tribune*, 12 May, 1953.

19. "Tornado Ripped Five-Mile Strip," *Waco News-Tribune*, 13 May, 1953.

20. "Waco Tornado Damage Is Set Between $10 and $25 Million," *Waco News-Tribune*, 13 May, 1953.

21. Smith, "Winds of Change."

22. "Behrens $400,000 Damage Leads Drug Trade's Loss," *Waco News-Tribune*, 19 May, 1953.

23. Charles D. Turner, *Turner's Notes*, hand-written book filled with the memories and stories told to Charles Turner.

24. "Dug Out With Bare Hands," *Waco News-Tribune*, 13 May, 1953.

25. "Damage Figures Continue to Rise," *Waco News-Tribune*, 14 May, 1953.

26. "BU Teacher, Wife Killed As Storm Hits Car," *Waco News-Tribune*, 13 May, 1953.

27. "Many Unaccounted For," *Waco News-Tribune*, 13 May, 1953; Reba Campbell, "Unsung Heroes Toil Till They Drop to Fine Victims Bodies," *Waco Times-Herald*, 14 May, 1953.

28. "Double Funeral Saturday For Rush, Ed Berry," *Waco News-Tribune*, 14 May, 1953.

29. Reba Campbell, "Many Work, Few Rest…Heroes All," *Waco News-Tribune*, 14 May, 1953.

30. Tom Caulfield, "Wacoan Had Amazing Birds-Eye View of Death-Dealing Storm," *Waco News-Tribune*, 15 May, 1953.

31. Sharyn Nourse, conversation with Andrea Turner, 31 July, 2009.

32. Smith, "Winds of Change."

33. "Life is Abounding in Desolation of Square," *Waco News-Tribune*, 15 May, 1953.

34. "Older Buildings On Bridge Street Torn Like Paper," *Waco News-Tribune*, 13 May, 1953.

35. "Every Building in Business Heart of City is Hit," *Waco Times-Herald*, 12 May, 1953.

36. "Deaths Pass 60; Many Bodies Still Lie in Wreckage," *Waco Times-Herald*, 12 May, 1953.

37. Smith, "Winds of Change."

38. "Older Buildings On Bridge Street Torn Like Paper."

39. "Negro Hotel Ruins Still Yielding Bodies," *Waco Times-Herald*, 14 May, 1953.

40. "Waco's Damage Reduced By High Tornado Funnel," *Waco News-Tribune*, 3 June, 1953.

41. "Woman Describes Shape of Tornado," *Waco Tribune-Herald*, 24 May, 1953.

42. "Witnesses Help Fix Waco Tornado Speed and Direction Of Its Destructive Path," *Waco News-Tribune*, 25 May, 1953.

43. "Wacoan Watches Tornado Return For Second Lick," *Waco Times-Herald*, 14 May, 1953.

44. Smith, "Winds of Change."

45. "Sergeant Says Waco 'Another Seoul, Korea,'" *Waco News-Tribune*, 13 May, 1953.

46. Ibid.

47. "Tornado Damage Looked Like Hit of V-2 Rocket," *Waco News-Tribune*, 27 May, 1953.

48. Ibid.

49. Earl Golding and Jules Loh, "Nearly

Neglected Crews Work on Square, Find Mass Graves," *Waco News-Tribune*, 14 May, 1953.

50. "Wacoans Recall Horror 25 Years Ago," *Waco Tribune-Herald*, 11 May, 1978.

51. Nourse, conversation with Turner.

52. Francine Parker, "5 Waco residents remember what took place that day," *Waco Tribune-Herald*, 11 May, 1988.

53. "Dennis Walls Crumbled, But God Stayed With Her," *Waco Tribune-Herald*, 17 May, 1953.

54. Betty Dollins, "'It was Awful' Survivors Say," *Waco Times-Herald*, 13 May, 1953.

55. "Dennis Walls Crumbled, But God Stayed With Her."

56. Dollins, "'It was Awful' Survivors Say."

57. Ibid.

58. Ibid.

59. Bill Miller, "Wacoan Just Rode er Out, Hit Five Flights Down, Safely," *Waco Times-Herald*, 14 May, 1953.

60. Ibid.

61. Ibid.

62. "Stop to Buy Food for Parakeet Is Fatal to Two as Third Looks On," *Waco Times-Herald*, 12 May, 1953.

63. Jim Dawson, "Quick Thinking Mother Heeds Warnings as Theater Crashes," *Waco Times-Herald*, 12 May, 1953.

64. "Deaths Pass 60; Many Bodies Still Lie in Wreckage," *Waco Times-Herald*, 12 May, 1953.

65. Fred A. McCabe, "Five-Year-Old Sandy is Waiting, But Daddy Will Never Come Home," *Waco Times-Herald*, 14 May, 1953.

66. Ibid.; "John Neelys Found Dead in Basement," *Waco News-Tribune*, 15 May, 1953.

67. Ibid.

68. "Pastor's Wife Dreamed; It Proved All Too True," *Waco News-Tribune*, 15 May, 1953.

69. Ibid.

70. "Trapped Woman Prayed Aloud, Then Help Came," *Waco Times-Herald*, 13 May, 1953; "Dennis Switchboard Operator Saved After 14-Hour Digging," *Waco Times-Herald*, 12 May, 1953.

71. "Trapped Woman Prayed Aloud, Then Help Came."

72. Ibid.

73. "Dennis Switchboard Operator Saved After 14-Hour Digging." *Waco Times-Herald*, 12 May, 1953.

74. Ibid.

75. Ibid.

76. Ibid.

77. Ibid.

78. "Trapped Woman Prayed Aloud, Then Help Came."

79. "Bus Driver Didn't Know of Wide Ruin," *Waco Tribune-Herald*, 17 May, 1953.

80. "Wacoans Recall Horror 25 Years Ago."

81. Clarence Weikel, "Had the Clock Been a Minute Fast, Scores of Douglas Co. Employees Might Have Died," *Waco News-Tribune*, 12 May, 1953.

82. "Famous Landmark," *Waco Times-Herald*, 12 May, 1953.

83. Woody Barron, "Unsung Hero is Found Amid Wreckage of Furniture Store," *Waco Times-Herald*, 12 May, 1953.

84. Smith, "Winds of Change."

85. "Wacoan Rushes To Rescue 'Man,' But He's No Hero," *Waco Times-Herald*, 13 May, 1953.

86. Clark Bolt, "Cotton Hardest Hit by Downpour," *Waco News-Tribune*, 13 May, 1953.

87. "Tornado Death Count Now 112," *Waco News-Tribune*, 15 May, 1953; "Tornado Brings Record Rainfall," *Waco Tribune-Herald*, 17 May, 1953.

88. "Whitney Dam Wards Off Second Tragedy," *Waco News-Tribune*, 14 May, 1953.

89. "Boats Needed to Get People Out of Homes," *Waco Times-Herald*, 12 May, 1953.

90. Jim Knight, "Four-Year Old Boy Missing In Flooded Bellmead Region," *Waco Times-Herald*, 14 May, 1953.

91. "Flooded Bellmead," *Waco Times-Herald*, 14 May, 1953.

92. "Sewer Lines Still Jammed At Bellmead," *Waco News-Tribune*, 16 May, 1953.

93. Betty Dollins, "Girl Reporter Climbs to Top of Dennis Pile," *Waco Times-Herald*, 12 May, 1953.

94. "Debris in South Waco Area," *Waco Times-Herald*, 14 May, 1953.

95. Harry Harelik, "A day I'll remember for Mom," *Waco Tribune Herald*, 11 May, 2008.

96. "Every Building in Business Heart of City is Hit," *Waco Times-Herald*, 14 May, 1953;" Smith, "Winds of Change."

97. "Every Building in Business Heart of City is Hit."

98. Ibid.; Smith, "Winds of Change."

99. "Bell's Hill Digs Out Rapidly From Tornado Debris," *Waco News-Tribune*, 14 May, 1953; "Life on Bell's Hill Far From Normal As Homeless Struggle With Storm Damage," *Waco News-Tribune*, 19 May, 1953.

100. "Debris in South Waco Area"

101. "Pint-Sized Hero Goes To Sleep on His Feet," *Waco Times-Herald*, 14 May, 1953.

102. Smith, "Winds of Change."

103. Ibid.

104. Leo Lyons, "Hospitals Overflow as Scores of Workers Care for Injured," *Waco Times-Herald*, 12 May, 1953.

105. Lynn Bulmahn, "Booklet sheds light on Waco's darkest day," *Waco Tribune-Herald*, 11 May, 1991.

106. Lyons, "Hospitals Overflow as Scores of Workers Care for Injured."

107. Smith, "Winds of Change."

108. "Free Chiropractic Aid Offered Storm Victims," *Waco Times-Herald*, 14 May, 1953.

109. "Waco Tornado Damage Is Set Between $10 and $25 Million," *Waco News-Tribune*, 13 May, 1953.

110. Smith, "Winds of Change."

111. "Report Insurance Claim To Your Agent Quickly," *Waco News-Tribune*, 15 May, 1953; "Adjuster Tells How to Collect On Insurance," *Waco News-Tribune*, 20 May, 1953.

112. "World War I Heroes Recall Waco Flood," *Waco News-Tribune*, 15 May, 1953.

113. "Red Cross Center Needs More Blood," *Waco Times-Herald*, 12 May, 1953.

114. "Steady Stream of Donors Rushes to Blood Bank," *Waco News-Tribune*, 13 May, 1953; "No Blood Donors Today," *Waco News-Tribune*, 14 May, 1953.

115. "Steady Stream of Donors Rushes to Blood Bank."

116. "No Solicitations Of Funds in Waco," *Waco News-Tribune*, 15 May, 1953.

117. "Sub-Stations Established To Give Need Clothing," *Waco News-Tribune*, 15 May, 1953.

118. "2,000 Sweet Rolls Made," *Waco News-Tribune*, 15 May, 1953.

119. "Cities, Groups Rushing Aid to Victims, Workers," *Waco Times-Herald*, 13 May, 1953.

120. "Limping Through," *Waco Times-Herald*, 13 May, 1953.

121. "Lucky Wacoans Opens Hearts to Destitute; Food Pours In As Gifts for Homeless," *Waco News-Tribune*, 14 May, 1953.

122. "Damage Figures Continue to Rise."

123. "Firemen, Grateful for No Fires, Join Rescue Work," *Waco News-Tribune*, 15 May, 1953.

124. "7,000 Airmen Join Crews Cleaning Up Devastated Area," *Waco Times-Herald*, 14 May, 1953.

125. "200 From Hood Dedicate Efforts To City's Square," *Waco Times-Herald*, 14 May, 1953.

126. "Heavy Earth-Moving Equipment Arrives From Wolters AFB to Help in Clean-Up," *Waco News-Tribune*, 13 May, 1953.

127. "Ft. Worth Crew Aids Dennis Rescue Work," *Waco Times-Herald*, 14 May, 1953.

128. "Deaths Pass 60; Many Bodies Still Lie in Wreckage," *Waco Times-Herald*, 12 May, 1953.

129. "Damage Figures Continue to Rise."

130. "24 Out-of-Town Embalmers Aiding Waco Funeral Homes," *Waco Times-Herald*, 14 May, 1953.

131. Samuel Adams, "The day downtown disappeared," *Waco Tribune-Herald*, 11 May, 1993.

132. "Tornado Brings Worst LD Phone Jam for Texas," *Waco Times-Herald*, 13 May, 1953.

133. "Phone Circuits Swamped; Situation Growing Worse," *Waco News-Tribune*, 13 May, 1953.

134. "Anxious Calls Pour Into City After Disaster," *Waco News-Tribune*, 15 May, 1953.

135. Ibid.

136. "3 Western Union Branch Offices Aid In Message Flow," *Waco Times-Herald*, 13 May, 1953.

137. "Special Delivery Letter Run Biggest in History," *Waco News-Tribune*, 15 May, 1953.

138. "125 More Light Company Men Called to Work," *Waco News-Tribune*, 13 May, 1953; "320 Crewmen Rush Power to Heart of City," *Waco Times-Herald*, 14 May, 1953.

139. "Electricity Still On Limited Basis," *Waco News-Tribune*, 14 May, 1953; "TP-L Makes More Progress," *Waco News-Tribune*, 15 May, 1953.

140. "Tornado Death Count Now 112."

141. "City Merchants Endorse Wednesday Reopening For Part of Storm Area," *Waco News-Tribune*, 19 May, 1953.

142. "Tornado Ripped Five-Mile Strip," *Waco News-Tribune*, 13 May, 1953.

143. Ibid.

144. "Transportation Remains Normal To, From Waco," *Waco News-Tribune*, 13 May, 1953.

145. "All Sections Now Being Served By Waco Transit Co.," *Waco News-Tribune*, 20 May, 1953.

146. "Tower Crumples," *Waco Times-Herald*, 14 May, 1953.

147. "Wacoans Sit in Shadow of Wreckage to Thank God," *Waco News-Tribune*, 18 May, 1953.

148. "Schools Will Stay Closed Until Monday," *Waco Times-Herald*, 14 May, 1953.

149. Ibid.

150. "Blocks around Katy Park, South Waco Badly Battered," *Waco News-Tribune*, 12 May, 1953.

151. "Quinn Holding Classes," *Waco Times-Herald*, 14 May, 1953.

152. "Auditorium, Gym Roofs Damaged at Paul Quinn," *Waco Times-Herald*, 13 May, 1953.

153. "Quinn Gets Storm Damage Repaired For Graduation," *Waco News-Tribune*, 27 May, 1953.

154. "Kiwanis Fences Are Down; Muny Stadium is Okeh," *Waco Times-Herald*, 14 May, 1953.

155. "Katy Park," *Waco Times-Herald*, 12 May, 1953.

156. "Blocks around Katy Park, South Waco Badly Battered."

157. Oscar Larnce, "Little Chance Seen to Build New Katy Park," *Waco News-Tribune*, 13 May, 1953.

158. "Much of Waco's History Buried in Rubble Heaps," *Waco News-Tribune*, 16 May, 1953; "Debris To Be Taken to Old Dump Ground," *Waco News-Tribune*, 19 May, 1953; "City Opens New Dump for Debris," *Waco News-Tribune*, 26 May, 1953.

159. "Garbage Trucks Do Double Duty," *Waco News-Tribune*, 19 May, 1953; "Grim Armed Guards Patrol City Dump Against Looters," *Waco Times-Herald*, 14 May, 1953.

160. Charles D. Turner, conversation with Bradley T. Turner, 20 June, 2009.

161. "40-Block Downtown Area Closed," *Waco News-Tribune*, 14 May, 1953.

162. "Police Guard Debris Dumps, Check Salvage," *Waco News-Tribune*, 21 May, 1953.

163. "Merchants Taking Over Salvage, Cleanup Tasks: Military Pulls Out as Rescue Operations End," *Waco News-Tribune*, 16 May, 1953.

164. "Merchants Of City Start To Bounce Back," *Waco Tribune-Herald*, 17 May,

165. "Tornado-Torn Autos Leave Parking Lots," *Waco News-Tribune*, 20 May, 1953.

166. "Highway Patrol Catalogues Cars," *Waco Times-Herald*, 14 May, 1953.

167. "Ask Quick Reply On Unified Plan For Rebuilding," *Waco News-Tribune*, 16 May, 1953; "Unified Plan For Building Gets Support," *Waco Tribune-Herald*, 17 May, 1953.

168. "Ideas Aplenty Buzzing On Future of City Square," *Waco Tribune-Herald*, 24 May, 1953; "Uncertainty Still Shrouds Unified Rebuilding Plan, *Waco News-Tribune*, 28 May, 1953.

169. "Tornado Cleanup Day Applauded," *Waco News-Tribune*, 26 May, 1953.

170. "Clean-Up Day Takes Shape," *Waco News-Tribune*, 27 May, 1953.

171. "Cleanup Trucks Rolling Today," *Waco News-Tribune*, 30 May, 1953.

172. "Storm Cleanup Called Success," *Waco News-Tribune*, 31 May, 1953.

173. "Free Labor In Tornado Saves City $850,000," *Waco News-Tribune*, 4 June, 1953; "City Overtime Pay Bill After Storm $10,641," *Waco News-Tribune*, 5 June, 1953.

174. "Methodical, Depressing Mop-Up

Replaces Rescuers," *Waco News-Tribune*, 16 May, 1953.

175. "38 Per Cent of Texas Patrolmen Rush to City," *Waco News-Tribune*, 22 May, 1953.

176. "Square Area Will Be Last One Cleared," *Waco News-Tribune*, 21 May, 1953.

177. "Rescue Tools Return to City Garage Asked," *Waco Tribune-Herald*, 17 May, 1953.

178. "Sight-Seers Clog Disaster Fringe," *Waco News-Tribune*, 18 May, 1953.

179. "Mayor Wolf, Central Disaster Group Extend Heartfelt Thanks to Workers," *Waco Tribune-Herald*, 17 May, 1953.

180. "Bishop Gomez to Speak On Tornado Over WACO," *Waco Tribune-Herald*, 17 May, 1953.

181. "Pastors Laud Mayor, Staff In Disaster Work," *Waco News-Tribune*, 22 May, 1953.

182. "Respite From Horror," *Life*, 25 May, 1953.

183. "Tornadoes Kill 9; Rip Midwest Town," *New York Times*, 11 May, 1953.

184. "Tornadoes Kill 34 In Two Texas Cities," *New York Times*, 12 May, 1953.

185. Ibid.

186. "87 Dead in Texas Tornadoes; Waco Faces a Flood Threat," *New York Times,* 13 May, 1953.

187. Ibid.

188. "Tornado Fells 6-Story Building: Two Texas Cities Hit By Twister; Three Dead," *Washington Post,* 12 May, 1953.

189. Aubrey Graves, "Waco Legend Of Immunity Blown Away," *Washington Post,* 13 May, 1953.

190. "Absolute Silence," *Time,* 25 May, 1953.

191. Ibid.

192. "Red Cross Units Speed Aid To Battered Areas in Texas," *Christian Science Monitor,* 12 May, 1953.

193. Bicknell Eubanks, "Heroes in Dungarees Dig Through Waco Rubble in Wake of Tornado," *Christian Science Monitor,* 13 May, 1953.

194. "Wacoan Watches Tornado Return For Second Lick."

195. "A Tornado and the Search for Miss Matkin," *Life,* 25 May, 1953.

196. "Tornado Havoc In Texas: Many Killed," *The London Times,* 13 May, 1953.

197. "Texas Tornado Death Roll Now 97," *The London Times,* 14 May, 1953.

198. "Damage Figures Continue to Rise."

199. "Tom Caulfield, "Rebuilding Job Begins Even as Loss Surveyed," *Waco Times-Herald,* 14 May, 1953.

200. "Funeral Biers Blanket City as Victims Are Laid to Rest," *Waco Tribune-Herald,* 17 May, 1953; The last tornado victim had not yet died at the time of this article, the total dead was 113 at that time.

201. "Waco 'Dry Run' for U.S. On Disaster Planning," *Waco News-Tribune,* 21 May, 1953.

202. "Dr. Feezor Says Wacoans' Duty to Seek God's Help," *Waco News-Tribune,* 18 May, 1953.

203. "22 Dennis Co. Employes Die, 23 Are Okeh," *Waco News-Tribune,* 16 May, 1953.

204. "Majority of 114 Killed in Waco Tornado Perished in Two Busy Downtown Areas," *Waco Tribune-Herald,* 24 May, 1953.

205. Smith, "Winds of Change."

206. "No Natural City Deaths Recorded in Four Days," *Waco Tribune-Herald,* 17 May, 1953.

207. "Waco's Death Toll Matches State Record," *Waco News-Tribune,* 21 May, 1953.

208. "Nation's '53 Tornado Rate Goes Over Twice Normal," *Waco News-Tribune,* 14 May, 1953.

209. "Blame Nature, Not A-Bomb Tests, for Foul Weather," *Waco News-Tribune,* 22 May, 1953.

210. "Weather Office Staff Reduced, Eyes Hour Cut," *Waco News-Tribune,* 23 May, 1953.

211. Smith, "Winds of Change."

212. Ibid.

213. Nourse, conversation with Turner.

214. Michael Babers, interviewed by Richard H. Fair, 31 July, 2008, Waco, TX, (Institute for Oral History, Baylor University, Waco, TX) 52.

215. "Graham Due At Memorial Rites Here," *Waco News-Tribune,* 11 June, 1953.

216. "Graham Urges Wacoans Heed Storm Lessons," *Waco News-Tribune,* 15 June, 1953.

217. "The day downtown disappeared."

218. "6,000 Donors Help Waco Rebuild After Tornado," *Waco News-Tribune,* 11 May, 1954; "978 Get Disaster Aid From Red Cross Funds," *Waco News-Tribune,* 11 May, 1954.

219. Smith, "Winds of Change."

A House Divided:
A Concise History of Integrating Commercial Waco

by Bradley T. Turner

The Housing Situation

*"Jesus knew their thoughts
and said to them,
'Any kingdom divided
against itself will be ruined,
and a house divided
against itself will fall.'"*
—Luke 11:17[1]

In 2009, just past the intersection of 6th Street and Austin Avenue, stands a clean brick building with freshly-painted white accents. Old show windows and multiple double doors likely date the structure's origins to the mid-twentieth century and the days of post-war progress. The building's smooth façade top and uniform design indicate the structure once housed a single business, but later developments likely divided the structure into four smaller sections to maximize rental profits. Lush trees mark the edges of the building's uniform design, and a spotless brick and concrete sidewalk combine with a vintage-style street light to illuminate the area during the evenings. The clean brick building, once home to the F.W. Woolworth Company, sits void from the bustling crowds that once gathered throughout its quarters for services varying from a snack at the lunch counter to a special gift from the countless racks and shelves that furnished the facility.[2] Some Wacoans might recall an occasional trip to Woolworth's when the old department store controlled this facility, but virtually nobody knows the importance of this building or about the time when these quarters played host to secret organizations that desired no public knowledge on the development of their agenda—an agenda that forever changed the social structure of Waco.

Throughout Waco's history, social, political, and cultural developments

The old F.W. Woolworth Company Building, 605 Austin Ave., Waco, Texas. *Photograph by Bradley T. Turner.*

commonly grew within the confines of staunch Southern conservatism and early twentieth-century conservative progressivism. Traditionally, many white Wacoans fought the vague liberal ideas of the federal government, except when the benefits involved monetary rewards and wartime patriotism, as demonstrated by Waco's response to the horrific global wars of the early twentieth century. Old pre-Civil War mentalities thrived in traditional Waco through local religious and fraternal organizations such as the African Methodist Episcopal (AME) Church, designated for only black Americans, and the Ku Klux Klan, an all-white hate-filled group of radical racial and religious supremacists.

On May 17, 1954, Chief Justice Earl Warren of the Supreme Court handed down one of the most pivotal judicial decisions of the twentieth century—*Brown v. The Board of Education of Topeka*.[3] *Brown v. Board* invalidated segregation and overruled the 1896 judicial decision of *Plessy v. Ferguson* which legally justified racial segregation in public facilities, provided that each facility was "separate, but equal."[4] After

half a century, segregationist states had achieved a total separation of the races, but had largely ignored the equality clause of the *Plessy* decision—a right guaranteed through the Bill of Rights and later amendments, particularly the Fourteenth Amendment of the Constitution of the United States.[5]

Segregation in Waco

In early May 1954, much of Waco matched the description of a Southern bi-racial society, largely barren of the racial equality mandated by the *Plessy* decision. When the Supreme Court announced the *Brown* decision, many Wacoans, both white and black, appeared anxious and tense, fearful to act on the new mandate. On Monday, May 17, 1954, the front page of the *Waco Times-Herald* averred the new regulation to the people of Waco by stating: "U.S. Supreme Court Strikes Down Race Segregation in Public Schools," but also included the placating conservative subtitle "Months May Pass Before Ruling Goes Into Effect."[6] State officials in Austin responded to the *Brown* decision with caution, saying the State of Texas would "comply" with the federal

decision, but only after State Education Commissioner J.W. Edgar personally reviewed the stipulations of the U.S. Supreme Court's decision.[7]

Locally, numerous questions emerged concerning the *Brown* decision, but most involved the extent of the decision's authority, the possibility of a desegregation timeline, a plan of non-violent action for integrating facilities, and determining the leadership of this radical new policy in conservative old Waco—each aspect providing an intricate riddle that needed response.

Waco's white citizens remained silent on the topic with hopes that Texas might recall the mandate, while many blacks refrained from speaking out about the decision because the white community controlled most of the economics in African-American neighborhoods through banks and employment opportunities.[8] People of all races watched the news, waiting for any negative or positive response to issues and questions created by the new desegregationist ruling, but no official answers or acknowledgement arrived for either group.[9]

In reality, the *Brown* decision was worth nothing in an extremely defiant

1950s Waco. State and local governments were required to enforce federal court decisions; but, with little oversight to see that they did so, it was up to the state and local governments themselves to actually enforce the law. In Waco, white leaders showed no immediate interest in changing the conservative system that had provided aristocratic whites with decades of tremendous economic and political power. Even if Waco's white political leaders had initially supported integration, the process of ending the deep bi-racial divisions required thoughtful timing and needed immense tact to placate constituencies. In 1954 Waco, the cynical leaders of old-Southern conservatism (both white and black) remained cautious, curious to see the reaction that other ethnic communities provided following the court decision.

Joseph Gomez, an AME Church bishop, believed that the *Brown* decision provided an open opportunity for African-Americans to obtain equality, saying:

America never does anything unless she is ready to meet the problems that will arise out of it. American people have always adjusted themselves. I am of the opinion that they will meet the issue with the same courage, moral will, and judgment that have characterized our united action in every great national issue … [Desegregation] places such a great burden on the Negro to be ready to move off on equal lines … I don't think it can happen overnight. There must be a period of adjustments and graduations.[10]

Gomez, a black minister, did not rely on the white community for his financial income. Gomez's economic independence from local white leaders allowed him the opportunity to discuss publicly the topic of integration without fear of financial retribution; however, Gomez still maintained the conservative stance that encompassed traditional Waco when he stated that the process would be gradual and require immense amounts of time. Other African-American community leaders such as F.M. Johnson, the leader of the local division of the National Association for the Advancement of Colored People (NAACP) in 1954, took a more liberal approach by affirming the belief that the ruling solidified the ideal that the NAACP held for years: equality.[11]

The national focus on segregation grew during the week following the *Brown* decision. On May 25, 1954, the Supreme Court ruled on other racially based cases involving colleges, universities, theatres, golf courses, and housing projects—each decision upheld desegregation and also included speculations on integrating other facilities, marking the beginning of a transition in the United States that linked the monumental decisions of *Brown v. The Board of Education of Topeka* with other racial cases involving desegregation.

Some people across America believed *Brown* only affected public schools, but the rulings during the following week debunked that mentality. The public school system represented a fraction of the bi-racial facilities located in the American South and the U.S. Supreme Court invalidated *all* public segregation because all segregation twisted American rights enumerated by the Fourteenth Amendment. Initially, the public school system provided the perfect location for exposing the nation's denial of natural rights to black

Americans, as schools were state-held, public entities that demonstrated the prevalent racism to Americans on a daily basis. National civil rights leaders agreed public schools provided the best means to begin integration and *Brown v. The Board of Education of Topeka* provided the perfect opportunity to implement a change because public schools received tax-based funding from both blacks and whites.

Waco and *Brown*

In 1954, most white Waco leaders remained set on the rejection of public integration and intrepid defiance of the U.S. Supreme Court's decision. White school administrators and business leaders decided to wait until federal officials forced local integration into effect. P.W. Shelton, described by the newspaper as "superintendent of one of McLennan County's richest school districts," believed that LaVega School District's black children would continue to "go where they are now going of their own free will and accord."[12] The *Waco Times-Herald* included an article on May 25, 1954 (one week after Brown's announcement) that proclaimed: "The

new decisions by the U.S. Supreme Court hitting at segregation in Texas will not immediately alter any practices in Waco, although the decisions do give a clear indication that the high court believes the unconstitutionality of segregation extends beyond the school issue."[13]

Reaction to the *Brown* decision did spark action across Texas. During June 1954 in San Antonio, Texas, the NAACP instigated their first municipal action since the *Brown* decision, requesting that the city provide African-Americans "unlimited free use of all municipal parks, swimming pools, and other public recreational facilities."[14] This study could not determine if the city of San Antonio approved the appeal, but the NAACP's request demonstrated that the *Brown* decision spurred quick, direct reactions.

As June 1954 approached, local race relations remained tense, with people wondering when or if the desegregation process would begin in Waco. Most thought some action, some mandate, or some event would occur during the following year responding in either favor or opposition to the federal decree—but nothing of any significance developed.

Most local white Wacoans simply ignored the decision and remained indifferent to *Brown*'s impact outside of an occasional public speech, newspaper article, or conversation during a family dinner. Many black Wacoans wondered if the judicial decision held any authority. According to the Associated Press in late May 1954, in the state of Texas, "Negroes, like white people, were restrained. There was no public celebration."[15]

By 1955, Waco news summaries slowly began including occasional reports on racial violence throughout the American South. Graphic images of rowdy protests and occasional martyrs filled nightly news broadcasts and papers. Throughout the United States, people steadily began engaging in protests to demonstrate their ideas, either for or against segregation. In Waco, a general apathy remained prevalent amongst whites during the late 1950s.

Though some places around the country instantly responded to desegregation, the years of 1956 through 1960 produced no events of great consequence in Waco regarding either educational or commercial desegregation.

Many white Waco community leaders ignored the racial problem, hoping the issue would simply abate and disappear. The attitude of local white leaders did not always originate from racism, however. Some local whites avoided desegregation because of the violence commonly associated with the social demonstrations across the American South. In general, the vague responses on desegregation from local white community leaders usually originated from the fact that many quiet desegregation processes failed to remain peaceful and Waco wanted to avoid dramatic scenes of public demonstrations. But avoiding the issue could only last so long.

In the African-American community, Waco's initial conservatism and cautiousness set the stage for postponing integration programs during 1954. When the prolonged delay extended past 1960, however, the black community became further disenchanted with the apparent political discrimination from local white leaders and many black community members shifted public opinion from a patient conservative stance to an eager liberal stance that promoted action.

The intentional, six-year delay sparked action from Waco's African-American community when no great changes in segregation occurred. The time for a new social order had arrived for Wacoans, and black citizens needed a political, civic, and social structure that provided the rights enumerated a century earlier by the Fourteenth Amendment and aligned local mentalities and policy with that of the federal government. That action would start by means of a "Committee of Fifty."

Taking Sides

By early 1961, many hesitant Wacoans accepted the fact that the time for a peaceful integration had arrived and community action for ending segregation needed to happen soon. Any further delay in integration could result in a locally violent uproar and create even greater tensions. The community's situation was obvious to local white elites—integrate before things got dramatic.

The Waco Chamber of Commerce, a giant in historic and current Waco civic ventures, traditionally addressed social topics through specialized committees that shared a loose affiliation with the all-white Waco Chamber of Commerce. Most of the specialized committee members originated from an elite group of local aristocrats that the Waco Chamber of Commerce described as "senior civic leaders"—members who paid additional fees to the Chamber. The local white elites formed an unofficial group that discussed the issues of the community behind closed doors and justified their secrecy by saying that their method averted public-relations problems. The unofficial group later became known by some as the "Committee of Fifty" because of the number of people in the unorganized group. The Committee of Fifty commonly acted as the selection pool for the Chamber's local projects between the late 1950s and the late 1970s. The Committee of Fifty stood completely sovereign from the Chamber of Commerce, though the Chamber of Commerce commonly acted on the will of the committee because of the prominence the committee members held within the white community.[16]

During May 1961, the constant postponing of integration emerged as an issue that needed attention. In June

1961, an unofficial sub-group called the "Inter-Racial Sub-Committee" of the Committee of Fifty slowly began discussing the issues associated with integration. The committee kept no official roster or minutes and answered to no one because the group worked on a strictly voluntary basis. Initially, the Inter-Racial Sub-Committee consisted of Earl Harrison (president of the First National Bank), Russell Cox (owner of R.E. Cox Co.), A.M. Goldstein (co-owner of Goldstein-Migel), Jack Kultgen (co-owner of Bird-Kultgen Ford), Harry Provence (editor of several local newspapers), Virgil Walker (president of Behrens Drug Company), Avery Downing (superintendent of Waco ISD), Abner McCall (president of Baylor University), Cullen Smith (law partner of Naman-Howell), Paul Marable, Jr. (manager of the Waco Chamber of Commerce), and Leon Dollens (representing the Waco Chamber of Commerce). Shortly after the Inter-Racial Sub-Committee formed, Harrison passed the leadership role of the group to Joe Ward, Jr., a local businessman, president of the Waco Chamber of Commerce, and former mayor of

Waco, though Harrison remained active in the group as a member.[17] In an interview, Jack Kultgen remembered that Ward provided "good leadership" for the group and Kultgen only spoke of Ward with the greatest respect.[18]

The reason for the group's sudden interest in integration and the formation of the Inter-Racial Sub-Committee remains fully unknown, but racial tension likely provides the best answer for motivation. Marvin Griffin, an African-American minister from New Hope Baptist Church, remembered that many black residents of East Waco wanted local companies to employ black delivery men and truck drivers to service businesses in East Waco. One specific example, Griffin recalled, involved the Pure Milk Company and a threat from some local African-Americans that included overturning the next milk truck they saw in East Waco driven by a white man.[19] Marcus Langley Cooper also remembered the tension that developed over the Pure Milk Company, maintaining that these tensions provided the forces needed to inspire the all-white Inter-Racial Sub-Committee to act.[20] Other ten-

sions likely originated from the anxious feelings of racial injustice and inspiring demonstrations across the South.

Talk of Protests

During the last week of November 1961, Paul Marable, Jr., received a phone call from Virgil Walker requesting a meeting with Marable to discuss something that "[Walker] said couldn't be discussed over the telephone."[21] During the meeting, Walker informed Marable that an anonymous "friend in East Waco" told Walker to expect seeing a combination of sit-ins and lie-ins across Waco beginning the week before Christmas 1961.[22] The unnamed source also informed Walker that these protests would occur at several of the most popular downtown venues: Williams' Drug, Pipkin's Drug, Woolworth's, Monnig's Drug Store, and Goldstein-Migel Department Store.[23]

Marable acted on the inside knowledge and called Joe Ward, Jr., the new chairman of the Inter-Racial Sub-Committee, to discuss a proper course of action. One of Ward's first strategies involved determining the identity of Walker's informant so Ward could personally converse with the source and determine an effective strategy. Next, the Inter-Racial Sub-Committee requested the *Waco News-Tribune* and *Waco Times-Herald* refrain from printing any information on the protests. This step was largely made possible by Harry Provence, a co-member of the Inter-Racial Sub-Committee, who worked as the editor for both the Waco newspapers. The Inter-Racial Sub-Committee believed local integration processes would happen with less resistance if most Wacoans remained ignorant of the committee's actions.

Soon, Marable and Ward discovered the identity of Walker's informant—Dr. J.H. Adams, president of Paul Quinn College. Paul Quinn College, an all-black school, moved to Waco in 1881 and established its grounds in the heart of East Waco on an area of the city traditionally associated with low-income and African-American Wacoans. When asked about the organization of the protests, Adams said the NAACP confronted him concerning the slow progress Waco had made toward integration. According to the NAACP, Waco remained the largest city in Texas yet to

integrate and something needed to instigate the change and force action.[24]

Integration Begins

As December 1961 began, the Inter-Racial Sub-Committee feared that protests during local Christmas shopping ventures would prove disastrous and cause an uproar that might spin out of control. The Inter-Racial Sub-Committee instead offered a counter plan to the NAACP and local leaders in the black community—cancel the December sit-ins and in the next few months each of the integration requests would be accomplished. Another committee stipulation involved limiting media interaction because they believed that public scenes and emotional demonstrations only hindered progress. As an additional olive branch, the Inter-Racial Sub-Committee arranged immediate integration at the lunch counter of Pipkin's East Waco Drug Store across from the all-black Paul Quinn College. Pauline Garrett, owner of Pipkin's East Waco Drug Store, agreed to integrate provided she could first communicate the details of the new arrangement to all of her employees and if the Inter-Racial Sub-

Committee promised the desegregation process would move in "an orderly manner."[25] After Garrett agreed to integrate, she also informed the committee that she did not appreciate being the Inter-Racial Sub-Committee's first desegregated business, especially when several members of the Committee of Fifty owned businesses that had failed to integrate.[26]

The committee's request that Garrett's business be the first to integrate stemmed from the business' proximity to the all-black Paul Quinn College. As 1961 unfolded, Paul Quinn College students provided the greatest supply of proposed sit-in participants, though many other members of the African-American community also desired to engage in protest activities, resenting the prolonged integration processes. The stores closest to the Paul Quinn College were the most likely targets for protests, so the college area received top priority from the Inter-Racial Sub-Committee. The committee realized that a liaison between Paul Quinn College and the Inter-Racial Sub-Committee was necessary to channel any frustrations and open the communication lines. The

committee placed Jack Kultgen as the official liaison to Paul Quinn College because Kultgen served on both the Inter-Racial Sub-Committee and the Paul Quinn College Board of Trustees. Further, Kultgen assisted Paul Quinn College by raising a large portion of money for the college to improve its library holdings and maintain its state accreditation.[27] Kultgen's status provided him the greatest opportunity to help alleviate any tension experienced at the college by funneling those concerns through a back channel.[28]

A few days after the integration of Pipkin's East Waco Drug Store, President Adams sent a new request to the all-white Inter-Racial Sub-Committee: integrate all downtown lunch counters by December 20, 1961. The committee responded to Adams' request with optimism, saying that the committee would reach an agreement with the stores soon. In the meantime, the Inter-Racial Sub-Committee requested that Adams organize a group of prominent African-American leaders with which the Waco Chamber of Commerce could interact to achieve the greatest amount of success with the process of integration.[29]

The Progressive Community Council

Adams obliged and requested that several prominent individuals form a council to act as representatives from the black community. The organization adopted the name of the Progressive Community Council and placed Rev. Marvin Griffin from New Hope Baptist Church, a well-educated moderate and strong leader, as chairman.[30] Other members included: Rev. Marcus Langley Cooper (president of the East Waco NAACP and pastor of the Second Baptist Church of Waco), Mrs. J.O.A. Connor, Van Pell Evans (leader of the Good Government League), Rev. L.F. Hardee, Dr. L.H. McCloney, and R.L. Penrice (an attorney). Throughout the American South, ministers and academics from all-black schools emerged as the greatest figureheads of the civil rights movement because those leaders held the highest levels of education, were trained in public speaking, and maintained salaries that originated from African-American patronage.[31]

Over the years, two primary factions emerged in Waco's black community: liberal and conservative. Conservatives demonstrated a cautious approach to integration and often refrained from protesting when it compromised the integrity of the law. Liberal demonstrators sometimes took a more hostile approach to the slow process of desegregation and regularly broke the segregation laws to demonstrate the injustice of racism.

As the years passed, Marvin Griffin proved an effective selection for chairman of the Progressive Community Council because of his cautious approach to problems and good oratory skills. Marcus Cooper, another leader of the council, presided over the East Waco Chapter of the NAACP and attempted to remain inside the confines of the law when protesting—a conservative idea in the late 1950s. Before moving to Waco in 1958, Cooper served as president of the Austin chapter of the NAACP. He tried to keep picketing within the limits of a tolerant society to avoid what he called "wildcat boycotts" that embraced violence and social disruption.[32] The NAACP, though nationally a liberal organization in 1960s America, obtained most of its support locally from money and financial incentives in

East Waco, but did not receive public support because of an economic dependence on the white community.[33] Both Griffin and Cooper provided a stable, steady leadership style which contrasted with the radical approaches of other local organizations.[34] Many times, the Inter-Racial Sub-Committee used the characteristics demonstrated by conservatives, like Griffin and Cooper, to show white business leaders that desegregation could be an organized process.

Another member appointed to the Progressive Community Council was Van Pell Evans, a part-time public relations worker for Mrs. Baird's Bread Company and a journalist. According to Evans' wife, Mary Evans, in an interview with historian Robin Bean in 1989, Van Pell Evans was a "fiery person" who approached the process of desegregation in an almost "militant" fashion.[35] Evans interacted with a liberal group (liberal by Waco standards) known as the Good Government League which met regularly at Iglegart's Funeral Home (Iglegart was a member of the Good Government League). The Good Government League collected data and information from local African-Americans who required political assistance. The group would then approach the City of Waco concerning the topics.

Cooperation

During early December 1961, within a week of its formation, the all-black Progressive Community Council met with the all-white Inter-Racial Sub-Committee. The Inter-Racial Sub-Committee promised that there would be no discrimination at any of the lunch counters in Waco if the protests were postponed until January 2, 1962.[36] The Inter-Racial Sub-Committee had agreed to desegregate by December 20, 1961, but the venture proved too complicated to organize in only a few weeks. The alternative proposal appeared fair, but created some internal rifts amongst the Progressive Community Council. Paul Marable understood the reason for the mixed sentiments: "It became obvious that the planners of the sit-ins and lie-ins had calculated that the week before Christmas would the optimum time to create the most hubbub."[37] Despite the split panel, the Progressive Community Council agreed to the Inter-Racial Sub-Committee's request on good faith, and the agreement provided the Inter-Racial Sub-Committee with two additional weeks to resolve the issue. Throughout the procedure, members of both committees kept the somewhat diplomatic meetings informal with the hope that the altered meeting styles would provide greater opportunities for bi-racial interaction.[38]

Perhaps another reason for the Progressive Community Council's reluctant agreement resided in the quiet means by which the Inter-Racial Sub-Committee operated. Shortly after the first joint meeting between the two, Harry Provence called a meeting of each newspaper and radio station in Waco, requesting that the media continue to ignore any news of protest activities in order to guarantee the transition moved as smooth as possible. Even Tommy Turner, the Central Texas correspondent for the *Dallas Morning News*, agreed to the voluntary code of silence, provided that the events did not become common knowledge to the community.[39] The committee believed that the best way to achieve full integration was to remain as quiet as possible and keep actions low-key and gradual.[40]

Initially, many members of the Progressive Community Council failed to understand the motivations for the secretive nature of the Inter-Racial Sub-Committee. Only later did M.L. Cooper state he believed the reason for the silent transactions centered on the potential problems, of which many black leaders were unaware, that the process of desegregation caused for white leaders' constituents, and the general desire for non-violent action. Most of the members of the Progressive Community Council believed the Inter-Racial Sub-Committee was now progressing as fast as possible and local facilities would desegregate quicker if potential protestors remained patient.[41]

The Inter-Racial Sub-Committee called a meeting with several managers of downtown lunch counters and informed the managers of the tense situation and the need to integrate. Most restaurant managers agreed initially, while some others needed a few days before deciding favorably.

The Progressive Community Council also had to abide by several stipulations before a trial integration. First, no more than four African-Americans could attend the first installment at each of the participating lunch counters. Second, the Progressive Community Council had to designate the participants in the attempt. Third, those chosen would arrive at a pre-determined time for the first installment (generally in the evening before the dinner rush crowded downtown locations), but could return at any other time following the first occurrence. Fourth, the agreement required that African-American participants dress in a manner complementing "the standards of dress and behavior [that] would apply to the regular clientele."[42] And last, the event would not be publicized. The Progressive Community Council agreed to the terms and, by agreeing, established the ground work for all the future integration exercises in Waco.[43]

Integration at Woolworth's
On January 2, 1962, two or three black Wacoans (sources conflict on the exact number) selected by the Progressive Community Council arrived at Woolworth's in downtown Waco at a pre-determined time. The participants sat at the counter and ordered a cup of coffee, and the attendant served their requests. After a short time, the participants paid their tabs and departed. The only negative response during the exercise at Woolworth's originated from a few whites dining at the end of the counter, who quietly moved to either a corner booth or down several seats in protest (sources dispute the white customers' second location).[44] Overall, participants considered the exchange a success.[45]

Over the next few weeks, lunch counters and restaurants became integrated one by one, using the method proven effective at Woolworth's. At each new integration exercise, the pattern remained the same: the Inter-Racial Sub-Committee discussed the need for integration with a business, a few weeks passed to prepare for the day, the business selected an approved time, the Progressive Community Council chose less than four people, the selected black participants arrived at the appointed time, the business served the group, the group left, and the media remained silent about the entire venture. Pipkin's Drug Store, Williams' Drug Store, and several other local businesses integrated using the quiet method with complete success.

Integration advocates understood the economic incentives associated with desegregation and commonly used the economics to their advantage. On May 20, 1963, the NAACP, spearheaded by Cooper, boycotted a 7-Eleven quick stop store on Elm Street. The store, across from Paul Quinn College, employed no African-American attendants and received delivery service from all-white drivers. The boycott lasted several months, through the month of July 1963. During that time, Cooper estimated that ninety-five percent of the black community participated in picketing the store on Elm Street.[46]

On May 21, 1963, the day after the 7-Eleven boycott began, Joe Ward, Jr., issued a new Four-Point Plan for integration. The plan's first step involved persuading the African-American community to cease all boycotts (including the one at 7-Eleven) because boycotts made persuasion difficult. Second, Ward requested the appointment of a truly bi-racial subcommittee by the Waco Chamber of Commerce. Third, the new bi-racial committee would meet with companies that caused tension in the black community (such as the Pure Milk

Company) and discuss compromises with the businesses' managers one-on-one. Lastly, local African-Americans could draft an official list of contentions that the new bi-racial board could address one at a time.[47]

Ward's strategy presented an alternative to other methods of desegregation that resulted in violent demonstrations and grueling processes. Throughout the entire process of integration in Waco, the transition occurred slowly, but smoothly, as the white businessmen persuaded each facility to individually integrate. The silent process required immense time, however, and soon the Chamber of Commerce received another request for a speedy integration, this time from the United States military.[48]

Integration and Connally Air Force Base

James Connally Air Force Base, located in North Waco (the present-day campus for Texas State Technical College Waco), relayed a message from Washington, D.C., that all servicemen should be treated equally in any town that housed a military base. James Connally Air Force Base contained a large number of

African-American soldiers and was a heavy contributor to the local economy. The base commander issued an ultimatum to the City of Waco: if the City of Waco refused to integrate, the military would relocate to a location that provided all soldiers with the same rights and privileges. The ultimatum provided the Inter-Racial Sub-Committee with its greatest weapon for persuading integration amongst remaining business owners. Joe Ward, Jr., president of the Inter-Racial Sub-Committee, remembered that the ultimatum made the process easier:

When word of this got around in the business community, it was quickly determined that, as unpopular as [integration] would be with the merchants involved as well as the general public, [integration] would be the better part of valor to bow to the inevitable and take the necessary steps to get [integration] done with as little turmoil as possible. Thus our efforts were made much easier.[49]

The government's mandate posed a larger threat to local commerce, and the almighty dollar began to soften public opinion toward integration.

The Inter-Racial Committee

Following the government's ultimatum, the Inter-Racial Sub-Committee adopted a new, official name and sponsor: the Inter-Racial Committee of the Waco Chamber of Commerce. This new committee provided official recommendations on desegregating Waco, something the Inter-Racial Sub-Committee of the Committee of Fifty could not do openly. The new committee originated as part of the second objective in Ward's Four-Point Plan. The Chamber refrained from appointing any prominent members of the black community to the board, however, and instead reappointed the same people from the Inter-Racial Sub-Committee with a few new white recruits.

Joe Ward remained the chairman of the new Inter-Racial Committee, with Avery Downing, Earl Harrison, Jack Kultgen, Abner McCall, Harry Provence, and Virgil Walker remaining in the group. The new recruits included: Glyndon Hague (manager of the Veterans Administration Regional Office), Brad Hoover (executive director of the Cooper Foundation), Paul Marable, Jr. (manager of the Waco Chamber of Commerce), and Leon Dollens (a member of the Waco Chamber of Commerce staff). The group consisted of all-white businessmen.[50] On some events, the Progressive Community Council and the Inter-Racial Committee worked together on public issues and used the name "Community Relations Committee" to demonstrate their joint alliance.

Desegregation in Other Parts of Waco

On May 31, 1963, the Progressive Community Council submitted an ambitious new list of places that required special attention in desegregation. The official statement from the Progressive Community Council to the Waco Chamber of Commerce read as follows, and though modified to appear as it does in Joe Ward's article, the opening statements are verbatim:

Pursuant to the direction of this group at the meeting on the 31st day of May 1963, we respectfully offer the following recommendations for your consideration in implementing a positive and rational program for the maintenance of racial harmony by; first, removing all racial discrimination in public accommodations; secondly, deliberately increasing employment opportunities for Negroes; and thirdly, providing representation at the policy making level in matter affecting community life:

DESEGREGATION
That the Waco Chamber of Commerce use its influence in the immediate desegregation of Waco Public Schools without further litigation.

That public facilities be desegregated as follows:

- *Desegregation of public facilities: parks (to include, but not limited to Cameron Park), swimming pools, playgrounds, YMCA, and YWCA.*
- *Desegregation of privately owned facilities coupled with a public interest: restaurants, theatres, hotels, motels, recreation facilities, Baylor University, business and other trade schools and hospitals.*
- *Unrestricted employment in such privately owned companies as: soft drink, milk, beer, bakery, wholesale grocery, potato chip, meat packing, department store, automobile and*

furniture, bank, savings and loan and public utilities.

- *Unrestricted employment in all tax supported entities: tax collector, police and fire department, court house, highway and public welfare departments and the Texas Employment Commission.*
- *Appointment of blacks to boards and commissions: Urban Renewal, Housing Authority, Zoning Board and Park Board.*
- *Promote black representation in local government by: electing councilmen from single-member districts and returning to the strong mayor form of government.*
- *Provide underpasses and overpasses on Interstate I-35 to provide free access to downtown.*[51]

In reality, many of these controversial issues already had entered a tedious process of reexamination by the Inter-Racial Committee. The desegregation of Cameron Park presented numerous problems that required special attention.[52] (Discussions of Cameron Park remain largely omitted from this chapter because a separate chapter in this study focuses on race-relations in Cameron Park). According to Ward, the primary issues surrounding desegregation centered on a defiant white public, integrated stores staffed with disgruntled white workers, and business owners who feared white locals would avoid their facility if it was the only integrated location.[53]

Other local whites decided to instigate mixed-race dining simply because the Waco Chamber of Commerce requested compliance. One of the most prominent establishments in Waco, George's Chef, sat, served, and attended African-American customers without any problems, largely because of the cooperative efforts of George Williams, the owner of the establishment.[54]

As the years passed, the Inter-Racial Committee and the Progressive Community Council agreed that the most effective means of desegregation involved continuing the process used at Woolworth's almost two years earlier and to integrate each business one by one. Meanwhile, Harry Provence, member of the Inter-Racial Committee and editor-in-chief of several Waco newspapers, continued keeping racial activities as soft as possible. On one occasion, a group of Paul Quinn College students decided to instigate a protest at Williams' Drug Store in East Waco, hoping to receive press coverage and start a public uproar, but the Waco newspapers (under order from Provence) ignored the incident and undermined the potential for a violent demonstration.[55]

The black community desired single-member districts because the process narrowed each representative ward to specific city districts. Even in 1970, the Waco city charter mandated that city council seats be at-large positions, which placed minorities at a disadvantage for election. In an at-large system, the city recognizes no districts/wards inside a city and the entire council can originate from the same neighborhood in Waco and ignore any outside community groups. East Waco and South Waco commonly contributed candidates for the Waco city elections, but never won an election because of the white majority that controlled the at-large positions. After a series of studies, prolonged work from the NAACP East Waco Branch, almost two decades, and a lawsuit, a judge finally ordered the City of Waco to adopt single-member districts for determining and electing a city council on April 19, 1976.[56]

Hotels, motels, theatres, and department stores each integrated using a means similar to the Woolworth's process started in January 1962. Still, some store owners chose not to assist the white Inter-Racial Committee and, according to Joe Ward, Jr., responded by saying, "No niggers better come into my place."[57] Most white business owners responded to the Inter-Racial Committee's integration request by saying they would agree to integrate their business when the City of Waco integrated its public places and schools.[58] The Inter-Racial Committee approached the management for the Interstate Movie House (the largest movie theatre in Waco) and received mixed reactions. The owner expressed interest in desegregating, but did not want to be the first theatre to integrate because he feared losing white patronage. The movie house owner expressed a common hurdle faced by the Inter-Racial Committee—nobody wanted to be the first or the last to integrate.[59]

Jobs for African-Americans

The Inter-Racial Committee responded to the Progressive Community Council's request for an increase in available jobs for African-Americans by sponsoring an employment program for the city titled "A Program for Increasing Job Opportunities for Blacks in Processing and Distributing Industries."[60] The program used voluntary participants and appealed to white employers by demonstrating the work experience and skill of "qualified Negroes."[61]

Eventually, the crusade for hiring African-American Wacoans developed into such a large program that the Waco Chamber of Commerce sponsored a separate committee for promoting black employment called the Major Employers Equal Opportunity Committee, which included representatives from some of Waco's most prominent employers: Universal Atlas Cement, Owens Illinois-Glass Co., General Tire and Rubber Co., the Veterans Administration Hospital, James Connally Air Force Base, and the City of Waco.[62] The Progressive Community Council saw some positive results at several large companies, but the process took time. Convincing traditionally all-white companies to hire African-Americans definitely proved the most complicated and difficult task for the joint Community Relations Committee. Some Wacoans might argue that the hiring process still remains a problem in 2009.

The Annual Report

In January 1964, the Inter-Racial Committee decided to go public with the process of desegregation and issued an *Annual Report to the Community Relations Committee, 1963*.[63] The Community Relations Committee released the report to the news media with full clearance to inform the general public about the occurrences of the last three years. The report stated that the first two years of the desegregation process occurred under the "auspices" of the Inter-Racial Sub-Committee of the Committee of Fifty and as an "official organ" of the Chamber of Commerce during the last year (1963).[64]

The report, intended as both a rallying point for integration and a source of information, began by proclaiming that segregation represented the greatest problem in the nation and in the City of Waco. The report explained that many reasons for conflicts were based on morals, traditions, and prejudices. The Community Relations Committee deviated from the emotional attachments of desegregation and adopted an economic approach by claiming that city-wide integration caused an increase in local revenues for white and black employees and employers.[65]

The Community Relations Committee also presented the first public statement that told locals, "Desegregation will take place to a degree in Waco, Texas."[66] Though liberal, the statement maintained a placid tone of compromise to the conservative segregationists in Waco by including the prepositional phrase "to a degree." Further, the Community Relations Committee wanted to avoid violent demonstrations, but still speculated on "how many heads [would be] bloodied in the process."[67]

The majority of the Community Relations Committee feared that local masses would still desire a series of violent and emotional demonstrations in either favor or opposition to desegregation, but the committee continued to justify local integration by using economics. The third contention of the annual report exemplified the committee's position, stating:

The favorable economic development of this city and conceivably the security of the life and property of its individual citizens will be materially affected by the orderliness of the process. Both our ability to attract new industry and to maintain and perhaps enhance existing governmental installations, each of which provides job opportunities for both whites and Negroes, is at stake.[68]

In the previous year, the federal government threatened to relocate James Connally Air Force Base because of racial segregation and discrimination in Waco facilities, but the ultimatum demonstrated the practical economic incentives of African-American employment in new areas of commercial development.

The key to the entire public campaign centered on a voluntary bi-racial accommodation structured in order and respect. One of the report's passages, similar to Gomez's initial reaction to the *Brown* decision printed in 1954, stated, "A situation created over a period of 400 years cannot be completely altered in four years or even, perhaps, in forty."[69] In short, the public needed time to adjust.

The report continued and informed the public that the Inter-Racial Sub-Committee of the Committee of Fifty (later the Inter-Racial Committee of the Waco Chamber of Commerce) and the Progressive Community Council occasionally formed the joint Community Relations Committee to establish communication between the two races during the time of adjustment. The Community Relations Committee mentioned that their members conducted a process of integration in cooperation with a "group of Negroes elected by the Negro community," which meant the Progressive Community Council.[70]

The Community Relations Committee's *Annual Report* concluded with a list of integrated achievements that occurred during the three-year period and the items still to be addressed. The list read as follows:

- *Institution of desegregation program by Waco Public Schools.*
- *Desegregation of Baylor University.*
- *Desegregation of all city park and recreation facilities except swimming pools.*

- *Desegregation of all lunch counter facilities and most suburban eating establishments.*
- *Desegregation of some suburban theatres.*
- *Desegregation of some hotels and motels.*
- *Institution of orderly desegregation programs in both major hospitals.*
- *Creation by several employer groups of equal job opportunity programs. Although the various plans vary somewhat in detail, each does attempt to remove race consideration from job qualifications in an orderly and as practical a manner as possible. Also in each plan no participating employer is expected to: dismiss any satisfactory employee in order to hire a Negro; create a new job not considered to be necessary and economically sound in order to hire a Negro; or fill any job with an unqualified person.[71]*

The Community Relations Committee knew the key to desegregating Waco rested in literally selling the idea to prominent white locals.

Desegregation and Piccadilly

Shortly after the optimistic report,
another predicament arose concerning the process of desegregation in Waco—Piccadilly Cafeteria. A special branch of the Veterans Administration (VA) had just moved to Waco, bringing 250 jobs to the downtown region. Piccadilly Cafeteria, down one block from the new VA office, invited the new employees for coffee and doughnuts but refused service to one new black employee, lawyer Billy Barrett. Once the employees arrived for their refreshments, a manager tapped Barrett on the shoulder and informed Barrett that the cafeteria was not integrated and Barrett needed to leave the restaurant.[72]

The following day, Piccadilly's headquarters in Baton Rouge, Louisiana, received a letter from George Nokes, president of the Lake Air Center (later Lake Air Mall), requesting the cafeterias integrate, but Piccadilly refused. Piccadilly did not integrate its Waco facility because, after conducting several economic studies, the cafeteria determined that integration would not be financially beneficial. The VA held the same opinion as James Connally Air Force Base and the federal government did not want its employees in a location that did not respect their workers. Over the following weeks, Nokes obtained a proclamation from the City of Waco and provided the Piccadilly headquarters with a copy of the 1963 report issued by the joint Community Relations Committee. The economics of the situation forced the local city government to respond in favor of the VA because the city did not wish to lose the 250 jobs created by the VA, and Piccadilly did not want to lose patronage. A few weeks later, Marvin Griffin and George Nokes visited Piccadilly Cafeteria and ate without problems from the management—the simple arm-twisting spurred another successful integration.[73]

The End of Commercial Segregation in Waco

By 1965, Waco emerged as a semi-progressive town boasting a fairly successful integration process. All public businesses and restaurants across Waco were integrated, but the biggest un-integrated area remained that which first spurred the process of desegregation—public schools.[74] One decade following the *Brown* decision, Waco Independent Schools had yet to desegregate. On December 3, 1964, Judge Homer Thornberry issued a court order for the systematic desegregation of Waco public schools. The integration process of Waco Independent School District still required attention—lots of attention.[75]

By the end of the official public desegregation process of the early and mid-1960s, many black Wacoans became disenchanted with the leadership of Marvin Griffin because of his conservatism, the same conservatism that the Community Relations Committee favored.[76] Jesse Sapp, a leader in the United Rubber Workers' Union at General Tire Company, believed that Griffin's low-key conservatism eventually worked against his progressive ideas because other, more-liberal leaders (like Van Pell Evans) believed that Griffin was too accommodating to the Community Relations Committee.[77] Van Pell Evans also went one step further than Griffin and established the Black Waco Chamber of Commerce with hopes of unifying the African-American community, but the small group contributed little to the integration process of Waco.[78]

A House United?

Despite a few angry locals, Waco's desegregation process went smoothly and excluded the stereotypical violence of other locations in the American South. By 1965, commercial integration was in place and functioning at a satisfactory level. When Waco's civic integration concluded, Jack Kultgen believed that Waco served as a model for other cities because of the lack of violence and the cooperation between progressive black community leaders and progressive white civic elites.[79] But several factors force a raised eyebrow: the silent press, the sluggish start of the integration efforts, and both the black and white perception of African-American expectations in a newly desegregated society.

First, with the request for the press to remain silent, some contemporaries believed that the lack of desegregation reports infringed upon the basic American right to a free press. However, the Waco Chamber of Commerce and the Committee of Fifty asked that the press refrain from including stories because the business group believed that more emotional and chaotic scenes would occur if the protestors received credit. Further, each news correspondent voluntarily refrained from reporting on the topic—no civic group legally mandated that the press exclude any civil rights information. The First Amendment of the Constitution of the United States does not say that people have a right to know information; rather, the Amendment states that the press can publish (or not publish) any news the press chooses (or does not choose) to publish. The specific wording of the First Amendment reads:

Congress shall make no law respecting an establishment of religion, or prohibiting the free exercise thereof; or abridging the freedom of speech, or of the press; or the right of the people to peacefully assemble, and to petition the Government for a redress of grievances.[80]

After the Community Relations Committee printed its 1963 report for all Wacoans to see, some claimed the secrecy infringed on locals' rights to the press and represented an act of deception, but every reporter who refrained from printing integration stories voluntarily did so. Leaders at the time believed that Waco would desegregate more easily if the majority of locals remained ignorant of the situation.

Waco had waited six to eight years to

begin desegregation officially, fearing a conservative backlash. In some cases, the situation appeared that Waco elites requested the exclusion of the press because the elites feared that the sluggish progress of Waco up to the early 1960s would make outsiders view the city with disfavor. In the end, Waco's quiet civic integration proved successful, but the conclusion ended about as slowly as it began, with reference to Waco public schools.

The objective of desegregation in Waco was not one of giving African-Americans the same rights as whites; desegregation meant that whites began to accept that blacks and whites were equals in a modern state. Integration finally provided an opportunity for all people to obtain true equality under the rights and privileges enumerated during the establishment of the United States of America some two hundred years previously; an opportunity to achieve equality did not always translate to guaranteed equality. The biracial tensions of American history required/require several generations before, if ever, achieving complete tranquility.

Throughout history, many of Waco's civic leaders prided themselves on playing an active role in demonstrating Christian love and morality, the best examples of this pride being the numerous churches constructed in the city and Baylor University, the largest Baptist university in the world. The demonstrated racism by the white Waco community—from the exclusion of African-American leadership in local civic projects to threatening violence against a delivery man because of his skin color—proved that old Waco did not completely find harmony in its Christian roots. But as the desegregation process continued and the years passed, both black and white community leaders evolved from a forced cooperation to a general collaboration of professional friendship. Perhaps several factors contributed to this process of social development: legal ramifications, economics, the desire to subscribe to the morality of Christian doctrine—or perhaps it was the perpetual disgust created from living in the crammed quarters of "a house divided."

Endnotes

1. Lk. 11:17, *NIV.*
2. 605 Austin Avenue, photograph by Bradley T. Turner, taken on 4 July, 2009.
3. Brown *v.* The Board of Education of Topeka, 347 U.S. 483 (1954).
4. Plessy *v.* Ferguson, 163 U.S. 537 (1896).
5. U.S. Constitution, amend. 14.
6. "U.S. Supreme Court Strikes Down Race Segregation in Public Schools," *Waco Times-Herald,* 17 May, 1954.
7. "'Sure Texas Will Comply' Edgar Avers," *Waco Times-Herald,* 17 May, 1954.
8. Robin Carlysle Bean, "The Role of the Commercial-Civic Elite in the Desegregation of Public Facilities in Waco, Texas" (M.A. thesis, Baylor University, 1990), 35.
9. "Negro Leaders Hail Court Ruling, Clergy Cautious," *Waco Times-Herald,* 18 May, 1954.
10. Ibid.
11. Ibid.
12. "Waco School District Lines Face Changes," *Waco Times-Herald,* 18 May, 1954.
13. "Race Decisions Studies by Waco," *Waco Times-Herald,* 25 May, 1954.
14. "Negroes Request Park, Pool Use At San Antonio," *Waco Times-Herald,* 20 May, 1954.
15. "Segregation Ban Gets Mixed State

Reaction," *Waco Times-Herald*, 18 May, 1954.

16. Joe L. Ward, Jr., *Quiet Desegregation of Waco's Public Facilities*, available from "The Waco History Project," found online at http://www.wacohistoryproject. org/firstperson/joeward.html [accessed 27 June, 2009]; Paul Marable, "Desegregating Waco, 1961–1963," presented to the Waco Philosophers' Club, 21 April, 1997; Jack Kultgen, *The Oral Memoirs of J. H. Kultgen*, (Institute for Oral History), The Texas Collection, Baylor University, Waco, TX, 155.

17. Ward, *Quiet Desegregation*.

18. Kultgen, 158.

19. Bean, "The Role of the Commercial-Civic Elite," 56; Marvin Griffin, *The Oral Memoirs of Marvin Griffin*, (Institute for Oral History), The Texas Collection, Baylor University, Waco, TX, 166.

20. Marcus Langley Cooper, Jr., *The Oral Memoirs of Marcus Langley Cooper, Jr.*, (Institute for Oral History), The Texas Collection, Baylor University, Waco, TX, 151–52.

21. Marable, "Desegregating Waco."

22. Ibid.

23. Ibid.

24. Ward, *Quiet Desegregation*.

25. Ibid.

26. Ibid.

27. Bean, "The Role of the Commercial-Civic Elite," 60–61.

28. Kultgen, *The Oral Memoirs*, 151–52.

29. Marable, "Desegregating Waco."

30. Ward, *Quiet Desegregation*.

31. Oscar DuConge, *The Oral Memoirs of Oscar Norbert DuConge: February 20, 1975-July 31, 1975*, (Institute for Oral History), The Texas Collection, Baylor University, Waco, TX, 271.

32. Bean, "The Role of the Commercial-Civic Elite," 37–38, 51; Cooper, *The Oral Memoirs*, 151–53.

33. Bean, "The Role of the Commercial-Civic Elite," 52; DuConge, *The Oral Memoirs*, 363.

34. Bean, "The Role of the Commercial-Civic Elite," 52.

35. Ibid., 40.

36. Ibid., Marable, "Desegregating Waco."

37. Marable, "Desegregating Waco."

38. Kultgen, *The Oral Memoirs*, 154.

39. Marable, "Desegregating Waco."

40. Kultgen, *The Oral Memoirs*, 160.

41. Cooper, *The Oral Memoirs*, 173.

42. Ward, *Quiet Desegregation*.

43. Ibid.

44. The sources on this subject conflict on the details associated with how the whites protested.

45. Ward, *Quiet Desegregation*; Marable, "Desegregating Waco." .

46. Cooper, *The Oral Memoirs*, 144–46.

47. Bean, "The Role of the Commercial-Civic Elite," 67–68.

48. Ibid.

49. Ward, *Quiet Desegregation*.

50. Ibid.

51. Letter to the Waco Chamber of Commerce from the Progressive Community Council, on the topic of desegregation, 31 May, 1963, Bean, "The Role of the Commercial-Civic Elite," Appendix B, 101–103.

52. Kultgen, *The Oral Memoirs*, 162.

53. Ward, *Quiet Desegregation*.

54. Ibid.

55. Ibid.

56. Jane Derrick, "Fighting for single-member districts," available from the "Waco History Project," found online at http://www.wacohistoryproject. org/firstperson/janederrick.html [accessed 1 July, 2009].

57. Ward, *Quiet Desegregation*.

58. Ibid.

59. Marable, "Desegregating Waco," 6.

60. Ibid.

61. Ibid.

62. Ibid.

63. *Annual Report of the Community Relations Committee, 1963*, "The Role of the Commercial-Civic Elite," Appendix C, 104–108.

64. Ibid.

65. Ibid.

66. Ibid.

67. Ibid.

68. Ibid.

69. Ibid.

70. Ibid.

71. Ibid.

72. Bean, "The Role of the Commercial-Civic Elite," 84–88; "Integration Issue Haunts VA in Waco," *Dallas Morning News*, 17 December, 1963.

73. Ibid.

74. Kultgen, *The Oral Memoirs*, 161.

75. The integration of the Waco public school system is extensive and is not within the scope of this chapter, which focuses on the desegregation process within Waco businesses.

76. Van Allen, "Black businesses—built from scratch," available from "The Waco History Project," found online at http://www.wacohistoryproject.org/firstperson/vanallen.html [accessed 1 July, 2009].

77. Bean, "The Role of the Commercial-Civic Elite," 44–46.

78. Ibid., 50.

79. Kultgen, *The Oral Memoirs*, 162–63.

80. U.S. Constitution, amend. 1.

For the Pleasure of Which People?
Race in William Cameron Park, Waco, Texas

by Mark Firmin

Cameron Park, the Early Years

In late May 1910 when the Cameron family donated the Proctor Springs property to the City of Waco as a memorial to the late lumber tycoon, William Cameron, they stipulated that the land be used exclusively as a public park for the "pleasure of the people" of Waco. To a twenty-first-century audience this appears to be a straightforward decree to allow the use of the park by all Wacoans regardless of class, race, ethnicity, or religious persuasion. It is necessary to consider the context in which this statement was made, however. Waco was a segregated city in 1910. Racial violence permeated the air, especially with Waco being a hotbed of activity of the Ku Klux Klan. This is not to say that the Cameron family held malice toward any race, nor is it a claim the Camerons meant to exclude a particular race from Cameron Park. The author is simply asking the reader to consider, how did Wacoans in 1910 interpret the gift of a *public* park? How did Wacoans interpret the phrase, "for the pleasure of the *people*," and how has this interpretation changed over time?[1]

One of the most enduring perceptions of Cameron Park is Wacoans' association of the land with some of the area's first settlers, the Waco Indians. In 1772, the Waco Indians, a sub-tribe of the Wichita Confederacy, established a village on the west bank of the Brazos River near the Waco Springs. The Waco Indians chose the land for its abundance of fresh water, fertile soil, and timber. Although they resided on the west bank of the Brazos, the Waco Indians did not fish. Instead, they thrived upon agriculture and hunting. With a heavy reliance on corn, the Waco Indian diet also consisted of squash, beans, watermelon, and peaches that were grown each spring. The Wacos hunted buffalo, turkey, bear, and deer. In *Waco: A Sesquicentennial History*, Waco historian Patricia Ward Wallace noted the Waco Indians revered the Brazos and the springs that fed into it because they considered the springs to hold sacred powers. The Wacos referred to the Brazos as the "Great Tohomoho" and believed a goddess named "Woman Having Powers in Water" resided there. By drinking the sacred water from the springs and river, the Wacos believed they would ensure their prosperity and security.[2] Vigilant for threats to their land from rival tribes and encroaching white settlers, the Waco Indians thrived under the protective powers of the Brazos.

With the arrival of the Cherokees—who had been driven west along the Trail of Tears by the U.S. federal government—in Central Texas in the 1820s, the Waco Indians faced a challenge to their security. In 1829, the resurgent Cherokees attacked, scalping at least fifty Waco Indians. By 1830, the Cherokee Indians established a temporary village of their own on the east bank of the Brazos River across from the Wacos. The appearance of the Cherokees marked the beginning of the end for the Waco Village, and by 1837 the village was abandoned. The Wacos migrated northwest along the Brazos, eventually settling in Palo Pinto County.[3]

While is difficult to ascertain how or if the Waco Indians used the land in Cameron Park, the white community that settled in Waco developed folklore of Waco Indians at Cameron Park in the form of the legend of Lovers' Leap.

Many years prior to the Camerons' acquisition of sixty acres of the White tract—widely known as Lovers' Leap—Wacoans routinely trekked to the bluff situated atop the Bosque River for picnics, romantic excursions, or simply to take in the breathtaking view of the Texas landscape. Decca Lamar West frequently included the story of Lovers' Leap in her historical sketches of Waco. West's rendition of the fable centered on the Indian maiden Wah-Wah-Tee.

Looking at Lovers' Leap, May 2009. *Photograph by Mark Firmin.*

Looking off Lovers' Leap, December 2008. *Photograph by Bradley T. Turner.*

Daughter of a Waco chief, Wah-Wah-Tee fell in love with a handsome brave of the Apache tribe, the Waco Indians' fiercest enemy. This white man's tale of star-crossed Native American lovers ended in much the same way as Shakespeare's *Romeo and Juliet*. Knowing the impossibility of being together, Wah-Wah-Tee and her Apache lover attempted to elope only to be thwarted by Wah-Wah-Tee's father and brothers. From the east bank of the Bosque River, Wah-Wah-Tee's father watched his beloved daughter kiss her lover just before the two leaped from the bluff. The bodies of the two washed up on the banks of the river near their original meeting place, still clasped in love's eternal embrace. University of Texas anthropologist Mariah Wade notes the irony that stories "romanticizing the Indians as noble savages" were penned by "the descendants or contemporaries of the Anglo-Americans who killed or exiled most of the Indians of Texas." Rooted in fiction and racial stereotypes, the tale nonetheless captured the romance and frivolity engendered by the beloved scenic spot.[4]

Selected as the county seat of McLennan County in 1850 and incorporated in 1857, the City of Waco prospered for much of its first fifty years. Proctor Springs—the first piece of land acquired and donated by the Cameron family to form Cameron Park—was a popular recreational and meeting spot for Waco citizens in the latter half of the nineteenth century. Celebrating emancipation day, African-Americans held Juneteenth festivities at Proctor Springs. More than 6,000 Confederate and Union veterans from across the United States camped on the beautiful one hundred acres for a reunion in 1896.[5]

The City Beautiful Movement

As the twentieth century dawned, the United States entered the "Progressive Era." Historian Jon A. Peterson characterizes the Progressive ethos as steeped in a "complex drift … away from competitive and individualistic ethics toward more altruistic, cooperative values; away from orthodox laissez-faire economics toward more socially interventionist policies;" and "away from inward-looking Christian pietism toward a more socially fulfilled Christianity." The City Beautiful movement, an expression of "urban pro-gressivism" and civic improvement, swept the nation like an epidemic. Acquisition and preservation of scenic, riverfront property for parks constituted a key tenet of City Beautiful ideology, which manifested itself in Waco through the donation and development of Cameron Park.[6]

During the City Beautiful movement, the elite class assumed the duty to educate the lower classes in matters pertaining to civic improvement. City Beautiful historian William H. Wilson asserts that by becoming educators and imparting their own value system on the lower classes, the elite class became "environmentalists." Wilson chooses the term environmentalists for two primary reasons. First, the elite sought to reform society within the social construct of the day. Conscious of class lines, the elite felt obligated as privileged and enlightened citizens to assert "cultural hegemony" over the lower classes by imparting their progressive views of morality and aesthetics. Beauty, the elite believed, served as a vehicle for instructing and refining the tastes of the poor. Beauty possessed the "capacity to shape human thought and behavior."

Sketch of Cameron Park depicting social elites enjoying Proctor Springs. *Courtesy of the Turner Collection.*

One must bear in mind that City Beautiful operated as a Progressive Era reform movement within the American social environment of the early twentieth century. Thus, one should not be surprised that City Beautiful did nothing to promote racial equality; rather, the City Beautiful movement perpetuated the rigid separation and discrimination that characterized the Jim Crow South by recognizing and seeking to improve social class relations, but not race relations. Moreover, the height of City Beautiful occurred during the apex of the racial tension and violence in Waco and McLennan County. The intent here is not to disparage the City Beautiful movement—for the movement profoundly shaped the development of the modern American city —but to highlight the context in which the City

An illustration, circa 1910, of Riverside Drive. *Courtesy of the Turner Collection.*

Beautiful movement took place and the atmosphere in Waco when the gift of Cameron Park was given to the people.[7]

In September 1920, the Cameron family donated another 191 acres to Cameron Park, including the land encompassing the park's picturesque bluffs, the confluence of the Brazos and Bosque Rivers, and the grounds of the Cameron Park Clubhouse. Following the gift, the people of Waco approved a $65,000 bond issue to improve the new parkland. In May 1921, Wacoans celebrated the eleventh anniversary of Cameron Park with a massive gala, highlighted by a track meet for boys, a number of dance routines by young girls, and capped with a dance for adults at the new municipal clubhouse. Waco photographer Fred A. Gildersleeve took aerial photographs of the celebration.

Jim Crow and Cameron Park

Thrilled at the development of Cameron Park over the past eleven years—including the addition of a playground, tennis courts, roads, colorful flower beds, and renovations to the clubhouse—the *Waco Times-Herald* claimed, "no giant baby has ever made such progress in the matter of growth and improvement as the park has made." On an aesthetic and physical level, the *Times-Herald*'s assessment rings true. On a social level, however, Cameron Park was not immune to the racial tensions that pervaded the South during the Jim Crow era. Although marketed as a park donated and developed for the "pleasure of the people," Cameron Park did not have a tradition of including African-Americans from the outset. At the 1910 dedication, blacks primarily drove the floats carrying white children and prominent Wacoans to the park. Although not officially sanctioned, the exclusion of African-Americans from Waco's chief playground became engrained in the social life of the park. This is not to say that blacks never visited the park, since it was impossible to keep someone from entering the extensive and heavily wooded park. When they did attend, however, they were not welcome. Cameron Park was not the only "white" park from which blacks refrained from visiting for fear they might incur the wrath of police or white park patrons. The construction of Edgefield Park next to Baylor University required the destruction of shacks owned by black families. The "separate but equal" philosophy of the Jim Crow era saw Mackey Park in East Waco converted into a park for African-Americans. During the Second World War, Mackey Park was renamed Bledsoe-Miller Park to honor two of the most famous African-Americans from Waco—musician, composer, and singer Jules Bledsoe, and Pearl Harbor hero and Navy Cross recipient Doris Miller.[8]

White Wacoans' determination to maintain Jim Crow policies came to the forefront in the public outrage over a racially charged murder in Cameron Park in 1922. The peace and serenity of Cameron Park evaporated on November 21, 1922, when nineteen-year-old Grady Skipworth was shot and killed at Lovers' Leap. Skipworth's corpse was tossed over the cliff and found at the base of Lovers' Leap. Miss Naomi Boucher—Skipworth's date—claimed that a "Negro" committed the murder.[9] Matching the description provided by the assaulted girl, unsuspecting Jesse Thomas, an African-American service car driver, agreed to accompany specialized deputy E.L. McClure under the false pretense that Thomas would be paid to do yard work. Instead, McClure took Thomas to the house of Sam Harris, father of the sexually assaulted girl. Upon seeing Thomas, Harris' daughter exclaimed that Thomas was the murderer. Harris quickly and brazenly emptied his gun into Thomas, killing the young man where he stood. Later that day, Thomas' lifeless body was dragged and burned in front of a crowd of 5,000 people.[10]

In February 1923, less than three months after the killing of Skipworth, Roy Mitchell was arrested for the murder of Skipworth and others. Mitchell, also an African-American, purportedly confessed to six murders, clearing the name of Jesse Thomas, accused just a few months before. In July 1923, Mitchell, sentenced to six death penalties, was hanged in the town square of Waco—the last legal hanging in Texas.[11]

The murder of Grady Skipworth did not deter visitors from frequenting Cameron Park. Might the crimes have further hardened and embittered whites toward permitting the already excluded black community from visiting the park? Regardless of whether

Skipworth's murder at the hands of Roy Mitchell solidified the white community's resolve to maintain racial hegemony over Cameron Park, the fact is that a park intended for and funded by all the people in Waco would not experience racial integration for several decades.

During the Great Depression of the 1930s, Cameron Park served as an escape from the harsh and bitter realities caused by the economic collapse of markets around the world—like a cool dip in the wading pools at Proctor Springs or a plunge off a rope swing into the Brazos River. Kids enjoyed picnic lunches brought from home or caught catfish for dinner on trot lines in the river. A trek through the dense woods of Cameron Park or games of tennis and baseball might occupy the rest of the afternoon. During the Depression a miniature zoo that sat atop the hill overlooking Proctor Springs was a favorite spot. Enclosed with chicken wire, the zoo held owls, rabbits, peacocks, birds, swans, and monkeys. A man-made pond with exotic ducks just inside the 4th Street and Herring Avenue entrance at the bottom of a hill drew curious visitors as

well. As a boy growing up in East Texas, future Waco City Manager David F. Smith, Jr., came to Waco with his Boy Scout troop and camped in Pecan Bottoms. Thick woods, grassy knolls, cold water springs, scenic bluffs, and a top notch playground made Cameron Park a recreational retreat for an increasing number of Texans as well as Wacoans.[12]

A Belated Christmas Gift

In late December 1942, the *Waco News-Tribune* announced that William Cameron and Company—now under the leadership of William Cameron's son-in-law, E.R. Bolton—had purchased and donated an additional 64.5 acres to Cameron Park as a belated Christmas gift to the people of Waco, providing a reprieve and morale boost from the strain of the Second World War. Accompanying the land was a check for $5,000 to be used at the discretion of the Board of Commissioners to aid in improving the park. A provision of the deed allowed for the commissioners to exchange part or all of the donated land for different property so long as it would be used for park purposes. Quick to implement this provision, park commissioners swapped some of the donated land for property occupied by a few homes and the Lovers' Leap Baptist Church, an African-American congregation, which voted to relocate the church at 3rd Street and Marlboro Avenue.[13]

With Waco service personnel fighting in the conflicts that raged throughout North Africa, Europe, and the Pacific during World War II, one might think the recently expanded Cameron Park experienced a decline in use. On the contrary, the U.S. Army Air Corps opened two air fields, Blackland Army Air Field and Waco Army Air Field, in McLennan County, which brought thousands of men and women into Waco. The military bases and wartime industries that flourished in Waco infused sorely needed people and money into a city and economy ravished by the Depression. Several veterans might disagree with Waco historian Patricia Ward Wallace's assessment that "there was not much to do by way of entertainment in Waco during the war, although the town swarmed with servicemen from the two Waco bases and from nearby Camp Hood"

in Killeen. For entertainment, soldiers frequented the United Service Organization (USO) club and Waco's four movie theatres. Soldiers also used the Kiwanis Pool on 4th Street—better known as the "Beach"—as well as Cameron Park. Numerous photographs reveal pilots, soldiers, and seamen recreating and relaxing in Cameron Park. Young women in Waco, like Margaret Smith Pauling, often went to the park on dates with servicemen. They played on the playgrounds, visited the Rose Garden, and even tried to throw rocks across the Brazos River from on top of Lovers' Leap. One young man actually managed to fling a rock to the eastern bank of the Brazos, costing Margaret a Coke since she bet the serviceman he could not accomplish the feat.[14]

Although everyone fought for a common cause, the policy of racial segregation was entrenched in the ranks of the military and the factories churning out ammunition, planes, tanks, and supplies. Segregation extended to entertainment as well, as African-American soldiers made use of the Negro USO and Elizabeth Lee Recreation Center. Along with black

servicemen, African-Americans from Waco continued to be barred from Cameron Park. Despite being warned by his parents that Cameron Park was a dangerous place for blacks, young Noah Jackson, Jr., occasionally rode his bike along Riverside Drive and into Pecan Bottoms. Each time, Jackson was asked to leave by either police or white park-goers. On one particular occasion, Jackson—with his sister sitting on the handlebars—was pedaling out of the park when a car came up from behind, and a passenger struck Jackson with a blunt object across his back, sending both children crashing to the ground. The African-American community was forced to wait several more years before exploring Cameron Park.[15]

Integration

By June 1954, the Parks and Recreation Commission faced a number of problems. For Chairman of the Commission Mrs. Rodney J. LeBlanc, the leading problem stemmed from the need for "a complete and thorough cleaning of Cameron Park." Before cleaning and improvements efforts in the park commenced, the Commission was compelled to address an even more pressing issue—racial segregation. At a July 1954 commission meeting—the same year as the landmark Supreme Court decision in *Brown v. The Board of Education of Topeka*—members of two separate African-American groups, the Citizens Committee on Recreation and the Waco Commission on Race Relations, demanded unfettered access to all tax-funded parks and recreation facilities in Waco. With Bledsoe-Miller Park largely reduced to ruins by the devastating tornado in 1953, African-Americans also requested that "immediate steps be taken" to remedy the unsatisfactory condition of the black community's primary recreational facility. A formal statement told how "several groups of Negroes have been forced by police to leave Cameron Park and a park at Lake Waco."[16]

Chief of Police Jesse Gunterman responded that until action was taken to reverse the traditional "policies of racial segregation" in Waco's parks and recreational facilities, he and the police force were compelled to ask African-Americans "to leave these areas not set aside for their use." Although providing little consolation to the black community, Gunterman stressed that if a new policy of desegregation were adopted the police would enforce it. With racial tensions on the rise across the country, Thomas Turner, Central Texas correspondent for the *Dallas Morning News*, reported that "many prominent Waco residents of both races are privately predicting a rash of 'incidents' if the city's parks, pools, and golf courses are thrown open to Negroes in the tradition-steeped Brazos River stronghold." The rest of the summer passed without incident, but changes to the entrenched policies of segregation did not occur just yet.[17]

The informal policy of racial segregation began to ease slowly in the same way that downtown businesses began to accommodate African-Americans. Testing the laxness of the policy, Rev. Marvin C. Griffin of New Hope Baptist Church started an annual church picnic for his African-American congregation in Cameron Park in the early 1960s. In April 1967, Reverend Griffin became the first African-American appointed to the powerful and prestigious Parks and Recreation Commission. Future park ranger Larry Simms remembers crossing from East Waco into the park with his friends to pick pecans, play ball games like "Strikeout," and ride their bikes all over the park.

As racial segregation in the park slowly dissipated, use of Cameron Park in general continued to increase in the 1960s. Over a ten-day period in December 1965, more than 11,000 cars viewed the Christmas scene near the Herring Avenue entrance in Cameron Park. An annual tradition for many Waco families, the scene included Santa's sleigh, reindeer, elves, gifts, and a workshop. In the spring, children went to the park to make Easter eggs. On Easter Sunday, "sunrise services" were often held at the Rose Garden. The Huaco Bowmen Archery Club—which entered into an agreement with the Parks and Recreation Department in December 1961—brought a new activity to the park. The sheer volume of people using the park in the 1960s became staggering. Favorite pastimes and locations such as the playgrounds, wading pools, bridle paths, beautiful vistas, and ball games brought Wacoans to the park each year in droves.[18]

Urban Renewal

Waco was not immune to the social and political upheaval of the 1960s and 1970s. In the throes of the Cold War, the American presence in the Vietnam conflict continued to escalate. The Civil Rights movement forced Americans to confront racial segregation and discrimination directly. The assassinations of the Kennedy brothers and civil rights icons Malcolm X and Martin Luther King, Jr., disillusioned Americans' psyche. The youthful counter-culture generation and anti-Vietnam War movement were in full swing, rebelling against the values and traditions of older Americans. Locally, the disastrous pedestrian mall on Austin Avenue and the Federal Government's Urban Renewal initiatives stoked economic turmoil and racial tensions in Waco. Constituting 5.2 percent of Waco's population in 1960, the Hispanic community bore much of the brunt of Urban Renewal efforts as barrios like Sand Town and Calle Dos were demolished, forcing the relocation of the Hispanic community. Black-owned businesses and communities also endured considerable suffering and dis-

location. The decay of downtown contributed to the "white flight" movement toward West Waco and the suburbs of Hewitt, Woodway, and Robinson.[19]

While there were setbacks, some progress was made. Respected local dentist Dr. Gary H. Radford—encouraged by his colleague and future mayor Oscar DuConge—won his 1966 campaign to become the first African-American elected to Waco's City Council. Still reeling from the 1953 tornado, Waco's recovery efforts received a boost from developments in the 1960s. Waco historian Patricia Ward Wallace notes that "the addition of McLennan Community College in 1964, an enlarged Lake Waco in 1965, Texas State Technical Institute in 1966, and most significantly … Interstate Highway 35" proved to be economic, educational, and transportation boons for the city.[20] After the passage of a 1967 bond issue, city officials announced their intentions to widen and extend Herring Avenue with the construction of a bridge across the Brazos. Perceived as a threat to the serenity and natural beauty of Cameron Park by bisecting the most historic and highly used areas of the park, the proposed Herring Avenue

Bridge generated considerable and vocal opposition. The controversy over the Herring Avenue Bridge marked the beginning of a period of slow decline for Cameron Park.

In recent years, the claim that the Herring Avenue Bridge controversy largely centered on heavily white West Waco wanting to deny largely black East Waco direct access to Cameron Park has emerged. While race was undoubtedly an underlying issue, it did not play as prominent a role in the opposition as has been suggested. On the contrary, some Wacoans suggest that racial tensions surrounding Cameron Park emerged more prominently only after the completion of the Herring Avenue Bridge and the increased access, traffic, and mixing of cultures.[21]

For most people opposed to the bridge, the primary issue centered on preserving the beauty and integrity of the Cameron Park entrance at Herring Avenue. The entrance gates donated by the Cameron family had welcomed visitors for nearly forty years. The big oaks inside the entrance provided not only beauty but also shaded picnic spots and the site for the annual Christmas

Spray Park near the Herring Avenue Bridge, May 2009. *Photograph by Mark Firmin.*

scene. With the widening and expansion of Herring Avenue, the Rose Garden and Proctor Springs would be bisected by a busy street that prohibited children from crossing from one area of the park to another without serious safety issues. Concern over an increase in traffic, noise pollution, and litter also pervaded the minds of opponents. While most agreed that increasing the ease of access to the park for all segments of Waco's population was needed, many Wacoans simply did not want to sacri-

fice the oldest, most beautiful, and most heavily used part of the park. Many Wacoans feared that the Herring Avenue Bridge would ruin Cameron Park.[22]

Racism did not motivate most critics of the bridge. Critics were clearly willing to consider increasing access to Cameron Park; they simply opposed locating the bridge at Herring Avenue—the heart of the park. Dr. Maurice C. Barnes, Congressman W.R. "Bob" Poage, and Walter G. Lacy, chairman of the Parks and Recreation Commission in 1968,

either suggested alternative routes, asked for a public hearing to discuss the issue, or stated that the project should be "postponed, not abandoned," so that Wacoans could reevaluate. If opponents truly did not want African-Americans in the park, they would have argued against any bridge regardless of the location or construction timeframe. The fact that the black community did not view the Herring Avenue Bridge controversy as a racial issue also seriously undermines the argument that the opposition stemmed largely from racial suspicions. Noah Jackson recalls that many in the black community saw the issue as being between two factions of whites, the city government and the old money of Waco that lived in the vicinity of the park and largely bankrolled the opposition.[23]

The Rise in Park Usage

During the 1960s and 1970s, young African-Americans unaware of the politics surrounding the Herring Avenue Bridge began riding their bikes in the park more frequently. As a young teenager, Walter Abercrombie, Waco native and legendary Baylor football player, regularly rode his bike to the park with friends all the way from his house on South 8th Street near Baylor University. After an exhausting ride to Lovers' Leap, the youths put their bikes aside to rest their legs and worked their arms by challenging one another to throw a rock to the other side of the river, a difficult feat for even the strongest of men. The young teenagers could not hurl the rocks any farther than halfway across the river. The arduous journey to Lovers' Leap on bicycle—which Abercrombie laughingly credits as developing all of the strength in his football legs—was worth it purely for the ride down. Smarter than their older counterparts sitting behind the wheel of a car, the rascally youths planted a lookout at the blind spot of each hill to watch for oncoming traffic. If Abercrombie got a thumbs up from the spotters, the coast was clear and he pedaled down the steep, sharply curving hills as fast as possible. The bike picked up so much speed that by the time he hit the straightaway near Jacob's Ladder, he could coast on his bike all the way through the North Pecan Bottoms past the Redwood Shelter.[24]

Organized sports activities began in the park in the late 1960s, introducing a new generation of young African-Americans to Cameron Park. The Parks and Recreation Commission granted the all-black Eastern Little League permission to establish fields on the old Waco High athletic field along 4th Street. Noah Jackson and other black leaders largely funded and constructed the facility themselves, helping to foster tremendous civic pride. Eastern Little League and the YMCA Elks—the pee-wee football team that used the fields in the fall—are classic models of well-oiled organizations. The Elks, which won nearly every city championship in three divisions for more than twenty years, instituted a "no pass, no play" rule long before it was implemented in schools. Eastern Little League also flexed competitive muscles by winning a state title in 1981. Both the YMCA Elks and Eastern Little League earned respect not just for their athletic prowess, but for the discipline and sportsmanship of both players and parents.

When the leagues were asked to relocate to make way for the construction of the Cameron Park Zoo, long-time director and coach Noah Jackson said he felt good about leaving Cameron Park because of the opportunities it furnished for people from all walks of life in the black community. Jackson credits the athletic organizations and the facilities in Cameron Park for fashioning children into well-disciplined and educated young men and women.[25]

With the completion of the Herring Avenue Bridge in the early 1970s, Cameron Park saw a surge in park use by African-Americans. Emmons Cliff became the favorite social spot for African-Americans. A convivial family atmosphere characterized the weekend gatherings at Emmons Cliff. Music by artists and groups such as Frankie Beverly and Maize, the Commodores, Lakeside, and Parliament poured out of car stereos, and boom boxes added to the festive mood. The heavy aroma of smoked barbeque and grilled burgers filled the air along with the laughter of children romping around. Cameron Park afforded African-American families a safe, inexpensive, and beautiful environment—essentially the same luxuries that whites in Cameron Park had enjoyed since the park's dedication more than sixty years earlier.[26]

As more people poured into Emmons Cliff, the area became overcrowded and unsafe. The traffic congestion and parking nightmare caused by the massive gatherings prevented emergency vehicles from reaching the point. Alcohol and drug use by a few ruined a good time for most, and many law-abiding African-American families opted to stay at home. The music played at deafening volume levels increasingly became a nuisance to families living in the vicinity. Noah Jackson and City Councilman Dewey Pinckney pleaded with the younger African-Americans to be respectful of people living in the area.

To alleviate the traffic problem, the Waco City Council banned parking on Cameron Park Road leading up to Emmons Cliff from the Mouth of the Bosque and for a short distance north of the cliff. Parking on a portion of the adjacent side street Merriwood Drive was also forbidden. Some members of the black community believed that parking restrictions were designed to force African-Americans to leave the park. Speaking on the behalf of two black organizations, the Northeast Neighborhood Council and the Grass Roots Organizations, Don Freeman acknowledged the traffic issue, but he concluded from his personal investigation that traffic and parking problems were pervasive in all areas of the park, not just at Emmons Cliff. City Councilmen Dewey Pinckney sought to assure the black community that no group was being targeted and that all groups should feel welcome in the city's parks. A *Waco Tribune-Herald* article reporting the parking ban also stated that harassment of both whites and blacks by police was occurring in parks throughout the city. Seeing the escalating racial tensions, Freeman concluded that the problem in the parks "boils down to the mixing of blacks and whites in Waco which has always been a problem." Eventually, several African-American leaders requested that the Parks and Recreation Department shut off the electricity to the Emmons Cliff area. The parking ban and loss of electrical outlets gradually ended the black community's use of Emmons Cliff.[27]

The Park in Decay

By the late 1970s, both whites and blacks faced a park plummeting into decay. The perception, and to a degree the reality, of Cameron Park was that it was becoming a haven for criminal activity. Inklings of problems in the park began to develop even prior to the 1968 Herring Avenue Bridge controversy. For the first few years after his arrival in Waco in 1963, Baylor professor Dr. Fred Gehlbach heard rumors of crime emerging in the park. While on a date with her future husband in Cameron Park on a warm night in 1964, Dorothy Head Powell remembers a police officer rapping on the window of her boyfriend's car. The police officer wanted the lovebirds to be vigilant because of reports of a man attacking people in the park. Although she literally lived next door to the park and had played there for eighteen years, Dorothy distinctly remembers the incident in 1964 as being the first time she ever feared for her safety in the park.[28]

Cameron Park's Dual Nature

The completion of Lions Park on Bosque Boulevard and New Road in 1965, the opening of several parks surrounding the new Lake Waco, changes in recreation patterns, new neighborhood parks, and the white population's movement to West Waco and the suburbs all contributed to creating a vacuum in Cameron Park that needed to be filled. The African-American community largely filled the vacuum created by the white community's gradual abandonment of the park. The completion of the Herring Avenue Bridge in the early 1970s certainly accelerated African-Americans' use of the park as well because of the city's stated purpose of the bridge—to create more access for all of Waco. On weekends, traffic congestion from massive numbers of people congregating at Emmons Cliff and later in the South Pecan Bottoms became so severe it might take a person anywhere from thirty minutes to an hour and a half to get from one end of the Bottoms to the other—a distance of three blocks. Waco resident Charles D. Turner said that if you were white and waiting in traffic, you did not even consider honking your horn out of fear. While stuck in the traffic line in Pecan Bottoms, Dorothy Head Powell remembers her truck being surrounded by a group of people and rocked back and forth. Traffic congestion, compounded by "racial suspi-

cions," played a major role in the white community's perception that they were no longer welcome in Cameron Park—a perception Noah Jackson suggests whites were correct to have. In Jackson's opinion, Cameron Park in the 1980s became a place of reverse discrimination. Jackson, who had been thrown from his bicycle by a blunt object wielded by a white motorist in the 1940s, lamented that by the 1980s some members of the African-American community were now guilty of a policy in the park they had fought to end.[29]

As a result of the white community's gradual abandonment of Cameron Park, the African-American community owned Pecan Bottoms on the weekends, especially on Sundays. Despite negative perceptions by segments of both the African-American and white communities, Parks and Recreation Director Max Robertson confidently stated that "99 percent" of the people in Pecan Bottoms were law-abiding citizens there to enjoy the social and recreational experience. The massive congregations in Pecan Bottoms occupied only a fraction of the total area of the park, leaving the heavily-wooded

and secluded areas open to illicit activity. Larry Simms, a former officer with the Waco Police Department, commented that on weekdays secluded areas such as Lovers' Leap, Circle Point, Lindsey Hollow, Proctor Springs, and the Mouth of the Bosque witnessed crimes such as prostitution, drug trafficking, and homosexual activity.[30]

During the 1980s, Cameron Park wore two different faces that changed with the rising and setting of the sun. Cameron Park's dual nature contributed to the park's already slumping reputation. A September 1984 *Dallas Morning News* feature on Lovers' Leap revealed that the park's poor reputations extended beyond the city limits of Waco. The article depicted a romantic point in the daytime as the reporter encountered Baylor students talking about engagement plans, a Hispanic couple, and Waco sculptor and artist James Lawrence all enjoying time at the bluff. Once a popular nighttime destination for dates and moonlight picnics, the park was nearly abandoned after dark. A nighttime excursion to the park seemed tantamount to a suicide mission to many Wacoans. With no money for rent, twenty-three-year-old Indiana native Lloyd Breeder, his wife Robin, and their friend Steve Gardner were forced to live in their car in Cameron Park for a few weeks. Breeder confided to reporter Kent Biffle that although he had lived in the Bronx for half a year, Cameron Park "'scares the hell'" out of him at night, because "muggers and rapists" infested the shadows of the park.[31]

Whether Wacoans' perception of Cameron Park as a dangerous place was justified remains debatable. At some level, however, perception is rooted in reality. Many Wacoans, regardless of race, felt uneasy and sometimes terrified in the park from the late 1960s to the 1980s. One of the most frightening experiences in Walter Abercrombie's life occurred one night when he and his girlfriend were at one of the scenic overlooks. For reasons he cannot fully explain, Abercrombie simply could not relax and take in the beauty of the park for fear he and his girlfriend were in danger. Whether compounded by recent criminal activity or not, the perception and distinct feeling of being unsafe kept Walter and thousands of other Wacoans from going to Cameron Park at night. Former officer Larry Simms concurs that many officers in the Waco Police Department also considered the park a dangerous place. Wacoans' fears and negative perceptions of Cameron Park at night had also transcended to the daytime. With fear's shadow engraining itself in the minds of Wacoans, the park had rapidly slipped into neglect and decay.[32]

Cameron Park Turns 75

The seventy-fifth anniversary of Cameron Park in 1985 presented an opportunity for city officials and concerned citizens to generate momentum for an effort to reassert the public's claim to Cameron Park. Parks and Recreation Director Max Robertson recognized the potential of the seventy-fifth anniversary to serve as a watershed moment in the park's history. The anniversary festivities held at Lovers' Leap attracted around seventy-five city officials and a few dozen interested citizens, including William Cameron descendents Mrs. Albert Clifton and Linda Reichenbach, who cited the need for new activities to draw people back into the park. They also urged support for renewed efforts at bringing the Waco Zoo to Cameron Park. Announcing future plans for the park, Jon Spelman, chairman of the Parks and Recreation Commission, named the members of the newly formed Cameron Park Study Committee, a diverse group of concerned and enthusiastic citizens tasked with researching ways to improve the park and address its sagging image in the community. To aid the committee in its endeavor, a $45,000 grant to fund a comprehensive plan for Cameron Park as well as the rest of Waco's park system was also announced.[33]

The thirteen-member Cameron Park Study Committee—chaired by Waco native and Baylor graduate Christi Breeding—quickly immersed itself in studying the problems hounding the beleaguered park. "Phase 1" of the revitalization efforts involved a dual focus of tackling the traffic and parking dilemma in Pecan Bottoms and providing recommendations on how to improve the park's image. Encompassed by a narrow two-lane loop with Cameron Park Road to the east and West Park Drive on the west, Pecan Bottoms was a veritable nightmare of traffic congestion on weekends. With hundreds of people flooding the Bottoms every Sunday, cars were parked on both sides of each road. Drivers moved at a snail's pace to flash their polished cars and wheels, and motorists often stopped their cars to holler at friends. Drivers often had to wait up to an hour to get through the Bottoms. The deplorable traffic conditions posed a safety concern, as congestion prevented police and emergency vehicles from reaching people who were ill or hurt. Preventing access to other areas in the park, congestion in Pecan Bottoms caused many frustrated Wacoans to stop visiting Cameron Park altogether.[34]

While members of the white community no longer felt welcome in the park and harbored racial suspicions of the massive gatherings of minority groups in the Pecan Bottoms, in contrast, new parking restrictions suggested by the Cameron Park Study Committee caused members of the black community to believe that they were being targeted for removal. African-Americans then leveled charges of discrimination at city officials. Delicately navigating the thin line of racial sensitivity and negative perceptions plaguing Cameron Park in the 1980s, the committee and city officials had two major tasks. On the one hand, the Parks and Recreation Department needed to convince African-Americans and Latinos using Pecan Bottoms that revitalization efforts were not intended to remove them. On the other hand, city officials needed to convince families from all ethnic backgrounds that Cameron Park was a safe place, and that the city was serious about improving the park. To assuage the fears and concerns of all sides, and to help establish a permanent, visible, and public presence in the park, the Cameron Park Study Committee suggested developing a mounted patrol by park rangers.[35]

Park Rangers Start to Work

Of the eighty-seven applicants for the Park Ranger program, Larry Simms was one of three chosen for the "Cameron Cavalry." Tasked with helping to enforce new parking regulations and provide security, the unarmed Rangers were invested with authority to issue citations and, when needed, radio the Waco Police Department, which provided great support and help for the program. As a native of Waco and former police officer, Simms knew the Rangers had their work cut out for them. Although Simms emphasizes that a huge majority of people in the Bottoms abided by the law, he also knew of the Bottoms' worst aspects. As a police officer and private citizen, Simms was well acquainted with the problems in Cameron Park, particularly Pecan Bottoms. Prior to the introduction of Park Rangers, Simms noticed that traffic congestion—which he asserts was often intentional—prevented police officers from breaking up fights and illicit activities such as gambling, dog fighting, and drug use. On horseback, the Park Rangers were not hampered the way police officers in vehicles were. The enhanced mobility and imposing image of authority of Rangers on horseback allowed for the clearing out of criminal activity and alleviation of traffic congestion. Rangers Nora Schell, Deke Dalrymple, and Simms worked together and the Park Ranger program made an immediate impact on Cameron Park. The Rangers roamed the park checking driver's licenses

Looking down Proctor Springs, about 1915. *Courtesy of the Turner Collection.*

and insurance cards, and even blocked off roads to prevent people from making the loop in the Pecan Bottoms. Eventually the loop was removed to allow park-goers better access to the Brazos River. Within the first year and a half of the Park Ranger program, police reports on offenses in Cameron Park were cut nearly in half from sixty offenses in 1986 to thirty-five in 1987.[36]

Reducing crime in Cameron Park, however, comprised only one facet of the Park Ranger program. *Waco Tribune-Herald* reporter Mike Copeland described the Rangers as donning "two hats: one for security and one for public relations." The Park Rangers' proficient skills as good-will ambassadors for the city and the park proved to be the most important aspect of their daily work. Simms agrees the main intent of the Rangers was to alter the way people viewed the park. For people who had refrained from using the park out of fear, the Rangers provided a desperately needed symbol that the park was safe and that all were welcome. Simms and Schell consistently provided reassurance to park-goers that Waco was not trying to run anyone out of the park except those

Looking down Proctor Springs, 2009. *Photograph by Mark Firmin.*

who engaged in criminal activities. Ultimately, the Park Rangers program was about reestablishing Cameron Park as a safe and inviting place for all Wacoans.[37]

By the mid-1990s it became apparent to most Wacoans that the successful revitalization efforts started in the mid-1980s had propelled Cameron Park to move far beyond the darkest chapter of its history. Even a double homicide in 1995 in Pecan Bottoms did little to dissuade throngs of Wacoans from flocking to Cameron Park in the afternoons and on weekends. *Waco Tribune-Herald* opinion page editor and staunch advocate of Cameron Park, John Young wrote in February 1993 that he was thankful his children were blessed with an opportunity to develop "precious childhood memories of Cameron Park" together with Wacoans of "many colors."[38] Young's words ring true. Through hard work, sacrifice, and an iron will, many Wacoans conquered the fear and prejudices that

The remnants of Proctor Springs, 2009. *Photograph by Mark Firmin.*

kept them from using the park in the 1960s, 1970s, and 1980s. With each year more Wacoans recognize how lucky they are to own a beautiful natural refuge in the midst of an urban jungle. Perhaps of paramount importance, most Wacoans now view Cameron Park as an invaluable asset, protected and set aside by the Cameron family. Now, Cameron Park truly is for the pleasure of all the people.

ENDNOTES

1. R.J. Tolson, *A History of William Cameron and Co., Inc., with a Biographical Sketch of Wm. Cameron and Others* (Waco, TX: J.S. Barnett, 1925); "Sketch of William Cameron Park," in Tolson, *History of William Cameron*; Patricia Ward Wallace, *Waco: A Sesquicentennial History* (Virginia Beach, Va.: Donning Company Publishers, 1999), 109.

2. Wallace, *Waco*, 13.

3. Wallace, *Waco*, 15; Kenna Lang, "An Environmental History: William Cameron Park, Waco, Texas" (M.A. thesis, Baylor University, 2007), 27; Frank H. Watt, "The Waco Indian Village and Its Peoples," *Texana*, 6, no. 3 (1968): 209.

4. "Lovers' Leap Park Gift," *Waco Times-Herald*, 28 June, 1917; Tolson, *William Cameron and Co.*, "Sketch of William Cameron Park;" Decca Lamar West, "The Legend of Lovers' Leap and An Historical Sketch of Waco, Texas," (Waco: Knight Printing Co., 1912); J.B. Smith, "Did Lovers Really Leap From Lovers' Leap," *Waco Tribune-Herald*, 14 February, 2009.

5. Wallace, *Waco*, 22-23; "Emancipation Celebration," *Waco Daily Examiner*, 17 June, 1896; "The Waco Reunion," *Dallas Morning News*, 5 August, 1896.

6. Jon A. Peterson, *The Birth of City Planning in the United States, 1840–1917* (Baltimore: Johns Hopkins University Press, 2003), 101, 116, 121.

7. William H. Wilson, *The City Beautiful Movement* (Baltimore: The Johns Hopkins University Press, 1989), 78–81.

8. "Cameron Park Given Birthday Party Friday," *Waco Times-Herald*, 28 May,

1921; Tolson, *A History of William Cameron & Co.*, "Sketch of William Cameron Park;" For reference to black float drivers see "Waco's Unanimous Tender of Appreciation of Princely Gift," *Waco Times-Herald*, 28 May, 1910; *Illustrated Municipal Handbook of Waco: The Happy Prosperous City of Central Texas* (Waco, TX: City of Waco, 1914), 25; Dayton Kelley, ed., *Handbook of Waco and McLennan County, Texas* (Waco, TX: Texian Press, 1972), 29, 189.

9. The case resembled the murder of Harrell Bolton and sexual assault of his date outside of Waco just seven months earlier in May 1922.

10. "Couple at Waco Attacked by Negro," *Dallas Morning News*, 22 November, 1922; "Negro Identified," *Waco Times-Herald*, 27 May, 1922; "Officers Link Road Tragedy with Cameron Park Shooting," *Waco Times-Herald*, 28 May, 1922.

11. "Couple at Waco Attacked by Negro;" "Charges Against Boucher Dropped in Waco Killing," *Dallas Morning News*, 1 February, 1923; "Admission That He Slew 5 Attributed to Negro at Waco," *Dallas Morning News*, 10

February, 1923; "Roy Mitchell to be Hanged Monday, *Dallas Morning News*, 29 July, 1923; Dayton Kelley, ed., *Handbook of Waco and McLennan County*, 192.

12. Dorothy Head Powell and Frank Curre, Jr., interview by author, 28 January, 2009, Institute for Oral History, Baylor University, Waco, TX; Johnny Appell and Beth Appell, interview by author, 3 November, 2008, Institute for Oral History, Baylor University, Waco, TX; David F. Smith, Jr., interview by author, 1 August, 2008, Institute for Oral History, Baylor University, Waco, TX.

13. "64 1-2 Acres Given By Cameron Firm to Enlarge Park," *Waco News-Tribune*, 30 December, 1942; "Trustees of Lovers' Leap Baptist Church to the City of Waco for use of William Cameron Park as shown in Vol. 502, page 475, Deed Records McLennan County," City of Waco Records and Archives, Cameron Park File, microfilm, reel 3, blip 0063.

14. Wallace, *Waco*, 111–14; Alva Stem, interview by author, 9 January, 2009, Institute for Oral History, Baylor University, Waco, TX.

15. Wallace, *Waco*, 115; Alva Stem

interview; Noah Jackson, Jr., interview by author, 28 May, 2009, Institute for Oral History, Baylor University, Waco, TX.

16. Mrs. Rodney J. LeBlanc to W.W. Naman, 24 June, 1954, City of Waco, Parks and Recreation Department, Minutes of the Parks and Recreation Commission; "Negroes Present Four Bids to Waco Recreation Panel," *Waco Times-Herald*, 22 July, 1954; "City Park Segregation Policy to Continue, Gunterman Says," *Waco Times-Herald*, 4 August, 1954.

17. "Police Policy Stated on Park Segregation," *Waco News-Tribune*, 4 August, 1954; "City Park Segregation Policy to Continue," Gunterman Says, *Waco Times-Herald*, 4 August, 1954; Thomas Turner, "Waco Negroes Bidding for Use of City Parks," *Dallas Morning News*, 6 August, 1954.

18. City of Waco, Parks and Recreation Department, Minutes of the Parks and Recreation Commission 22 January, 1965; City of Waco, Parks and Recreation Department, Minutes of the Parks and Recreation Commission, 13 December, 1961; "Where Buffalo Clover Bloomed," *Waco Times-Herald*,

31 May, 1959; City of Waco, Parks and Recreation Department, Minutes of the Parks and Recreation Commission, 16 May, 1967; Marvin C. Griffin, interview by author, 12 August, 2008, Institute for Oral History, Baylor University, Waco, TX; Larry Simms, interview by author, 13 May, 2009, Institute for Oral History, Baylor University, Waco, TX.

19. Wallace, *Waco*; Noah Jackson, Jr., interview.

20. Wallace, *Waco*, 161.

21. David F Smith, Jr., interview; Dorothy Head Powell and Frank Curre, Jr., interview; Charles D. Turner, interview by author, 19 March, 2009, Institute for Oral History, Baylor University, Waco, TX.

22. Fred Gehlbach, interview by author, 12 August, 2008, Institute for Oral History, Baylor University, Waco, TX; David F. Smith, Jr., interview; Charles D. Turner interview; Johnny Appell and Beth Appell interview.

23. "A Chronological History," Nell Pape Papers, The Texas Collection, Baylor University, Waco, TX, 9, 12; Maurice C. Barnes to H. Malcolm Louden and City Council, 13 July, 1968, Nell Pape Papers; W.R. Poage to Mrs. G.H. Pape, 21 December, 1968, Nell Pape Papers; Noah Jackson, Jr., interview.

24. Walter Abercrombie, interview by author, 23 March, 2009, Institute for Oral History, Baylor University, Waco, TX.

25. Noah Jackson, Jr., interview. Mr. Jackson says that the Eastern Little League and YMCA Elks began playing in Cameron Park in the 1960s, but the earliest documentation in the Parks and Recreation Minutes is August 1972, Parks and Recreation Commission Minutes, 18 August, 1972, Parks and Recreation Department, Waco, TX.

26. Walter Abercrombie interview; "Emmons Cliff Area Parking Banned," *Waco Tribune-Herald*, 4 May, 1977.

27. Noah Jackson, Jr., interview; Walter Abercrombie interview; "Emmons Cliff Area Parking Banned;" Larry Simms interview.

28. Fred Gehlbach interview; Dorothy Head Powell and Frank Curre, Jr., interview.

29. "Cameron Park Merits New Life," *Waco Tribune-Herald*, 19 May, 1985; Larry Simms interview; Max Robertson, interview by author, 29 October, 2008, Institute for Oral History, Baylor University, Waco, TX; Noah Jackson, Jr., interview.

30. Lynn Bulmahn, "William Cameron Park Enjoys Ceremony Marking Service to City," *Waco Tribune-Herald*, 19 May, 1985; Walter Abercrombie interview; Larry Simms interview.

31. Kent Biffle, "Lovers' Leap Still Attracts Young Hearts," *Dallas Morning News*, 30 September, 1984; Charles D. Turner interview; Dorothy Head Powell and Frank Curre, Jr., interview; Larry Simms interview.

32. Walter Abercrombie interview; Larry Simms interview; Charles D. Turner interview.

33. Lynn Bulmahn, "William Cameron Park Enjoys Ceremony Marking Service to City;" Mike Copeland, "Wacoans Urged to Enjoy Park," *Waco Tribune-Herald*, 20 May, 1985.

34. Lynn Bulmahn, "Officials Mull Cameron Parking Rules," *Waco Tribune-Herald*, 22 May, 1985; Ann Cervenka, "Officials Seek Help with Park parking," *Waco Tribune-Herald*, 29 July, 1985; Walter Abercrombie interview; Ernesto Fraga, interview by author, 26 March, 2009, Institute for

Oral History, Baylor University, Waco, TX; Charlie Jaynes, interview by Dave Sikkema, 26 July, 2008, Institute for Oral History, Baylor University, Waco, TX; Dorothy Head Powell and Frank Curre, Jr., interview; Max Robertson interview; Larry Simms interview.

35. Ann Cervenka, "Officials Seek Help with Park Parking," Charlie Jaynes interview; Dorothy Head Powell and Frank Curre, Jr., interview; Max Robertson interview; Larry Simms interview.

36. Mark England, "Cameron's Cavalry," *Waco Tribune-Herald*, 1 December, 1986; Rebecca Zimmermann, "Riders Show Off Horse Sense to Apply for Park Ranger Jobs," *Waco Tribune-Herald*, 19 January, 1986; Larry Simms interview; Walter Abercrombie interview; Mike Copeland, "Rangers Cut Crime at Park," *Waco Tribune-Herald*, 19 November, 1987.

37. Mike Copeland, "Park Rangers Cut Crime at Park," Max Robertson interview; Larry Simms interview.

38. Mark England, "Park's Image a Concern," *Waco Tribune-Herald*, 21 March, 1995; John Young, "Park of Many Colors," *Waco Tribune-Herald*, 2 February, 1993.

What Are They Fighting For?
Reaction to the Vietnam War in Waco

by Bradley T. Turner

BAYLOR–1967

Baylor Students and Vietnam

Birds sing and flowers grow around the statue of Judge R.E.B. Baylor on the Baylor University campus.[1] The oversized, bronzed figure of the early Texas leader Baylor sits atop a granite throne with his back to the iconic Pat Neff Hall while his eyes stare at Waco Hall. Many visitors stop and pose in front of the memorial to Judge Baylor, while some even crawl in his lap for a comedic cameo. But few visitors remember previous eras on campus, when the tranquil areas surrounding the granite effigy were anything but placid.

The Judge Baylor statue, November 2006. *Photograph by Bradley T. Turner.*

Americans faced multiple college movements during the 1960s, many originating from social issues like the Civil Rights movement or the Vietnam War. When Baylor integrated in 1962, the amount of local Civil Rights protests declined, but Vietnam remained an unresolved issue. Most national historians do not regard Baylor's protest activities with the same enthusiasm as those of larger or more radical schools, but Baylor's protesting experiences present a common example of what protesting around the country was like in 1967.[2]

The conflict in Vietnam represents a change in the characteristics of warfare since modern villains are not always kings, emperors, or Kaisers, but also ideologists, nationalists, radicals, or terrorists. Often, these newer, complex wars gradually develop and do not begin with an exact date or incident. The nature of a modern war's beginning follows with intricate American interpretations and presents an entirely new definition of conflict.

In the early 1960s, most Texans viewed Southeast Asia as irrelevant, so the average student at Baylor held little interest in the Vietnam situation.[3] The first formal discussion involving the status of the Vietnam dilemma occurred in a debate between the Young Republicans and Young Democrats in 1964. Both political groups agreed that containment represented the best solution, though few details about Vietnam were discussed.[4] As a generalization in 1964, most Baylor students and faculty favored intervention in Southeast Asia as a preventative measure against communist threats where war appeared inevitable.[5]

During 1965 and 1966, Baylor students became involved with on-campus movements that supported the soldiers overseas and several organizations contributed audio Christmas cards specifically designed for American troops in Vietnam.[6] KWBU-FM, Baylor's on-campus radio station, recorded Christmas greetings from students on audio cassettes and shipped the messages to the soldiers in 1966.[7] These thoughtful actions demonstrate that Baylor students acknowledged the sense of growing anxiety in Southeast Asia, but most likely did not believe the war would greatly impact their lives in Waco, Texas.[8]

Baylor students in 1966 remained largely apathetic about the politics surrounding the struggle in Vietnam, even during the Christmas card program. Some religious clubs focused their efforts on supplying humanitarian and financial assistance to the various peoples of Southeast Asia, and a few community clubs and organizations followed by sponsoring similar drives.[9]

The Draft

Faculty and student involvement in Vietnam assistance programs lulled for several months after the Christmas campaigns of 1966, until the government introduced the possibility of a mandatory military service draft for the conflict in Vietnam. The concept of a military draft was not a new idea for the era. Since 1940, every man older than the age of eighteen and younger than twenty-six registered for selective service or faced legal repercussions such as fines or possibly prison, though during peaceful years, this policy was not strictly enforced. The discussion of the nationwide draft created immense tension in the public spectrum, though it was possible to avoid the draft by successfully passing a selective service draft deferment exam.

The deferment exam assessed a man's mental, social, and physical abilities. The exam detailed the applicant's reactions to hostile environments and listed his college attendance and grades, medical history, marital/parental status, and IQ. Other deferments originated from conscientious objectors—people who religiously opposed war—but these deferments were some of the most difficult to acquire. Through a variety of methods, a potential draftee could receive a deferment and simply continue his life unaffected.[10]

The Baylor University bookstore began to stock books filled with strategies on passing the deferment exam. Abner McCall, president of Baylor University during this time, stated publicly that positive results on the selective service draft deferment test ensured personal stability because a good score cleared the student from military service.[11]

The medical deferment served as the most common method of avoiding the draft outside of the college-attendance deferment. Charles D. Turner, a Waco High School student in 1967, said he knew of several men who took blood

pressure medications to avoid the draft between 1967 and the early 1970s. Other men bribed medical doctors to falsify records or prescribe medicines that caused harsh reactions. Turner stated that draft-dodging represented a fairly "common thing" for several local men.[12]

One thing is certain about the draft—it made Vietnam a significant topic with many young Waco residents. Despite the reality that a fellow student may be drafted at any moment, most college students still supported the draft, believing that an American presence in Vietnam hindered communist expansion. Perhaps the largest reason why so many Baylor students in 1966 and 1967 supported the war in Vietnam originated from the belief that most college students would be spared from selective service.[13]

The First Peace Vigil

Not every student and faculty member viewed the war in Vietnam as a just cause. In April 1967, several individuals at Baylor decided to initiate a protest against intervention in Vietnam—an activity that seemed largely un-Ameri-

can in conservative Waco, Texas. Hope Bronough, an instructor who taught German, and Don Donham, a Baylor University senior, spearheaded the movement by sponsoring a series of peace vigils as a non-aggressive Vietnam protest.[14] A series of dates were chosen and Bronough sought permission from President McCall to hold four peace vigils during the month of April 1967. McCall agreed and cleared Bronough to conduct a peace vigil each Wednesday of the month, from 10:00 a.m. until 11:00 a.m., near the statue of Judge Baylor across from Waco Hall.[15]

As planned, at 10:00 a.m. on Wednesday, April 5, 1967, several students and two faculty members held the first peace vigil, standing silently in a circle around Judge Baylor for one hour. Other volunteers distributed literature and encouraged passing students to join the silent circle. The protest went well until about 10:50 a.m.[16]

A small group of hecklers approached the silent group near the end of the vigil and began to ridicule the participants by throwing pennies, tossing wadded paper balls, and placing an active water sprinkler directly behind the protesters. These actions did not mark a large backlash from the Baylor masses, but still caused the members of the vigil some grief. Don Donham responded to the incident by calling it "one of the most tragic aspects of the war [because of] the de-humanization of the American people. I can cite no better example than what happened to us."[17] Perhaps Donham exaggerated the impact of the hecklers' actions during the first peace vigil, but the group did experience a hostile response.

Hope Bronough did not accept the harassment and went to President Abner McCall's office requesting campus police/security in case similar events occurred at future vigils. McCall explained that no protesting policies existed at Baylor, but they could distribute all of the "legal material" they desired.[18] McCall also stated to Bronough that "a person has the right to pay the consequences for what he [or she] says."[19] In essence, the administration would make no attempts to stifle activities so long as the demonstrations remained within the confines of the law. According to McCall, the only types of people who protested in large, violent protests were "show-offs."[20]

In his private life, President McCall made few secrets of his political opinions. In 1964, McCall claimed to be a Democrat, but voted a split ticket and publicly supported George Bush, the Republican candidate, for the senatorial race in Texas. McCall endorsed Bush because of Bush's conservative politics and traditional views on social issues. In an article written in 1964 and appearing in Baylor University's campus newspaper, the *Baylor Lariat*, McCall explained, "My policy as president of Baylor is to encourage both faculty members and students to actively participate in partisan politics." McCall further explained, "I am in favor of individual liberty; … I want to live as I want to."[21]

The Campus Response

In the April days that followed the first peace vigil, the topic of Baylor allowing the protest became as controversial as the actual Vietnam War. Numerous Baylor students wrote letters to the *Lariat* criticizing the actions of the Baylor vigils, citing the irony of protestors using freedom to protest the expansion of freedom in Southeast Asia. Other students wrote that they did not agree with the vigil's message, but did not want hecklers to harass participants for exercising their rights.[22]

The *Baylor Lariat* published several letters to the editor expressing feedback on the Baylor peace vigils. The following letter appeared in the *Baylor Lariat* on Friday, April 7, 1967:

It would be an understatement to say that Mrs. Bronough and her followers are guilty of the same error that most of the "peace" demonstrators commit. Always, it is the condemnation of the U.S. policy in North Vietnam. But one never hears from this group the same concern concerning the terror and murders committed against South Vietnam by North Vietnam.

One of the "peace" demonstrators, Mr. Donham, not only reveals his ignorance of history, but also his ignorance of what Christianity really is. He assumes that because Baylor University is a Christian University, many, if not most, of the students would rally to his cause. He also considers the Viet Cong his brothers. If Mr. Donham were to seriously study the Bible, he would discover that he has made five serious mistakes:

1. *Only those who have a personal relationship with Jesus Christ can*

ever be considered Christians.
(Many students at Baylor are not
Christians).

2. Jesus' "pacifistic attitude" before
Pilate was not connected with war,
but was connected with His purpose of dying to reunite men with
God.

3. The Christian life is not one of our
trying to imitate Christ. It is rather
allowing Him to control our lives, to
the point that attention is directed
to Him, not us.

4. All men are not to be considered brothers to Christians just because they
exist. In the spiritual sense the only
brother a Christian has is another
Christian. (It is really quite an exclu-
sive group).

5. The Christian's first responsibility
is to point other men to Jesus
Christ.

What is missing in the "peace" demonstrations is a show of concern for those men
who daily sacrifice their lives so groups similar to Mrs. Bronough's can use their costly
freedom to voice their dissent on any issue.
Next, Wednesday morning (the date of the
second peace vigil) would be an opportune

time to do this.[23]

The above letter, composed by Earl
Stewart, demonstrates the tension
existing between the preferred religion of
Baylor University (Southern Baptist) and
other Protestant denominations. Other
letters commended the group for
demonstrating their beliefs in the face of
opposition. The following letter, written
by eight students, appeared in the Baylor
Lariat on Tuesday, April 11, 1967, the
day before the second peace vigil, and
demonstrated another point of view
prevalent on the Baylor campus:

Last Wednesday a group of Baylor men
valiantly upheld the good old Americanis-
tic way by crudely attempting to deny four
people their right to free expression on the
issue of the Vietnam War. We would like
to express our view on the silent vigil of
last Wednesday.

First, we publically uphold the right of
the demonstrators to express their views,
and we denounce crude, childish attempts
to ridicule these people.

Second, we commend Mrs. Bronough,
Mr. Baker, Don Donham and Curtis
Clogston for thinking through the question

of Vietnam and taking a serious public
stand. Regardless of our disagreement
or agreement, we admire them for doing
what so many others lack the courage to
do—taking a public stand which is a minority viewpoint. If more Baylor students
had such fortitude of personal expression,
the academic atmosphere of our university
would definitely be improved.

Furthermore, all Americans would do
well to contemplate and study seriously
the Vietnam situation. No matter how
just any war may be, there is always a
great degree of evil in the killing of other
human beings. We affirm that our under-
standing of the whole Biblical message is
that all men are brothers. Therefore, we
all could well spend an hour's silent vigil
in contemplation and repentance, whether
we are pacifists or not. Finally, reducing
the Christian faith to a completely individualistic matter as was done in a letter
to the editor last Friday [Stewart's letter]
is completely unscriptural [sic] and at
odds with the Biblical concept of proph-
ecy. One of the tasks of the Church is to
speak to great social problems. Therefore,
we commend the silent demonstrators for
fulfilling their prophetic function as they
see it.[24]

These letters to the editor demonstrate a small portion of the high level of differing opinions that encompassed the Baylor student body—aggressive, pro-war; passive, pro-war; apathetic; passive, anti-war; and aggressive, anti-war.

The Second Peace Vigil and the YAF

Tensions only continued to escalate as the second peace vigil approached. The members of the peace vigil organized the second event to begin at 10:00 a.m. and continue until 11:00 a.m. on April 12, but most sensed this occurrence would be different.[25] The past week's publicity made the protest a popular subject, and on the day of the protest the large amount of people gathered near Judge Baylor's statue only confirmed this vigil would not conclude like the first.

Seven new anti-war protestors, consisting of both faculty and students, joined the original four in an attempt to demonstrate an increase in public support since the first vigil. At this protest, anti-war participants wanted to remain completely silent and used a card table in front of Judge Baylor's statue to supply onlookers with peace literature. A sign instructed passers simply to take one of the pamphlets.[26]

In an effort to recognize the varying opinions on Baylor campus, the members of the vigil changed the focus of the second vigil to the "suffering of people in Vietnam."[27] This new stance softened the previous message of immediate withdrawal from South Vietnam, and instead held the potential to be completely accepted by both pro- and anti-war groups; however, the hecklers would not accept the new message.

Estimates indicated that during the hour, one thousand people swarmed into the vicinity of Judge Baylor's statue.[28] A new organization, the Young Americans for Freedom (YAF), sponsored a booth across the street in front of Waco Hall, titled "Victory in Vietnam!" as a rival protest organization. The group consisted of Baylor students, but represented a national chain of pro-war sponsors who funded pro-war rallies on college campuses.[29]

Individual reactions to the peace vigil varied. Earl Corbitt, a Baylor sophomore and military veteran, wore an old-fashioned sandwich sign that read: "Silent Vigil for Minorities under Communist Domination Who Dare Not Protest!"[30] During the hour hundreds of pro-war activists began chanting: "We Want War! We Want War!" and an enigmatic "War Meat! War Meat! War Meat!" A large counter-protest emerged and the hecklers became more obnoxious while other, sympathetic onlookers joined the silent members of the vigil who stood quietly inside the hostile crowd.[31]

Rufus Spain, history professor at Baylor University and member of the second peace vigil, stated that there were two times in his life when he personally witnessed large masses develop crowd hysteria. One of the occasions occurred during the Second World War in Paris, France, when Charles de Gaulle returned; the other occasion occurred at Baylor University's second peace vigil protest. In fact, Spain remarked that in that moment he was truly afraid.[32]

Somewhere between the screams and constant wave of movement, someone threw a cherry bomb firecracker at Judge Baylor's statue. It exploded, startling both the vigil participants and the pro-war rally. In the passing moments, the impact of the surprise explosion wore thin, and the prior energy of the crowd began to swell once more. The majority of the peace vigil participants, though startled, anxiously remained still and silent.[33]

The energy regained its previous magnitude and an unnamed Baylor football player grabbed the protestors' literature from the table, threw it into the air, flipped over the card table, and proceeded to level the "Silent Vigil" sign to the ground. The crowd roared, and another loud pop rang out as a second cherry bomb exploded near the statue.[34] This firecracker was met with pro-war enthusiasm. A third cherry bomb exploded, injuring a protestor's leg with minor third-degree burns. The injury caused the crowd to panic suddenly. Fearing repercussions, the crowd dissipated soon after the injury and the voices grew softer.[35]

Response to the Second Peace Vigil

The next afternoon, Curtis Clogston, a student from Houston and participant in the peace vigil movements, discovered a note on his door warning: "If you even begin to know what is good for you, you better make yourself scarce before tomorrow." The note was signed, in handwritten pen, "The Patriots."[36]

The peace vigil became a complete catastrophe. Ironically, many of the participating faculty members found more fault with the administration than with the students. Rufus Spain stated that he saw W.C. Perry, Dean of Students, standing on the edge of the crowd doing nothing to stop the growing violence.[37] Other faculty members proved susceptible to vague and complex reactions when attempting to enumerate what defined an appropriate level of free expression—when was free expression chaotic disorder?

For Spain, free expression did not involve scare tactics and social hysteria that harmed students. Hope Bronough joined Spain's opinion and the two faculty members went to Abner McCall's office to speak about the problem. McCall, staying true to his previous policy of tolerance, told the teachers that anyone who participated in the protest movement now did so at his or her own risk.[38] McCall's stiff policy came as a surprise to Borough, who likely expected the president of the school to take a proactive stance toward avoiding conflict and not allow for such chaos on campus

grounds.[39]

Numerous pro-war organizations gained support following the second peace vigil. The Veterans for Victory represented veterans who attended Baylor and took an active role in providing support for the Vietnam conflict by sponsoring pro-war veteran speakers to discuss the significance of Vietnam with Baylor students.[40] The most prominent group, the Young Americans for Freedom, received its official charter from the Student Congress on April 27, 1967, and used its power to counter the actions of the anti-war proponents.[41] The pro-war movement appeared to be gaining support at a rapid pace on Baylor campus.

The Public Debate on Vietnam

Borough, fearing another disastrous episode, recommended canceling the next silent vigil scheduled for April 19, 1967, and instead suggested sponsoring a series of public debates on topics centering around the Vietnam conflict. Bronough speculated that a discussion would provide an open forum, allowing more students to speak and give greater insight into the various problems associated with the war.[42] The group agreed, and on the day representing the originally scheduled third vigil, a public discussion of the war was held with both anti-war and pro-war supporters invited. Specifically, the peace vigil members welcomed the Young Republicans and Young Americans for Freedom to engage in the intellectual assessment of the Vietnam situation. Only an estimated 110 students viewed the debate in Kayser Auditorium (a building adjacent to the statue of Judge Baylor), a substantial reduction in participants since the second peace vigil only one week earlier. The following day, April 20, 1967, the newspaper summaries reported no disturbances.[43]

Earl Corbitt, the man who donned the sandwich sign during the second peace vigil, held his own pro-war vigil in an effort to match the anti-war organization "demonstration for demonstration."[44] He told passersby: "I am protesting those individuals who upgrade the communist movement in our country by taking their information from communist sources, and using this information to sway a student body into a way of thinking."[45] Corbitt, father of three and a veteran,

had returned to school at Baylor University in 1967 after his military service.[46]

One week later, in late April 1967, another group of students began distributing pamphlets obtained from the Episcopal Peace Fellowship, Fellowship of Reconciliation, and the Friends Peace Committee (Quakers) to educate students on conscientious objection. The information told students of different jobs inside the military that, once drafted, allowed the objector to serve in various other positions (cooking, medic, etc.).[47]

The Third Peace Vigil and the Pro-War Event

The reduced attendance at the public debate on April 19 sparked a belief that the peace vigils could resume without significant consequences; thus students organized an unofficial third vigil on May 4, 1967, at 10:00 a.m. in front of the Tidwell Bible Building (diagonally across the street from the Judge Baylor statue) in an attempt to catch students en route to chapel. The third vigil hosted a guest speaker and distributed literature, but the amount of participants only averaged about fifteen during the

majority of the service, swelling to about 150 after chapel. The Young Americans for Freedom manned a table on the other side of the street, but all remained quiet with only a few exceptions.[48]

Several days later, on May 9, 1967, the Young Americans for Freedom responded to the anti-war peace vigils by sponsoring a public, pro-war event in Kayser Auditorium. The event entertained some sixty people and spotlighted a military speaker, a movie explaining the reasons why Americans were fighting in Vietnam, and another movie on the importance of "Operation Golden Fleece"—a movement sponsored by the United States to win the support of the Vietnamese people through agricultural development. On this occasion, it was the anti-war protestors who placed a card table outside the building, counterprotested, and distributed literature.[49]

The summer of 1967 proved rather quiet on the Baylor campus. Protests continued intermittently without impact because most of the students left campus for summer break. In the fall of 1967, the anti-war protestors and peace-vigil members reunited and established a name for their group—the Committee to End the War in Vietnam (CEWV). President Abner McCall recognized the CEWV as a legitimate, formal organization and provided the group with the opportunity to open a reading room in the Student Union Building. The new room left the group's leaders with optimism. Hope Bronough stated: "We don't expect as much opposition as last [school] year … We do expect more interest."[50]

The CEWV

During late September 1967, however, the Baylor Student Congress faced problems when pro-war students accused the Congress of co-sponsoring a speaker with the CEWV. Instead, the student body president clarified that the Student Congress only assisted in the endeavor, but did not co-sponsor the event because the CEWV lacked a recognized charter from the Student Congress. The CEWV was only a group of people that did not host a treasury, hierarchy, or structure related to official charters. The CEWV represented special interest at Baylor—not a formal organization.[51]

In the same week as the predicament

with the Student Congress, the CEWV did not receive official permission from the assistant director of the Student Union Building to post announcements for an upcoming event. The group found all of their event-announcement posters and papers removed from every area in and near the Baylor Student Union Building (SUB) near the date of a scheduled guest lecture. According to the assistant director of the SUB, a surge in recent flyer postings placed around the building had created a jumble on all bulletin boards and now any future posters required administrative clearance before displaying.[52]

The CEWV invited guest speakers to discuss Vietnamese topics in the SUB. Dr. Robert Palter, of the University of Texas at Austin, spoke in October 1967 about his disapproval of Dean Rusk, the U.S. Secretary of State, and the Vietnam War. Palter believed that the U.S. government demonstrated no substantial reasoning for becoming involved in an emerging Vietnamese civil war.[53] President Abner McCall responded to the entire event and others sponsored by the various groups by saying: "I think the educational value is minimal."[54]

The increase in guest speakers created tension between the various student groups associated with the politics of the Vietnam War and the Baylor University administration. Each organization generally required facilities for guest lectures and Baylor found much of its auditoriums being used by ad hoc student groups. In response, the school attempted to establish a standardized rule for extracurricular use of Baylor facilities, but struggled to determine any permanent fixations.[55]

Protests, demonstrations, guest speakers, and literature soon reached a plateau of apathy, and most students grew tired of hearing the same people quarrel over the same issues. The Tet Offensive in January 1968 shook the American public, as did the full implementation of the military selective service draft in 1969. Community-based protest vigils and moratoriums grew in popularity around the country and in Waco, spreading a series of organized nationwide protests beginning in 1969.

In March 1968, Baylor polls indicated most students still supported war, but the anti-war movement had grown significantly on campus over the past year. The *Lariat* concluded that most Baylor students remained pro-war, despite the impending draft and the Tet Offensive. The majority of Baylor students also believed the government needed to begin reducing American troop levels. The CEWV interpreted the shift in public opinion as a sign of the increase in anti-war interest and decided to sponsor bigger drives with more literature.[56]

The year of 1967 was one of confusion, violence, and expression at levels rarely seen in more-recent times. Some students looked to the principles of Christianity to determine the proper balance between war and pacifism, while other individuals relied on secular ethics. The Baylor University administration held to the early platforms of free expression and non-bias as best as they could during 1967. Though the war in Vietnam would not be resolved for several more years, the standard for collegiate protesting in Waco had been established by each person involved—a legacy still in effect at Baylor today. But, the question remained—what were they fighting for?

WACO–1971

The Waco Delegation to Paris and the Freedom Fountain

In 2009, a large fountain between the Waco Convention Center and the Waco Hilton sits dry and dirty amidst the trees.[57] The mineral deposits on the concrete walls and lining of the pool stand as testament to a time when the monument proudly stood adjacent to Waco's greatest gathering locations. Leaves and trash clutter the basin, as the eroded concrete and granite stones stand devoid of water. Skateboarders, loiterers, and businessmen often frequent the plaza surrounding the fountain because of its proximity to downtown Waco. Mounted along the plaza's perimeter are colored-stone symbols in numerous languages repeating the same word—"freedom." But in 2009, less than forty years after the dedication of the Freedom Fountain in 1973, few Wacoans know its origins or why the fountain stands in its present location.

As the 1960s ended and the 1970s began, one thing became obvious—the reasons for the war in Vietnam remained murky, at best. The controversy of Southeast Asia did not stop local residents from taking an interest in the war; however, most people did not know how to address the issues effectively. For a long time, Wacoans waited for a neutral rallying point that provided both pro-war and anti-war locals with an equal opportunity to assist in the war effort. But in 1971, few locals realized that a call already existed, just waiting for their aid.

In 1965, the North Vietnamese imprisoned George Robert Hall when his plane crashed somewhere in enemy territory. Though Hall was in fair health at the prisoner camp, the Viet Cong/Provisional Revolutionary Government of South Vietnam (PRG) and North Vietnamese government failed to notify the U.S. military of Hall's status and capture. When Hall's family learned of his accident, they remained uninformed of anything other than his crash and missing-in-action status.

Hall's family, living in Waco, informed the public of the crash, hoping that by exposing the incident more information could be obtained about Hall's fate. Numerous other families in the area also faced the same dilemma

The Freedom Fountain in April 2009. *Photograph by Bradley T. Turner.*

regarding their loved ones, including two pilots with connections to Central Texas: Ronald Bliss and William Elmo Powell. As these stories became more frequent, a public sentiment slowly began to grow around Waco—regardless of one's support of or opposition to the war, someone needed to provide local families with closure.[58]

The "Write Hanoi" Campaign

As a means of protesting the treatment of POWs, local Wacoans used two methods, both loosely affiliated with the American Red Cross, to request information from North Vietnam. First, Wacoans became involved in the "Write Hanoi" campaign which sent letters requesting that the North Vietnamese government in Hanoi or the North Vietnamese embassy in Paris, France, provide American families with the known status of captured soldiers. Second, other Wacoans protested by signing a petition to be sent to the PRG embassy in Paris, France. Both programs centered on the status and treatment of American POWs serving in North and South Vietnam.

Thousands of people mailed letters and signed the petition supporting both campaigns as the year continued. On April 7, 1971, Boy Scout Troop 548 submitted more than 1,000 signatures while other participating banks, theatres, and stores also received petitions around Central Texas. Local response reached record levels with more than 50,000 signatures.[59]

During late 1970, Linda Hamilton and Pat Hall (wife of George Hall) approached Cullen Smith, a local attorney and military veteran, about the prospect of organizing an awareness program concerning POWs. Smith agreed and began to develop a strategy for delivering the petitions to the North Vietnamese and PRG.[60] In early March 1971, H. Ross Perot of Dallas suggested that the locals simply go to the PRG embassy and hand-deliver the petition. After some discussion, local leaders decided that, despite the slightly outlandish nature of the concept, a personal visit might prove the most effective means for achieving their goal—desperate times call for desperate measures.

The Waco-to-Paris Committee

During the early months of 1971, Cullen Smith journeyed to Washington D.C. to discuss the idea of personally going to Paris. Since the beginning of the war, the federal government disappointed many Americans because of a lack of information concerning the status of POWs, a perceived ineptitude in acquiring any knowledge or results, and an exhibition of a sense of apathy concerning immediate action. The federal government lacked public confidence and many locals felt that entrusting the petition to the federal government would be the worst solution. One popular theory in 1971 stated the Vietnamese were a tribal people, and perhaps the representatives of a town would make greater progress than the federal government. Local leaders decided the best option was to deliver the petition personally and instigated a search to locate qualified delegates to go to Paris.[61]

To meet the criteria for the Waco-to-Paris committee, delegates had to: pay their own way to Paris, France; be respected by the community; and be a concerned citizen. The delegation was not concerned with the politics of a pro-war or anti-war faction in the community; instead, the group focused on the sincerity of each member. Ironically, during the week the delegation formed, the country celebrated a "National Week of Concern for Americans Who Are Prisoners of War or Missing in Action."[62]

Twelve people were chosen for the eclectic team, each with differing backgrounds. Later called "The Waco Dozen," the group consisted of: Nadine Baldwin (teacher from Richfield High School), Carroll Fadal (student at Richfield High School), Gary Jinks (student at McLennan Community College), Harry Provence (editor of the *Waco News-Tribune* and the *Waco-Times Herald*), Karl May (mayor of Waco), Dr. Jack Flanders (chair of the Baylor religion department), Cullen Smith (local attorney), Linda Hamilton, Richard Hill, Ed Brigham (representing the Baylor University student body), Willie Hobbs, and Manuel Gonzales. The group included a diverse make-up to provide the Vietnamese with officials of differing demographic and ethnic origins.[63] The delegation's objective was to discover the status of American POWs and request either better care for the soldiers or an immediate release.

The group met frequently during the weeks before the trip to Paris. Christian missionaries and military officials assisted in teaching the delegation about Vietnamese culture and customs. The specific importances of body posture/positioning and drinking tea became apparent to the group. Each member prepared for diplomacy because the group remained unsure of who (or if anybody) would gain an audience.[64]

Political support for the delegation remained strong. The City of Waco

The Waco Dozen catching a connecting flight in Dallas. *Photograph courtesy of Cullen Smith.*

supported the delegation as Mayor Karl May was one of the delegates. The Texas State Senate passed a resolution recognizing the Waco-to-Paris delegation for their support in objectifying the local commitment to the principles of the American Red Cross.[65] The McLennan County Commissioners condemned the North Vietnamese in a proclamation supporting the delegation.[66] Earlier in

the year, Cullen Smith visited the State Department in Washington, D.C., and received official support from the federal government, allowing the Wacoans to push for definitive answers.[67]

The Dozen in Paris

The delegates left Waco on Saturday, April 10, 1971 (the day before Easter Sunday), and traveled to DFW Airport to board a connecting flight from New York City to Paris. Before departing, the group wired a telegraph to the Delegate General of the PRG and North Vietnam in Paris to prepare for their arrival and request an audience. The telegraph read:

Delegate General
    of North Vietnam
2, rue Leverrier
Paris 6, France

Official twelve member delegation from Waco, Texas, will arrive Paris, Sunday, April 11. Request audience as soon as possible to discuss questions of peace, prisoners of war and other problems of mutual concern. Delegation includes Mayor, newspaper editor, students and other representatives of town. Staying at Paris Hilton.

Cullen Smith,
Chairman of Delegation
Waco, Texas, USA

The group intentionally sent the telegraph shortly before departing because the limited time prevented a negative response from the PRG and North Vietnamese governments.[68] The plan somewhat backfired when the group failed to

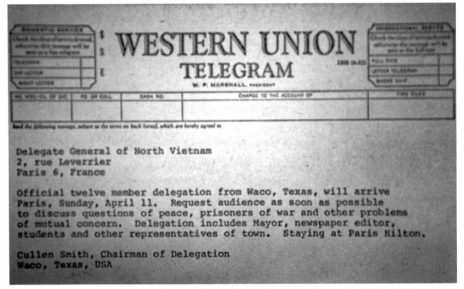

One of the Waco Dozen's telegraphs to the Delegate General of North Vietnam. *Photograph courtesy of Cullen Smith.*

receive any response from the embassies because of the Easter holidays.[69] In addition, over the prior few months, several other American communities had sponsored similar groups to Paris, but were not granted an audience with either embassy.[70]

The holidays placed a damper on spirits, and instead of conducting diplomacy, the delegation fought the pessimism by spending their first full day in Paris, April 11 (Easter Sunday), praying for a successful visit while participating

in an Easter service at the famous Notre Dame cathedral. Following the message, the group returned to the Paris Hilton Hotel, where they spent the week waiting for word from the PRG or North Vietnamese embassy and made arrangements with their interpreter, an Englishman named Stanley Goulston, to be ready at a moment's notice if the Wacoans received a call.[71]

Also on Easter Sunday, Cullen Smith wired another telegraph to the Delegate General of North Vietnam to inform the North Vietnamese embassy of the Wacoans' arrival. The telegraph read:

Delegate General
of North Vietnam
2, rue Leverrier
Paris 6, France

Twelve member Waco, Texas, USA, delegation has arrived in Paris for conference with you to discuss mutual problems including termination of conflict and prisoners of war and betterment of mankind. We are awaiting word at Paris Hilton Hotel. Delegation includes Mayor of town, newspaper editor, students, teachers, and other concerned representatives.

Cullen Smith
Chairman of Waco, Texas Delegation
Paris Hilton Hotel[72]

The Wacoans would persist until receiving some response.

On Monday, April 12, 1971, the group ventured to the American embassy in Paris and discussed strategies with U.S. Ambassador and negotiator at the Paris Peace Talks, David K.E. Bruce. Harry Provence reported the event was "a very pleasant chat," but the delegates

did not learn of any new information during the meeting.[73] The local delegates continued to phone and telegraph the PRG and North Vietnamese embassies for a meeting, but received no reply or acknowledgement from either Delegate General.[74]

Along with the petition containing more than 50,000 signatures, the Waco delegates carried a photo album documenting the organization of the

petition, pictures of a POW's family, and other photos showing the formation of the delegation to Paris. Harry Provence believed the album was an effective tool because it provided the Vietnamese with proof that local residents cared about the fates of the POWs.[75]

At the culmination of the second full day in Paris, the delegates became frustrated at the group's lack of progress. The committee had not planned on

The Waco Dozen meets with Ambassador Bruce in Paris. *Photograph courtesy of Cullen Smith.*

spending more than a few days in Paris because each member privately paid for the trip and many of the travelers could not afford another week in France. They originally had hoped to spend three or four days negotiating diplomacy, but by the second day the delegates had failed to arrange a single meeting. Sunday and Monday both proved to be holidays for the North Vietnamese and the repeated contacts between the interpreters and the embassies only resulted in multiple messages, some simply saying, "they are not here."[76]

Tuesday morning did not prove fruitful either as the dozen Wacoans sat

Stanley Goulston speaks with the North Vietnamese embassy as Gary Jinks patiently waits for news.
Photograph courtesy of Cullen Smith.

around their hotel. Lunchtime approached, and still no response from the Vietnamese groups. Wednesday started like the previous days—slow and uneventful. Then at 3:20 p.m., the phone in Room 1135 of the Paris Hilton rang—it was the North Vietnamese embassy.

A Meeting is Set

The North Vietnamese Delegate General, who had received the numerous messages, became intrigued by the Texans' motivations. North Vietnamese officials decided to meet with three of the Waco delegates at 5:30 p.m. at the North Vietnamese Embassy, just two blocks from the Wacoans' hotel. The group chose Cullen Smith (because he was the chair of the delegation), Karl May (because he represented the City of Waco as mayor), and Harry Provence (because of his experience with news reporting).[77] The pre-conditions prohibited cameras, recorders, local (Parisian) press, and broadcasters.[78]

The two-hour intermission provided the three men with time to prepare for the event. Dr. Jack Flanders, one of the delegates, led the group in prayer for a

successful mission. Afterward, the Wacoans' interpreter took the three chosen delegates to Luxembourg Gardens to wait the remainder of the time under a bushel of chestnut trees before traveling the remaining distance to the embassy.[79]

After the group arrived at the North Vietnamese embassy early (5:10 p.m.), a Vietnamese man opened a glass panel on the door to screen the solicitors. Following a brief conversation with the Wacoans, a French woman appeared at the door who later allowed the three delegates inside. The three Texans traveled upstairs to a parlor, where the woman seated the group, offered them cigarettes, and left the room. Mindful that their hosts might be spying on their conversation, the visitors discussed their preference of tile flooring versus carpet while inspecting the room. On the wall hung a picture of Ho Chi Minh (communist leader of North Vietnam and the New Liberation Front/Viet Cong/PRG) and a large Rand McNally map of China and Indochina.[80]

After about an hour, three Vietnamese men entered the room: an interpreter representing the North Vietnamese embassy, one unnamed, and a man

Karl May, Cullen Smith, and Harry Provence walk to the North Vietnamese embassy. *Photograph courtesy of Cullen Smith.*

known as Mr. Lieu. The Vietnamese officials began by asking if the Texans had any questions or opinions about the Vietnamese situation. Cullen Smith responded first by asking if any American POWs could be transferred to a neutral country—the answer to Smith's question took almost an hour.[81]

Lieu began by explaining how the Americans had been involved in Vietnamese affairs since 1950 when the French controlled Southeast Asia, known then as Siam/Indochina. After a verbose, communist diatribe explaining how the Americans instigated the Asian conflict, Lieu added the only person who could grant the full wishes of the Wacoans was President Richard Nixon. Lieu also, at one point in the discussion, referred to the American prisoners-of-war as captured "barbarians" and "war criminals."[82]

The North Vietnamese representatives remained argumentative through-out the duration of the visit, insisting that American politicians placed the soldiers in the POW camps. Both factions became frustrated. Karl May grew tired of the Vietnamese avoiding questions about the treatment of POWs and asked why the North Vietnamese did not allow any inspections of POW camps for American soldiers. The North Vietnamese officials responded by saying they did not allow for inspections because the PRG held the Americans captive and not the North Vietnamese.[83]

The Wacoans then took another approach and spun the conversation by suggesting that if the North Vietnamese and PRG released all of the soldiers, the American public might not care about who had imprisoned the troops and instead rejoice at the POWs' release. The North Vietnamese provided no response. Smith continued later by asking if the delegates could obtain any information concerning several Wacoan POW's (George Hall, Ronald Bliss, and William Elmo Powell), and the un-named Vietnamese man wrote down their names—the delegates never received a reply. When the session concluded, the three Wacoans asked Mr.

Lieu if he would like to meet the other Waco delegates over dinner or tea, but Lieu declined by saying his schedule was full for the week.[84]

The delegation next presented the North Vietnamese with the petition and photo album, but the North Vietnamese refused to look at the items. As Smith and Provence left the room, each man noticed that Karl May was missing. Smith returned quickly up the stairs to search for May in the negotiating room, where he discovered May hiding the petition and album under a chair. Once the petition was deposited, the delegates left the embassy and returned to the Luxemburg Gardens, where the remaining Waco delegates anxiously waited.[85]

The Last Days in Paris

The following days proved uneventful as the Waco delegation failed to receive an audience with the PRG in Paris. The delegates called the number listed for the PRG daily, but a Vietnamese interpreter refused to give the Wacoans any information and every attempt proved futile.[86] By Friday, April 16, 1971, the dozen Texans questioned the true impact of their week in Paris, but maintained the optimism of knowing that at least they tried to help their neighbors.[87]

Other volunteer groups and reporters in Paris were fascinated that the Wacoans received an audience with the North Vietnamese. A similar group of delegates from the city of Dayton, Ohio, and a writer from *Ladies Home Journal* did not receive an audience with the officials. In fact, estimates guessed that only one in twenty groups who requested a visit to the North Vietnamese embassy received an interview with the Delegate General.[88]

Before leaving for the return to Waco, Carroll Fadal searched the galleries and shops of Paris for a painting to give to Richfield High School as a token, thank-you souvenir. Gary Jinks and Dr. Jack Flanders assisted Fadal. One picture the group located cost a mere $1.50—a bargain for most shoppers, but Fadal

Propaganda given to Provence, May, and Smith by the North Vietnamese after their visit. *Photograph courtesy of Cullen Smith.*

Carroll Fadal and Karl May exit their plane during the return trip to Waco.
Photograph courtesy of Cullen Smith.

rejected the discounted item, saying, "I can't take back a $1.50 picture to Richfield after all those students have done for me."[89]

Other Waco delegates struggled with Fadal's dilemma—what should be the public legacy of the trip? Somewhere over the Atlantic Ocean, on the return flight from Paris, Karl May and Cullen Smith gave substantial thought to memorializing the trip to Paris with a monument to POWs along the Brazos River as part of the developing Lake Brazos Project. The most difficult subject became how to memorialize the journey and what the monument should promote and achieve. Most of the delegation agreed that a fountain served as the best type of monument because of the tranquility associated with running water and because of the beautiful fountains each delegate viewed while touring Paris.[90]

As the conversations continued to transform, so did the reason for the journey. On the return flight, the reason for the Waco-to-Paris delegation shifted from POWs to include all Americans, and from all Americans to the value of freedom. According to the leaders of the delegation, freedom—freedom for POWs, freedom for the struggling South Vietnamese, freedom for the entire world—arose as the true theme for the trip.

The Freedom Fountain
Suggestions on how to memorialize the trip varied during the flight, ranging from a floating fountain in the Brazos River to renaming the famous Waco Suspension Bridge "Freedom Bridge," where a fountain could be added as part of the bridge's structure. Instead, the group agreed on constructing a new fountain as a memorial of their journey that would be called the "Freedom Fountain."[91] The delegation thought the fountain should awe viewers and stand near the newly constructed Waco Convention Center.[92] As 1971 passed, the inertia of the delegation began to slip out of the forefront and, to some extent, so did support for the Freedom Fountain.

Harry Provence, one of the three who met with the North Vietnamese embassy in person, worked as the editor of both the *Waco News-Tribune* and *Waco Times-Herald*. Provence decided to assist in obtaining donations for constructing the fountain using advocacy journalism—a concept that uses the news to endorse subjects or objectives. The technique spurred mixed reactions. In the September-October 1972 edition of the *Columbia Journalism Review*, Preston Lewis, a former reporter for Provence's newspapers, published a brief synopsis detailing Provence's uses of advocacy/new journalism in Waco concerning the Freedom Fountain. In the article, Lewis criticized Provence for placing stories about donations to the Freedom Fountain on the first page and moving important local news to page 10-A. Lewis expanded by saying that few critical letters-to-the-editor made the press, and when Provence did include a critical letter, he commonly printed a rebuttal directly under the submission.[93]

One critical letter dated July 2, 1971, indicated the opposition to the Freedom Fountain:

Building fountains in honor of desirable concepts could eventually become ridiculous. We could next have a fountain in honor of good health, one for happiness, another for higher education, and one dedicated to a mother's love. But the most annoying thing to me is that the large sums of money being donated by private citizens and businesses alike could be better used as donations to really worthy causes …

Anyway, Waco's proposed "Freedom Fountain" isn't going to help bring back U.S. prisoners one bit. Only the end of the Vietnam war can do that. It should be abundantly clear now that what the prisoners need and what all people of the world need is freedom not fountains.[94]

A response, written by one of the younger Waco delegates to Paris working for the paper over the summer, stated:

Because the members of the delegation realized that too many Americans take our numerous freedoms for granted, we felt that Waco needed a reminder to its populace and visitors of the liberties U.S. citizens possess. I do not believe that money dedicated to this principle is wasted.[95]

The fountain emerged as controversial in some realms when some local residents did not understand why the area needed a monument to freedom when the delegation had originally organized to support prisoners-of-war. Lewis expanded on this issue by saying that "few newsroom employees—and relatively few members of the community—backed the drive," and that privately, Provence confessed that the program lacked the donations he had expected to receive.[96]

The Reality of the Freedom Fountain

Over the next two years (and over fifty front-page articles later), the Waco delegates who envisioned the symbol constructed the fountain using less money than initially proposed.[97] A sum totaling $55,000 in donations trickled in and the group dedicated the Freedom Fountain on May 26, 1973.[98] Provence's *Waco Times-Herald* proudly proclaimed the fountain as the first public project to freedom since the Statue of Liberty.[99]

Designs for the fountain represented a blend of materials and modern aesthetics. When completed, the primary

A few of the "freedom" translations in Freedom Plaza, April 2009. *Photograph by Bradley T. Turner.*

structure of the fountain stood twenty-three feet tall and was composed largely of concrete to signify power. The basin that housed the fountain measured forty-four feet in diameter and was also constructed using concrete in a circular shape to signify humanity's constant struggle for freedom. Granite originating from South Dakota (similar to the stone found on Mount Rushmore) adorned the top of the fountain, while the front and back of the fountain used bricks whose ingredients originated from the silt and clay of the Brazos River. The fountain required about two million gallons of recycled water per day to achieve the full effect of its waterfall.[100]

At the official dedication of the Freedom Fountain, Harry Provence acted as the Master of Ceremony, while the Jefferson-Moore High School Band performed music. The project committee awarded a twelve-year-old student from North Waco Elementary School named Carrie Taylor the honor of signaling the first official water flow in return for all of the fund-raising she conducted at her school. Guest speakers included two of the three POWs referenced in Paris with the keynote speaker being George

Hall—the pilot shot down in 1965. Hall was released from captivity in the spring of 1973 and returned to Waco soon thereafter.[101] Hall told the onlookers, "You, the people of Central Texas, have shown that you have the spirit which prizes liberty. You have shown that you care about freedom. And you have shown that you care about us, the service men who fought and died and were prisoners in Vietnam."[102] Seated in the front row of the dedication was Ronald Bliss, another returned POW. William Elmo Powell's family also attended the ceremony, though Powell died in Vietnam.[103] Over the next year, other donations and volunteers landscaped the surrounding areas with oak trees, concrete, and stone, naming the location "Freedom Plaza." The word "freedom" appears in fifty-three translations throughout the plaza to represent the global struggle for freedom.[104]

Decades passed and eventually the fountain fell into disrepair. On July 4, 2001, the *Waco Tribune-Herald* printed an article explaining the significance of the Freedom Fountain between the Waco Hilton Hotel and the Convention Center, since many Wacoans had

forgotten the motivations for the fountain, though it was less than thirty years old at the time. Ronald Bliss, who attended the dedication of the Freedom Fountain, also attended the dedication of a memorial plaque in front of the Freedom Fountain in 2000.[105]

On December 3, 2008, the *Waco Tribune-Herald* announced that the Waco City Council favored moving the Freedom Fountain because new plans for expanding the area between the Waco Convention Center and the Waco Hilton might crowd the beauty of the fountain. Plus, the fountain needed cleaning and a working water pump, estimated at about $170,000—three times the cost of original construction. Estimates to fix the fountain in 2009 included adding new parts and cleaning existing pieces, not to mention relocating the fountain to a spot where it could continue as a reminder of freedom to the public.[106]

An exact resolution of the issues involving the fountain remain undecided. A suggestion was made to replace the current Freedom Fountain with a spray fountain on one of the abandoned pillars of the Interurban Bridge support

The Freedom Fountain's dedication plaque, April 2009. *Photograph by Bradley T. Turner.*

(between the Suspension Bridge and the Iron Bridge). Another proposition was to construct a new monument on a vacant lot east of the Waco Convention Center. Or, the existing structure could be rebuilt and fixed at its current location. Reactions to the proposed ideas varied, largely because no conceptual images were released. Fundraising efforts for the new fountain were slowed until the Waco City Council decided its exact course of action.[107]

The subject of the Vietnam War, however, remains as controversial today as its motives were in the 1960s and 1970s. Baylor students and faculty, delegate leaders and supporters all struggled to define the best means for properly addressing the situation in Vietnam. Each Wacoan involved with the Vietnam War chose some means of action, possibly involving vigils, cherry bombs, pamphlets, petitions, trips, fountains, or newspapers. But despite the level of participation, the question still remains—what should Waco's legacy of the Vietnam War be?

The Freedom Fountain, November 2006. *Photograph by Bradley T. Turner.*

ENDNOTES

1. Statue of Judge Baylor on Baylor Campus, 11 November, 2006, photograph by author.

2. Mostafa Bahloul, "Student Protest Against the Vietnam War on the Baylor Campus between April 1967–January 1971" (M.A. thesis, Baylor University, August 1988), 69.

3. Kevin Michael Brady, "Baylor at War" (M.A. thesis, Baylor University, August 2002), 76.

4. Ibid., 77.

5. Bahloul, 69.

6. Brady, 82.

7. "KWBU plants vocal cards for Vietnam," *Baylor Lariat*, 15 November, 1966.

8. Brady, 84.

9. "Care Drive Raises $600," *Baylor Lariat*, 15 December, 1965.

10. Brady, 86.

11. Ibid.

12. Charles D. Turner, interview by author, 20 October, 2006, tape in author's possession.

13. Ibid.

14. Rufus Spain, interview by author, 2 October, 2006, tape in author's possession.

15. Ibid.

16. Bahloul 71.

17. Ibid., 71–72.

18. Ibid., 72.

19. "Protestors begin peace vigils," *Baylor Lariat*, 6 April, 1967.

20. "Vigils Not Restricted by University Policy," *Baylor Lariat*, 6 April, 1967.

21. Carol Spencer, "McCall Backs Bush, Participates Actively," *Baylor Lariat*, 23 September, 1964.

22. Bahloul, 72.

23. "Letters to the Editor: Stewart Says Demonstrators Err," *Baylor Lariat*, 7 April, 1967.

24. "8 Defend Demonstrator's Rights," *Baylor Lariat*, 11 April, 1967.

25. Bahloul, 73.

26. Spain interview.

27. "Bahloul, 74.

28. "Observers Watch 11 in Vigil Heckled, Counter Protested," *Baylor Lariat*, 13 April, 1967.

29. "2 groups organize peace vigil protests," *Baylor Lariat*, 12 April, 1967.

30. Ibid.

31. "Observers Watch 11 in Vigil Heckled."

32. Spain interview.

33. Bahloul, 74.

34. Ibid.

35. Ibid., 75.

36. "Observers Watch 11 in Vigil Heckled."

37. Spain interview.

38. Bahloul, 76.

39. Spain interview.

40. "Reactions to Vigil Continue," *Baylor Lariat*, 14 April, 1967.

41. Louise Later, "Peace Vigil May Be Held Today," *Baylor Lariat*, 3 May, 1967.

42. Bahloul, 78.

43. Ibid., 79.

44. "Corbitt Has Lone Vigil Wednesday," *Baylor Lariat*, 20 April, 1967.

45. Ibid.

46. Ibid.

47. "Protestors Pass Out Pamphlets," *Baylor Lariat*, 27 April, 1967.

48. Bahloul, 80.

49. "YAF Met By Group For Peace," *Baylor Lariat*, 10 May, 1967.

50. "'Committee to End War' to Open Reading Room," *Baylor Lariat*, 14 September, 1967.

51. "Moffatt: SC Not Sponsor For Palter," *Baylor Lariat*, 30 September, 1967.

52. Mike Phillips, "Anti-War Group Removed from Student Union Lobby: Mrs. York Says Signs Not Cleared," the *Baylor Lariat*, 30 September, 1967.

53. Bahloul, 82.

54. Preston Kirk, "Meeting Policy for All 'Not Workable'-McCall," *Baylor Lariat*, 3 October, 1967.

55. Ibid.

56. "Baylor students have taken stands on war," *Baylor Lariat*, 14 March, 1968.

57. Freedom Plaza in Waco, TX, 25 April, 2009, picture in author's possession.

58. "Let Freedom Ring," *The Waco Heritage Foundation*, Fall 1999, The Texas Collection, Baylor University, Waco, TX, 2–7.

59. "More Names Requested in POW Project Here," *Waco Times-Herald*, 7 April, 1971.

60. Cullen Smith, interview by author, 30 April, 2009, recording in author's possession.

61. Ibid.

62. Ibid.

63. Ibid.

64. Ibid.

65. "Resolution Backs POW Delegation," *Waco Times-Herald*, 9 April, 1971.

66. "County Commissioners Blast POW Treatment," *Waco News-Tribune*, 1 April, 1971.

67. "Let Freedom Ring," 2–3; Smith interview.

68. Smith interview.

69. "12 Wacoans Keep Trying," *Waco Times-Herald*, 12 April, 1971.

70. "Let Freedom Ring," 2–3.

71. Ibid., 3; "12 Wacoans Keep Trying;" "Wacoans Hold Fruitful Talks With Key Red," *Waco Times-Herald*, 14 April, 1971.

72. Western Union Telegram to Delegate General of North Vietnam, 2 rue Leverrier, Paris 6, France, sent by Cullen Smith, 11 April, 1971, telegraph copy in Smith's possession.

73. "Bruce Sees 12 Delegates from Waco," *Waco Times-Herald*, 13 April, 1971.

74. Ibid.

75. Ibid.

76. "No Luck With Cong For Waco Delegates," *Waco Times-Herald*, 15 April, 1971.

77. Smith interview.

78. "Wacoans Hold Fruitful Talks With Key Red."

79. Ibid.

80. Ibid; Smith interview.

81. "Wacoans Hold Fruitful Talks With Key Red."

82. Ibid, Smith interview.

83. "Let Freedom Ring," 5.

84. "Wacoans Hold Fruitful Talks With Key Red."

85. Smith interview.

86. "No Luck With Cong."

87. "Let Freedom Ring," 6.

88. "Waco Delegates Head For Home," *Waco Times-Herald*, 16 April, 1971.

89. "POW Group Discusses Plan for Memorial," *Waco Tribune-Herald*, 18 April, 1971.

90. Ibid; Smith interview.

91. Ibid; Smith interview.

92. "Waco's Expression of Freedom," *Waco News-Tribune*, 29 September, 1971.

93. Preston Lewis, "Advocacy Journalism in Waco," *Columbia Journalism Review* (September/October 1972): 50–51.

94. Ibid.

95. Ibid.

96. Ibid.

97. Lewis, "Advocacy Journalism in Waco," 50–51.

98. "Freedom Fountain Stands as Reminder to Centexas," *Waco Tribune-Herald*, 7 January, 1974.

99. "Dedication Today, Freedom Fount to Flow Here," *Waco Times-Herald*, 26 May, 1973.

100. "Freedom Fount to Flow Here," *Waco*

Times-Herald, 26 May, 1973.

101. "Let Freedom Ring," 7.

102. "Fountain Dedicated Today as a Sign of Liberty," *Waco Tribune Herald*, 27 May, 1973.

103. Powell's remains were returned to the United States in 1988; "Home at last," *Waco-Tribune Herald*, 20 April, 1988.

104. "Officials Name It Freedom Plaza," *Waco Tribune-Herald*, 2 May, 1973.

105. "Where Freedom Flows," *Waco Tribune-Herald*, 4 July, 2001.

106. "City to Proceed with Fountain Relocation Plan," *Waco Tribune-Herald*, 3 December, 2008; Freedom Plaza in Waco, TX, 2006, 11 November, 2006, picture in author's possession.

107. "City considering 3 sites for Freedom Fountain," *Waco Tribune-Herald*, 17 August, 2009.

INDEX

Note: Page numbers in bold denote a photograph or illustration.

A

7-Eleven (quick stop store), boycott of, 192

Abercrombie, Walter (football player), 214-215, 218

Acker, R.A. (telephone company manager), 162

Adams, J.H. (president of Paul Quinn College)
  role he played in integration efforts, 188-190

Adams, Meyer (businessman)
  opens a retail beer store, 31-32

Adams, Mollie (legendary madam), 25-37
  biography, 25
  court cases and, 29-30, 31
  entrepreneurship of, 25-26
  house, **27**, **28**
  one of the last madams operating in 1918, 36-37
  photograph, **25**

Adams, Rosa (sister of Mollie) (prostitute), 35

Adsit, Robert (eyewitness to Waco tornado), 150

advertisements targeting soldiers and patriots, **106**

African Americans
  1900 census and employment demographics, 34
  black madams operating brothels, 36
  boycott local stores, 192
  Cameron Park as place for celebrations, 206
  Civil Rights movement and, 213
  elected to local offices, 213

employment opportunities as part of integration, 193-194, 197

factions and their approach to integration, 189-190

funeral homes, 161

"good colored citizens" as "victims, 57

James Connally Air Force Base and, 192

lynchings, 55, 56, 58-61

lynchings in Central Texas, 56

Methodist circuit riders and, 10

plan protests and sit-ins of commercial businesses, 187-189

policy of racial segregation in Cameron Park, 211-212

popularity of Cameron Park with, 212, 217

population in McLennan County, 55

racial tension and violence, 207

segregation in Waco, 183-187

as "troublemakers," 57

Waco tornado, impact on, 172-173

William Brann's attitude towards, 43-44

alcohol

  moral crusaders outlawing sale of, 38

Alexander, Maggie (prostitute), 26

American Protective Association (Clinton, Iowa), 43

  anti-Catholic, anti-Semitic group, 43

American Red Cross,

  prisoners of war and, 239

  social functions involving WWI military, 100-101

  and Waco tornado, 160

  Write Hanoi campaign and, 238

Amicable Building (Waco) and tornado, 139, 150, 152, 158

  also known as the Alico Building, 158

Anderson, C.A. (weather bureau chief), 142

Andrews, Captain C. F. (commanding officer), 81-83

Artesian Manufacturing and Bottling Company, 26

Asbury, Francis (circuit rider), 11-12

Austin (TX), 59-60
   Guy Town (red-light district), 23

Austin, F.H. (Western Union superintendent), 163

Aviation Hall at the Lions Den, 108, 109, **109**

B

Bakanowski, Adolf (circuit rider), 12

Baker, Newton (Secretary of War), 36

Baldwin, Nadine (teacher), 238

Baptist churches
   Columbus Avenue Baptist Church, 148
   Emmanuel Baptist Church, 165
   First Baptist Church, 26, 171
   Lone Star Baptist Church, 154
   Lorena Baptist Church, 14
   New Hope Baptist Church, 187, 189

Barcus, E.R., Sr. (circuit rider), 13-17
   assets of, 17
   biography, 13-14
   friendship with Thomas Stanford, 14
   importance of education, 16
   photograph, **15**
   Stanford Chapel (church) and, 13

Barcus, George (defense attorney), 60, 61, 64

Barcus, J. Sam (son of E.R. Barcus), 16

Barcus, John (son of E.R. Barcus), 16

Barcus, Mary Frances (wife of E.R. Barcus), 15

Barcus, Thomas Stanford (Reverend), 17

Barnes, Maurice C. (doctor), 214

Barnes, Ralph (program organizer), 99

Barrett, Billy (African American lawyer), 197

Barron, Woody (reporter for *Waco Times-Herald*), 156

Baylor Lariat (Baylor University campus newspaper), 236

  runs student letters on peace vigils, 230-232

Baylor, R.E. B. (Judge). *See* Judge Baylor statue

Baylor University, 187

  administration sets standard for collegiate protesting, 236

  Baylor students and response to the Vietnam War, 227-228

  Chamber of Commerce and call for integration of, 193, 196, 199

  Committee to End the War in Vietnam (CEWV), 235-236

  damage from the Waco tornado, 165

  demands *Iconoclast* boycott, 43

  embittered relationship with William Brann, 42-45

  given bear as mascot by soldiers, 107-108

  impact of gasoline rationing on, 120

  integrated in 1962, 228

  Kayser Auditorium and peace vigil, 234

  medical deferment strategies and students, 229

  military service and the draft, 228-229

  minor mention in *London Times* article, 170

  new curriculums introduced during WWII, 116

  Pat Neff Hall, 227

  peace vigils, 230-236

    campus response to, 230-232

    first peace vigil (April 1967), 229-232

    hecklers and disruptions of, 229-230

    letters published pro/con in *Baylor Lariat*, 230-232

locations of, 229
   second peace vigil (April 1967), 232-233
   third peace vigil, 234-236
   Young Americans for Freedom (YAF), 232-233
pre-med students helping out following tornado, 159
pro-war events held on campus, 234-235
protest activities in the 1960s, 228
public debate on Vietnam, 233-234
religious tension because of campus unrest, 231
Student Congress, and Vietnam protests, 235
Student Union Building (SUB) and Vietnam protests, 235
students kidnap William Brann, 45-46
Tidwell Bible Building, 234
used as shelter during tornado, 170
Bean, Robin (historian), 190
Behrens Drug Company, 187
  damage done by the Waco tornado, 143-147
  The Lofts (present day use for building), 147
  photographs of damage, **144-147**
  urban legend of "armless man" haunting, 147
Bellefant, Hunt (Waco police officer), 50
Bell's Hill (TX)
  path of 1953 tornado, 143, 163, 173
Bell's Hill School, and tornado damage, 165
Bengal, William E. (president of veteran's group)
  offers help on behalf of WWI vets following tornado, 160
Bernstein, Patricia (historian), 61, 62, 64
Berry, Edward, victim of 1953 tornado, 148
Berry, Rush, victim of 1953 tornado, 148, 152
Biffle, Kent, 218

Bird-Kultgen Ford (Waco business), 161, 187

Birkhead, J.C. (salesman), 30-31

Black Waco Chamber of Commerce, 198

Blackland Army Air Field, 211

Bledsoe, Jules (musician, composer and singer), 209

Bledsoe-Miller Park, 209, 212

Bliss, Ronald (prisoner of war), 237, 243
  attends dedication of Freedom Festival, 248

Bluebonnet Ordnance Plant (BOP), 124-125

Bolton, E.R. (son-in-law of William Cameron), 210

Bourcher, Naomi, 209

Bowmen Archery Club, 212

Boy Scout Troup 548 (signature gathering effort), 238

Branch Davidians (religious cult), 56

Brann-Baylor war, 42-43, 44-47, 50, 53

Brann, Inez (daughter of William Brann), 42
  commits suicide, 42

Brann, Noble (reverend), 41
  father of William Brann, 41

Brann, William Cowper, **42**, **46**
  attacks Baylor University in writing, 41, 42-45
  birth of, 41
  character of, 53
  children of, 42
  Colt .41 used in shootout, **50**
  death of, 41, 50-53
  early years of, 41-42
  editor of *Waco Daily News*, 42
  editorial career, 41-42
  endnotes, 53-54

    fatal confrontation with Davis, 41, 50-52

    gravestone headstone, **52**, **53**

    kidnapped by Baylor students, 45-46

    modern opinion of, 53

    monument at Oakwood cemetery, 41

    mother's early death, 41

    physically attacked by the Scarboroughs, 46-47

    racism of, 43-44

    response to Joseph Slattery's denunciation, 43

    runs away from foster home, 41

Brazelton, William B. (Waco businessman), 65

Brazos River, 21, 169, 211, 222

  construction of bridge across the, 21, 213

  Great Tohomoho (nickname), 204

  record rainfall impacts after Waco tornado, 157, 164

  reverence by Waco Indians and, 204

Breeder, Lloyd and Robin, 218

Breeding, Christi, 218

Brigham, Ed (Baylor University student), 239

Bronough, Hope (Baylor University instructor)

  protests against the Vietnam War, 229, 230-235

brothels. *See* prostitution

Brown, Hildy (madam), 33, 34

Brown, Richard Maxwell (historian), 55, 56, 58

Brown, Stanton (member of tire rationing board), 116

Brown v. The Board of Education of Topeka, 212

  African American leaders response to, 184-185

  impact on Waco, 185-186

  importance of judicial decision, 183-185

  Plessy v. Ferguson invalidated by, 183

public schools in Waco ordered to desegregate, 197-198

reaction to across Texas, 185

ruling, how affected public schools, 184

segregation in Waco, 183-185

white leaders response to, 183-184

Bruce, David K.E. (U.S. Ambassador), **241**

Burger, Margaret (prostitute), 32, 33

Burger, Maria, 32

Burger, Sarah, 32

Burleson, Rufus T. (Baylor University president), 44-45

Burton, Viola (prostitute), 30

   lawsuits for debts, 30-31

Bush, George H.W. (president)

   candidate for Senate in 1964, 230

C

Caldwell, Charles T. (pastor), 71

Cameron Cavalry (park ranger program), 219, 222-223

Cameron Park, 203-226

   11th anniversary, 209

   75th anniversary, 218-219

   African Americans and, 206, 211, 215-216

   Cameron Park Study Committee, 218-219

   Cameron Park Zoo, 215

   City Beautiful movement and, 206-209

   criminal activity in park, 217-218, 219, 222

   decay of in late 1970s, 216

   Depression era and, 210, 211

   dual nature of, 216-218

   Emmons Cliff, 215, 216, 217

endnotes, 223-226

favorite leisure pastimes, 212

Herring Avenue Bridge controversy, 213-214

integration of, 193, 211-212

Jacob's Ladder, 215

Jim Crow era and, 207, 209-210

land donated by Cameron family, 203, 209, 210

murder of Grady Skipworth, 209-210

overcrowding at the park, 216

Park Ranger program and, 219, 222-223

Pecan Bottoms, 215, 217, 218-219, 222

"pleasure of the people" (phrase), 203, 209, 223

popularity of park in the 1960s, 212

Proctor Springs, 206, **207**, 210, 217, **220-222**

Redwood Shelter, 215

reverse discrimination and, 217

rise in usage, 214-216

Riverside Drive, **208**

sports activities and, 215

traffic problems and, 216, 218-219

World War II and popularity of, 211

Cameron, William (lumber tycoon)

family donates land for Cameron Park, 203

Camp Hood, 211

Camp Logan (Houston, TX), 83

Camp MacArthur (army camp)

acreage of, 80

after the Armistice, 96

American Red Cross Convalescent House, **100**

bayonet school, 87

boost for local economy, 79, 102

camp life at, 96-102

Christmas Eve celebration, 102

closing of, 107

cost to complete, 79

endnotes, 110-112

entertainment activities, 99, **103**

gas school, 87, 94

historical marker, 77, **78**

hospital and grounds, **80**

musical band used to sell war bonds, 148

named for Arthur MacArthur, 79

officers' club chimney, **108**

officers' school at, 94

opening the camp for training, 84

parade down Austin Ave., **101**

scenes of Camp life, **87-95, 99**, **103-105**

statistical data, 80

tent city, **94**

training routines at, 86-87, 94

troop capacity, 80

Waco wins bid to build, 79

Camp MacArthur Riot, the, 80-83

Carrigan, William D. (historian), 56, 57, 61, 62

Catholic Church, verbally attacked by Joseph Slattery, 43

cattle

economic importance of, 21, 23

Central Texas, reputation for vigilante violence, 56

CEWV (Committee to End the War in Vietnam), 235-236

Cherokees

conflict with Waco Indians, 204

China Spring, (TX), 107

Chris's Café (Waco), damaged in Waco tornado, **156**

Christian evangelicalism

   rise of religious individualism and, 7, 9-11, 17

Christian Science Monitor, coverage of 1953 tornado, 170

circuit riders (traveling preachers), 7-19

   average day of circuit rider, 11-12

   decline of, 9, 17

   duties of, 12

   education, importance of self-improvement, 15-16

   endnotes, 18-19

   evolution into stationary preachers, 12-13, 17

   legacies of local circuit riders, 12-17

   life of a circuit preacher, 9, 11-12

   literacy and general academics, 15

   lonely nature of profession, 12

   low wages of profession, 12, 17

   Methodist church and, 7, 9-11

   revivals and, 15

   rise of religious individualism and, 7, 9

   routes traveled, 9, 12

   Sabbath (Sunday) services, 12, 14-15

   services provided to rural areas, 9

Citizen National Bank (Waco), 160

City Beautiful movement, 206-209

   impact on race relations and, 207

City Hall building (Waco) and 1953 tornado, 158

Clark, Winnie (madam), 27, 34, 36

Claypool, R. H., 97

Cleveland, Kate (alias Kate Coleman) (madam), 27, 31

Clifton, Mrs. Albert (descendant of William Cameron), 218

Clinton, Eva (prostitute), 27
  stabbing death of fellow prostitute, 27

Clogston, Curtis (Baylor University student), 231, 233

Coates, John (killed in 1953 tornado), 154, 171

Coates, Patsy (husband killed in tornado), 154

coffee rationing during WWII, 127-128
  coffee production levels, 127
  ration books issued, 128

Collins, Kate (prostitute), 34

Columbia Journalism Review, 246

Committee to End the War in Vietnam (CEWV), 235-236

Committee of Fifty, 186-187, 193
  specialized committee of white community leaders, 186-187

Commodores (musical group), 215

Community Relations Committee
  disenchantment with by African Americans, 198
  issues Annual Report on process of desegregation, 195-197, 198
  major achievements in integrating Waco, 196-197

Community State Bank (Waco), 160-161

Conger, Roger (historian), 99

Connor, Mrs. J.O.A., 189

Cooper, Marcus Langley (Reverend), 187, 189, 191
  leadership and work for the local NAACP, 189, 192

Copeland, Mike (reporter), 222

Corbitt, Earl (Baylor University student and veteran)
  pro-war student protestor, 232, 234

Corpus Christi (TX), 99

Cotton Belt Railway, 80

cotton, economic importance of, 21, 23
Cotton Palace, 99, 106
Cotton Palace Grounds' Sun Pool, **143**
  damaged by Waco tornado, 143
Cox, Russell (owner of R.E. Cox Co.), 187

D
Daggett, Dot (madam), 25
Dallas Morning News
  agrees to voluntary code of silence, 190
  article about Brann-Davis shooting, 50
  reminiscence about William Brann, 53
  reporting on Jesse Washington lynching, 59, 60-61
Dallas (TX), 63
Dalrymple, Deke (park ranger), 219
Davis, Morris, 57
Davis, Tom E.
  accuses Witt Ward of firing at him, 52
  fatally shot by G.B. Gerald, 50
  gun that killed, **50**
Davis, W. J. "Joe," 66
Dawson, Joseph Martin (pastor), 71
Dennard, E.N. (school superintendent), 165
Dennard, Floyd (tornado survivor), 142-143
Dennis Building. *See* R.T. Dennis Building
desegration. *See* integration of Waco
Diddie, Jack (eyewitness to tornado), 148-149, 152
Diddie, Kathryn (elementary school teacher), 172
Dixie Appliance Company, tornado and, 143
Dobrovolney, Gloria Mae (eyewitness to tornado), 153

Dollens, Leon (Waco Chamber of Commerce), 187, 193

Dollins, Betty (reporter for *Waco Times-Herald*), 157

Dollins, John (mayor), 69

Donham, Don (Baylor University student)
  protests the Vietnam War, 229-231

Douglas Company (Waco), and 1953 tornado, 156

Douglas, Ray (madam), 34-35

Downing, Avery (school superintendent), 187, 193

Downing, Henry (vigilante), 58

Dr Pepper Museum, 26

DuConge, Oscar (mayor), 213

Dudley, J.W., and Waco tornado, 163

Dunnam, W.V. (chairman tire rationing board), 116

Dupree, W.E. (landlord), 30-31

Durie, Dave (Waco police officer), 50

E

East Waco
  1918 flood, 160
  damage done by Waco tornado, 150, **151**, 163

East Waco NAACP, 189, 194-195

East Waco School, and Waco tornado, 165

Eastern Little League, 215

Edgar, J.W. (State Education Commissioner), 183

Edgefield Park, 209

Edwards, Alice (prostitute), 26

Eide, H.L. (hatchery owner) and tornado, 149-150

El Paso (TX)
  Utah Street (red-light district), 23

Elmore, Edna (madam), 26

emancipation, effects of, 56

Emergency Price Control Act of 1942, 115

Emmons Cliff, 215, 216, 217

Episcopal Peace Fellowship, 234

Eschenburg, C.J. (died from tornado-related injuries), 172

Eubanks, Bicknell (eyewitness to tornado), 170

Evans, Mrs. Oscar (injured in tornado), 142

Evans, Mary (wife of Van Pell), 190

Evans, Van Pell (Good Government League), 189

  leadership on behalf of African Americans, 190, 198

extralegal groups

  as juries, 55-56

  violence disapproved of, 56

F

Fadol, Carroll (high school student), 238, 244, **245**

Fall, John (undertaker), 61

Falls County (TX), 56, 60

farm life

  during World War II, 128

Fee, Joe (newspaperman), 66

Feezor, Dr. Forrest C. (pastor of First Baptist Church), 171

Fellowship of Reconciliation, 234

Fetherlin, David (eyewitness to tornado), 151

Field, Eugene (eyewitness to tornado), 148

First National Bank of Waco, **121**, 149, 187

  disaster headquarters following 1953 tornado, 167

Fisher, Ella (prostitute), 25, 26

Flanders, Jack (chair of Baylor religion department), 239

  Waco-to-Paris delegation member, 239, 242, 244

Fleming, Sheriff, 62-64, 65, 66, 69

Flemmons, Jerry (playwright), 52

Ford, Dan (former county sheriff), 61

Fort Hood (Killeen)
  rescue efforts during the Waco tornado, 150, 161

Fort Worth (TX)
  Hell's Half Acre (red-light district), 23

Fourteenth Amendment of the U.S. Constitution
  and *Plessy v. Ferguson*, 183

Frankie Beverly and Maize (musical group), 215

Franklin, Eugenia (kitchen supervisor) and tornado efforts, 159

Franks, Alice (madam), 34

Freedom Fountain (memorial to freedom), 236-237, 245-250
  controversy surrounding, 246
  cost of, 246
  current condition of, 236
  dedication ceremonies, 248, 250
  dedication plaque, **249**
  design of, 246, 248
  endnotes, 251-253
  fountain falls into decay, 248
  fountain repaired, cost of, 248
  granite from stone from South Dakota, 248
  guest speakers at dedication, 248
  how idea for emerged, 245-246
  letter written in opposition to, 246
  modern view of, **237**, **249**, **250**
  moved to new location, 248
  rededication of, 248, **249**
  relocation efforts, 248, 250

    Statute of Liberty and, 246
    waterfall feature, 248
    word "freedom" translations, **247**, 248
Freeman, Don, 216
Freeman, Elizabeth (reporter), 66
Friends Peace Committee (Quakers), 234
Fryer family, 56, 63
Fryer, George (husband of Lucy Fryer), 62
Fryer, Lucy (murder victim), 62, 64, 66, 72
Fryer, Ruby (daughter of Lucy Fryer), 62
funeral homes
    Compton's Funeral Home, 154, 161, 162
    Connally Funeral Home, 161
    Iglegart's Funeral Home, 190
    Wilkerson and Hatch Funeral Home, 161

G

Gaiety Hotel (Waco), tornado and, 150
Gainesville (TX), 56
Galveston (TX)
    Post Office Street (red-light district), 23
Gardner, Sam (relief efforts of), 161
Gardner, Steve, 218
Garrett, Pauline (drugstore owner), 188
    agrees to have Pipkin's be first to integrate, 188-189
Garrettson, Freeborn (circuit rider), 11
    unique preaching style of, 11
gasoline rationing during World War II, 117, 118-121
    gas rationing violators, 120
    hoarding of gasoline, 119-120

McLennan County Gasoline Rationing Board, 118-119
   price freeze on cost of gasoline costs, 118
   Ration Books and, 119
Gehlbach, Fred (professor), 216
   damages from 1953 tornado, 165-166
General Tire and Rubber Co., 195
Gerald, Colonel G.B., **48**, **49**
   attacks J.W. Harris in writing, 48-49
   fights with William Brann opponents, 48
   wounded by W. A. Harris' gunshot, 49
   wounds J. W. Harris with gunshot, 49
Germany, Congress declares war on, 77
Gibson, Lester (County Commissioner), 71
Gildersleeve, Fred A. (photographer), 209
   photographs taken of downtown Waco, **149**
Goldberg, Deputy Sheriff Barney, 66
Goldstein, A.M. (department store owner), 163-164, 187
Goldstein-Migel Dept. Store, 187
   newspaper notice, **163**
   targeted for protests, 187
   water damage from tornado, 163-164
Goliad tornado of 1902, 172
Golinda (TX), 59, 60
Gomez, Joseph (African American church leader)
   on the issue of desegration, 184, 196
   and Waco tornado relief efforts, 169
Gonzales, Manuel (part of the "Waco Dozen"), 239
Good Government League (civil rights group), 190
Gorham, John (member of tire rationing board), 116
Gorham-Jones (Waco business), advertisement, **168**

Goulston, Stanley, **242**
Graham, Billy (Christian evangelist), and Waco tornado, 173
Grant, Mrs. Truett, and tornado relief efforts, 161
Graves, Aubrey (reporter for *Washington Post*), 169
Gray, Sallie (madam), 35
Great Hanging at Gainesville, 56
Greater East Asia Co-Prosperity Sphere, 115
Greyhound bus, and 1953 tornado, 165
Griffin, Marvin C. (African American minister), 212
    African American leaders become disenchanted with, 198
    appointed chairman of Progressive Community Council, 189
    leadership of, 189-190, 197
    recalls racial tension in Waco, 187
grocery stores
    contemporary stores, well stocked, 113
    store shelves during WWII, 113-114, 131
Gunterman, Jesse (Chief of Police), 212

H
Hague, Glyndon (manager of VA regional office), 193
Hall, George Robert (prisoner of war), 236-237, 238
    attends dedication of Freedom Fountain, 248
    imprisoned in North Vietnamese prison, 236-237, 243
Hall, Jacquelyn Dowd (historian), 64
Hall, Pat (wife of George), 238
Hall, Sam S. (Waco police officer), 50
Halve, Max (eyewitness to tornado), 153
Hamilton, Linda, 238, 239
Hardee, L.F. (Reverend), 189
Harelik's Mans Shop (Waco) and tornado, 158

Harrington, Lee (Waco Fire Chief), 150
Harris, J. W., **48, 49**
  editor of *Waco Morning Times-Herald*, 48
  fires shot at Gerald, 49
  fights with Gerald, 48
Harris, Myrtle (madam), 35
Harris, Sam, 210
Harris, W. A.,
  brother of J. W. Harris, 49
  wounds G.B. Gerald with gunshot, 49
Harrison, Earl (bank president), 187, 193
Harrison, Guy B. (history professor), 113
Hawkins, William and Mary (foster parents of William Brann), 41
Heart O'Texas Coliseum and Fair Grounds, 108, 109, 110
Heart O'Texas complex (site of memorial), 173
Heart, Thomas (clerk), 34
Herring Avenue Bridge, **214**, 215
  controversy centered on, 213-214
Hessdoerfer, Oscar (Waco resident), 96, 102
Hewitt (TX), 142
  path of tornado, 143, 173
Hickman, T.M. (eyewitness account of tornado), 155
Higgins, Captain (Army captain), 82-83
Hill, Richard, 239
Hillsboro (TX), 62
Hispanics
  population growth in 1921-1922, 37
  rise in immigration (1910 census), 35, 36
  urban renewal of barrios and, 213
  use of Cameron Park, 219

Hobbs, Willie, 239

hogs

    hog production during WWII, 128-129

Holmes, William F. (historian), 57

Homer Martin Feed Store and 1953 tornado, 165

Hoover, Brad (director of Cooper Foundation), 193

hospitals and response to Waco tornado, 159-160

    Hillcrest Hospital, 159

    James Connally Air Force Base (hospital), 159

    Providence Hospital, 159

    Veterans Hospital, 159

Houston, (TX), 83

Howell, Maggert (pastor of church), 164

Huaco Indians (legend of), 169

Hubbard, Elbert

    editor of the *Philistine*, 52

    writes William Brann's epitaph, 52

Humphries, Will (saloon owner), 35

Hunt, Warren (court stenographer), 66

hurricanes, spur hoarding behavior, 131

Hutcheson, J. J. (newspaperman), 66

I

Iconoclast, the (newspaper)

    apology to Baylor University ladies, 47

    failure of, 42

    founding of, 42

    negative articles in, 41, 42

    response to Scarborough incident, 47

    revival and success of, 42

integration of Waco
   Annual Report (list of major achievements), 196-197
   background on, 183
   Bill of Rights and, 183
   Brown v. The Board of Education of Topeka, 183-186
   commerical desegregation of, 185-199
   Committee of Fifty and, 186-187
   concise history of, 181-201
   conservative viewpoint of community on, 184-185
   desegration efforts (1956-1960), 185-186
   dining establishments integrated, 194
   drugstores targeted for protests, 187
   end of commercial segregation, 197
   endnotes, 199-201
   first drugstore is integrated, 188-189
   Fourteenth Amendment and, 183
   lunch counters, strategy for non-violent integration, 191, 197
   news summaries on racial violence, 185
   newspapers refrain from printing news about protests, 188, 198
   objective of desegration, 199
   Piccadilly Cafeteria, 197
   Plessy decision and, 183
   public schools ordered to desegregate, 197-198
   race relations in the 1950s, 185-186
   racism in Waco, 199
   resistance by some white business owners to, 195
   summary of efforts, 198-199
   talk of protests and sit-ins escalate, 187-188
   slow to implement after *Brown* decision, 186, 198-199
   strategy used by civic leaders to avoid protests, 187-188, 190-192

white majority and Waco city elections, 194-195

white Waco community leaders and, 186

Woolworth's, 181, **182**, 191-193

Inter-Racial Sub Committee, 186-187, 195

Annual Report (1964) on process of desegregation, 195-197

list of committee members, 187, 193

new official name to reflect bi-racial makeup, 193

Progressive Community Council and, 189-193

strategy used by civic leaders to avoid protests, 187-188

Interstate Highway 35, 213

Interstate Movie House, integration efforts and, 195

Interurban Bridge, 248

and Waco tornado, 164-165

J

Jackmon, W. T. (Hays County sheriff), 59

Jackson Noah, Jr. (community leader), 211, 215, 216, 217

James Connally Air Force Base, 195

hospital efforts after tornado, 159

integration of, 192, 196, 197

rescue efforts after Waco tornado, 155, 161

James, Keith (Baylor philosophy teacher)

killed along with wife in Waco tornado, 147

Japan, World War II aggressions against U.S., 115

Jasper, Shepherd (African American drayman), 50

casualty of the Gerald-Harris shooting, 50

Jaworski, Dr. Hannibal (eyewitness to tornado), 152

triage efforts in hospital to save victims, 159

Jefferson-Moore High School Band, 248

Jenkins, Lee (deputy sheriff), 62, 66

Jim Crow era, 207
    and impact on Cameron Park, 209-210
Jinks, Gary (student), 238-239, **242**, 244
Johnson, Barbara (eyewitness to tornado), 153
Johnson, Lawrence (city councilman), 71
Johnston, Chester A. (Merrill Lynch investor), 120
Jones Construction Company
    military facilities builder, 80
Jones, Liza, 31
Jones, Myrtle (prostitute), 26
Joy Hotel Building (Waco), and tornado, 150
Joy Theatre and Waco tornado, 153-154
Judge Baylor statue (memorial), **227**, 234
judicial equality, 58

K
Kakin, Benjamin (circuit rider), 12
Karem Shrine Temple (site of memorial), 173
Katy Depot, **82**, 101
    initial arrival of troops, 83
Katy Park, 142, 143, 159, **166**
    damage done by Waco tornado, 166
Kelly, Don E., and Waco tornado, 163
Kelly, Mr. and Mrs. Jon T. (parents of Don), 163
Kendrick, Bruce (vigilante), 58
Kendrick, James (farmer), 58
Kiddieland (amusement park), 108, 110
Kilgore, Patsy (Lucy Fryer relation), 72
King, Will (executed African-American), 61-62
    effects of retrials, 62

trial of, 61-62

Knights of the White Camelia, 57

Koresh, David (Branch Davidian leader), 56

Krogstad, Major Arnold K. (pilot), 84

Ku Klux Klan, 203

   desegregated South and, 183

   role in vigilantism and, 55, 57, 71

Kultgen, Jack (co-owner of Bird-Kultgen Ford)

   Inter-Racial Sub-Committee activities, 187, 193

   viewpoint on integration of Waco, 198

   works as a liaison to help integration efforts, 189

KWBU-FM (Baylor University radio station), 228

L

labor disputes, 57

Lacy, Walter G. (parks commissioner), 214

Lacy, Walter, Jr. (bank president), 120, 122

   and Waco tornado, estimates cost of, 159-160

Ladies Home Journal, 244

Lake Air Center, 197

Lake Waco, 108, 109, 213

   Bosque River, flood problems after tornado, 157

   Lake Waco Dam, 157

Lakeside (musical group), 215

Lanham, Samuel L.M. (Texas Governor), 59

Lavender, Jackie (student), 123

Lavender, Luther L. (grocery store employee), 123

Lavender, Nell (farmer), 128

Lavender, Wallace (student), 129

Lawrence, James (sculptor), 217

LeBlanc, Mrs. Rodney J., 211

Ledbetter, John, helps deliver embalming fluid, 161

Leed's Clothiers (Waco), and tornado cleanup efforts, 168

Lewis, Preston (reporter), 246
    criticizes Harry Provence for advocacy journalism, 246

Liberty Bond Campaign, 97-99, 102,
    advertisements, **97, 98**

Lieu, Mr. (Vietnamese official), 243-244

Life magazine, coverage of Waco tornado, 170

Lindsey brothers, lynched for horse theft, 41

Lions Park, 216

Liveley, Mike T. (county attorney), 63, 66

Lockhart (TX), 59

London Times
    coverage of Waco tornado, 170

Long, Fred (county sheriff), 62, 66

Lorena (TX), 64
    Waco tornado and, 142

Lovers' Leap, **204, 205**, 211, 217
    75th anniversary celebrations, 218
    murder of Grady Skipworth, 209-210
    popularity of, 215

Lovers' Leap Baptist Church, 211

Lundsgaarde, Henry P. (writer), 58

lynch law
    defined, 55
    history of, 55

lynchings, 55
    endnotes, 72-75
    extra legal hangings and, 58-61

fostering atmosphere of hysteria, 59

"good colored citizens," 57

Great Hanging at Gainesville, 56

and huge crowds, 59

Jesse Washington, 56, 65-71

lack of accountability following, 62

resolution condemning, 72

Sank Majors, 58-61

variations in frequency of, 57

M

MacArthur, Arthur (father of Douglas MacArthur)

Camp MacArthur named for, 79

MacArthur, Douglas (General), 79

Mackey family (Sank Majors mother's employer), 59

Mackey Park, 209

renaming of, 209

Majors, Polk (Sank Majors' brother), 60

Majors, Sank (lynching victim), 58-61, 65

claims innocence, 60

extralegal lynching of, 58-61

Marable, Paul, Jr. (Waco Chamber of Commerce), 187, 193

actions to avoid sit-ins and protests, 187-188, 190

Mart (TX), 65

Martin, Carrie Bell (wife of William Brann), 42

Matkin, Lillie (eyewitness account of tornado), 154-155

rescued from wreckage, 154-155, 170

May, Karl (mayor of Waco), 239, **243, 244**

Waco-to-Paris delegation efforts, 242-244

May, Maggie (madam), 25

Mayfield, Wetona (nurse) and response to tornado, 159

Maynard, J. H. (Lucy Fryer's examiner), 62, 66

McCall, Abner (president of Baylor University), 187, 193

  student protests/vigils, actions taken, 229-230, 233, 235

McCloney, L.H. (Dr.), 189

McClure, E.L., 209-210

McDaniel, Douthit Y. (judge), 125

McGregor (TX), 65

  Bluebonnet Ordnance Plant (BOP), 124

McLennan Community College, 213, 238-239

McLennan County, 41

  circuit riders and rural areas of, 15

  Community War Chest established, 122

  decline of African-American population, 55

  defense industry jobs during WWII, 124-125

  Democratic Executive Committee, 48

  farm life during WWII, 128

  founding of, 55

  gas rationing during WWII, 120

  passes resolution condemning lynchings, 72

  prone to mob violence, 58-61

  racial tension and violence, 207, 209

  rainfall and flooding after 1953 tornado, 157

  selected as county seat, 206

  Sheriff's Office, 46, 48, 52

  white supremacy in, 61

  whitecapping attack in, 57-58

  World War II home front, 113-137

McLennan County Bond Board, 120, 121, 122

McLennan County Commissioners, 239

McLennan County Gasoline Rationing Board, 118-119

  issues stamps and tokens, 119

McLennan County Jail

  broken into by mob, 60

  Jesse Washington brought back for trial, 65

  Jesse Washington taken to Dallas for safety, 64

  Sank Majors removed from by mob, 61

McLennan County Medical Society, 159

McLennan County Tire Rationing Board, 116-118

McNamara, Guy (Police Chief), 65, 66, 69, 83

McNamara, J.B. (county attorney), 66

meat rationing during WWII, 128-129

  beef and pork substitutes, 129

  horse meat substituted, 129

Mecca Drug Company (demolished by tornado), 150

Methodist Church

  African Methodist Episcopal (AME) church, 10, 169, 183

  circuit riders and, 9-18

  early history of in America, 10

  emergence in Waco, 9-11

  First Methodist Church and the Waco tornado, **164**, 165

  First United Methodist Church of Hewitt, 17

  First United Methodist Church of Temple, 14

  Lorena United Methodist Church, 14, 17

  theology debate over slavery and, 10

  use of circuit riders to reach rural areas, 10-11

Michigan, Camp MacArthur troops originating from, 84

Middleton, Madge (madam), 27, 37

  lawsuit filed by landlord against, 30-31

military draft, brief history of, 228-229

Miller, Doris (Pearl Harbor hero), 209

Miller, Ella (madam), 31, 34

Miller, LaNell (Lyn), poem written by, 249

Miller, Pearl (prostitute), 29-30
   court case for unpaid doctor's fees, 29-30

Minnesota, Camp MacArthur troops originating from, 84

Mitchell, Roy, last legal hanging in Texas, 210

MKT (Katy) Railroad, and the Waco tornado, 165

Montgomery Ward, advertisement, **124**

Monnig's Drug Store (drugstore), 187

Moody, (TX), 65

Moore, A. J. (African-American educator), 62

Morris, Silas (Reverend)
   Rufus Burleson's son-in-law, 44

Morris, Steen, 44
   named as her rapist by Antonia Teixeira, 44

Mrs. Baird's Bread Company, 190

Mrs. Caroline Miller Mexican School, 37

Munroe, Richard I. (District Court judge), 65-66

Murphy, Lilly (prostitute), 27
   stabbed to death by another prostitute, 27

N

NAACP and racial equality
   Brown v. The Board of Education of Topeka, 184
   role group played in integrating Waco, 188, 189-190, 192, 194-195

Naman-Howell (lawfirm), 187

National Guard, and presence in Waco following tornado, 168

National Weather Bureau
   provides climate information to U.S. Army, 80

weather prediction before 1953 tornado, 142

Neely, Mr. & Mrs. John (victims of 1953 tornado), 154, 171

Neff, Pat (governor), 17

   objection to retail beer store, 32

   president of Baylor University, 120

New Hope Baptist Church, 212

New York Times, coverage of Waco tornado, 169, 170

Nixon, Richard (president), 243

Nokes, George (president of Lake Air Center), 197

Nolan, Stella (madam), 25, 26, 36

North Waco (TX)

   location of Camp MacArthur, 86

   Officer Club chimney still standing, 108

North Waco Elementary School, 248

Nourse, Sharyn (eyewitness to tornado), 152

O

O Dammit! (play about William Brann), 52

O'Daniel, W. Lee "Pappy" (U.S. senator), 119

  protests gas rationing during WWII, 119

O'Henry. *See* Porter, William Sydney

Oakwood Cemetery

   William Brann's headstone, **52, 53**

   William Brann's monument at, 41

Office of Price Administration (OPA), 116

oil industry in Texas

  rise of during World War II, 118

Owens-Illinois Glass Company, 125, 195

P

Palacio, Dave (Waco resident), 108

Palter, Robert (faculty member University of Texas), 235

Parker, James (Brigadier General), 83

Parliament (musical group), 215

Parnell, Jeanette (4 year old survivor of tornado), 153-154

Parnell, Mrs. Jack (eyewitness to tornado), 153-154

Parton, Mrs. Cecil (husband killed in tornado), 154

Patton, Carrie (eyewitness to tornado), 152-153
  injuries sustained in tornado, 152-153

Paul Quinn College (African American college), 165-166
  is liaison between Inter-Racial Sub-Committee and, 188-189
  role college played in integration of Waco, 188-190, 192
  tornado damage to auditorium and gymnasium, 165-166

Paul Tyson Football Field, 109-110

Pauling, Margaret Smith, 211

Pearl Harbor, Japanese attack on in 1941, 115

Pence, Belle (madam), 27
  lawsuit against for unpaid rent, 31

Penland, James (Waco Chamber of Commerce), 81, 83

Penrice, R.L. (attorney), 189

Perot, H. Ross (business)
  prisoners of war and petition, helps with, 238

Perry, Minnie (prostitute), 34

Perry, W.C. (Dean of Students, Baylor University), 233

Peterson, Jon A. (historian), 206

Philistine (newspaper), 52

Phillips family house, 56

Piccadilly Cafeteria (Waco)
  initial resistence to integration efforts, 197

Pinckney, Dewey (city councilman), 216

Pipkin's Drug (drugstore), 187

  first drugstore to be integrated in East Waco, 188-189, 191

Plessy v. Ferguson (1896 Supreme Court decision)

  invalidated by *Brown v. Board of Education of Topeka*, 183

Poage, W. Robert "Bob" (congressman), 80, 214

Porter, William Sydney (writer), 42

  buys the *Iconoclast* from William Brann, 42

  lets William Brann revive the *Iconoclast*, 42

  popularly known as O. Henry, 42

Powell, Dorothy Head, 216, 217

Powell, William Elmo (prisoner of war), 237, 243

  family attends dedication of Freedom Fountain, 248

PRG (provisional government of South Vietnam), 236

  petition sent to in regards to prisoners of war, 238

  Waco-to-Paris delegation and, 244-245

Pringle, Dixie Dick (factory worker), 125

Proctor Springs, 206, **207**, 217, **220-222**

  Depression era activities, 210

Professional Building (Waco, TX)

  damage suffered by 1953 tornado, 148-149

Progressive Community Council (black community leaders), 189

  calls for hiring more African American workers, 195

  council's role in integration efforts, 189-191, 193-195

  integration of Woolworth's and, 191-192

  Inter-Racial Sub-Committee and, 189-193

  list of members names, 189

  statement on desegration, 193-194

prostitution, 21-40. *See also* Two Street

  age trends of prostitutes, 32-33

average number of years working in business, 33

business relationship of madam and girls, 29-32

call for abolition of, 23

census demographics and, 32-36

clothing typically worn, 29

court cases by landlords for unpaid rent, 30-31

dangerous business of, 27-28

end of red-light district, 38, 83

endnotes, 38-40

and growing economy, 23

interior furnishings/layout of typical brothel, 30

interracial relationships between prostitutes, 33

modern era streetwalkers, 38

occupation of men visiting brothels, 33

progressive reform movement and, 23

red-light districts in other Texas cities, 23

rise of in 1890s, 23-24

structural plans of typical brothel, 26

transient nature of, 29, 32

typical age considered too old, 27, 33

venereal disease and, 29

why women entered the profession, 33

Provence, Harry (newspaper editor), 187, 193, **243**

   Freedom Fountain and, 246, 248

   helps keep news of protests out of papers, 188, 190, 194

   practices advocacy journalism, 246

   Waco-to-Paris delegation efforts, 239, 241-245

Pure Milk Company, racial tension involving, 187, 192

Purple Cow (diner), and Waco tornado, 161

R

R.T. Dennis Company (Waco furniture store)
  eyewitness accounts of tornado, 152, 153, 154-155
  rescue efforts following tornado, 155
  salvage operations, 158
  statement issued by, 158
  suffered greatest devastation from tornado, 147-148
  victims of tornado, 148, 154, 171
  Waco tornado and, 141, 142, 147-149
  wreckage caused by tornado, **148**
racial violence and extreme torture, 59
racism
  integration efforts and, 199
  racism in post-Reconstruction Texas, 44
Radford, Gary H. (dentist), 213
radio stations (Waco)
  KWTX, and 1953 tornado, 169
  WACO, and 1953 tornado, 169
Ramirez, Beatrice (eyewitness to tornado), 152-153
rape
  accusations of, 56
  and fear of black men, 56
  as threat to white male authority, 64
rationing during war. *See* war rationing
Reconstruction era, 57
Red Cross
  relief efforts after the Waco tornado, 154, 160, 170
red-light district. *See* prostitution
Red Men Museum and Library, 50-51
  Colt .41 that killed Tom Davis, **50**

display of three pistols, **51**
Reichenbach, Linda (descendant of William Cameron), 218
religious denominations
  Baptists, 9-10
  Methodists, 9-11
Rice, Lula (madam), 35
Rich Field (Army air field), 83, 85, 86
  Army Flight School, 107
  cadet pilot, **84**
  closing of, 107
  description of, 85-86
  entertainment activities at, 99
  flight school, 85
  initial arrival of planes, 84
  named for fallen officer, 79
  requirements in constructing, 79
  top ranked flying school, 85
  training plane, **85**
  Waco provides roads & amenities, 80
  YMCA at, **86**
Rich Field Flyer, 102
Rich Field Vaudeville Company, 99
Richfield High School, 238, 244
Richfield Veterans' Association
  response in the aftermath of Waco tornado, 160
Ridgewood Country Club and Waco tornado, 161
rifle clubs, 57
Riley, Irene (madam), 35
Riley, Maude (madam), 31, 35
Robert, Ben (husband of Clinnie Robert), 59

Robert, Clinnie (alleged sex assault victim), 59-60

Robertson brothers (lynching victims), 57

Robertson, Max (parks and recreation director), 217, 218

Robinson (TX), 56, 62-63, 64, 65, 69

Rodriguez, Ysabel (Hispanic restaurant owner), 36

Rolling Stone (William Sydney Porter publication), 42

Roosevelt, Franklin (President)

  scrap rubber drives and, 117

  war bond advertisement, **121**

Roosevelt Hotel (Waco) and Waco tornado, 158

Ross, Deputy Sheriff Harvey B., 60

rubber and tires. *See* tires and rubber rationing

Rusk, Dean (U.S. Secretary of State), 235

S

Salvation Army, and 1953 tornado, 160

San Antonio (TX)

  The District (red-light district), 23

  reaction to *Brown* decision, 185

Sanders, J. J.(County Sheriff), 59

Sandler, Evant (lynching victim), 57

Sapp, Jesse (African American community leader), 198

Scarborough, George (son of John Scarborough), 46-47

  beats William Brann with a gun, 46-47

  son of Judge John Scarborough, 46-47

Scarborough, Judge John

  assaults William Brann with a cane, 47

Schell, Nora (park ranger), 219, 222

Schotlz, Airman Dennis (tornado rescue efforts), 155

Schwartz, Katy (madam), 35

Scott, Milton W. (architect)
  designed brothel, 26
Scott, Samuel R. (District Court Judge), 58
scrap drives during World War II
    children enthusiastic embrace of, 125-**126**
    community embraces the effort, 125-126
    heyday of in Waco, 126
    scrap metal drives, 114, 117, 125-127
    scrap rubber, 117
    slogans used to encourage donations, 126
Select Beer Distributing, tornado and, 143
Sendon, Mary, 107
Seton, R.C. and Waco tornado efforts, 162
Sheppard, Morris (Texas senator), 83
Sibley tents, 96
Simms, Larry (park ranger), 212, 217, 218, 219, 222
Simon, Chris (Fryers' neighbor), 62
Simpson, Matthew (circuit rider), 10
Sinclair Mattress Company, tornado and, 143
Six Shooter Junction (early nickname for Waco), 41
Skipworth, Grady, murder of, 209-210
Slattery, Joseph, verbally attacks William Brann, 43
slavery
    theological debate over by Methodist church, 10
Smith, Benny Frank (eyewitness to tornado), 149, 173
Smith, Cullen (law partner of Naman-Howell), 187, **243**
    chair of Waco-to-Paris delegation, 242-244
    helps with POW efforts, 238, 239
    telegrams sent to PRG, 240-241
Smith, David F., Jr. (Waco City Manager), 210

Smith, Della (madam), 35

Smith, J.D. (tornado rescue efforts), 155

Smith, Les (actor), plays William Brann in play, 52

South Waco
  Waco tornado and, 143, 158-159, 163

Southwestern Bell Telephone Co., and Waco tornado, 162

Southwestern University (Georgetown), 16

Spain, Rufus (history professor at Baylor University)
  comments on student protests at Baylor, 232-233

Spanish Influenza outbreak, 94-97

Spark, Milton (eyewitness account of tornado), 155-156

Spelman, Jon (park commissioner), 218

Spotts, Robert (tornado rescue efforts), 155

Spray Park, **214**

St. Mary's Parish, and Waco tornado, 161

Stanford Chapel (Methodist church), **14**
  baptisms, number of, 17
  cemetery, 13, 17
  communities served, 13
  congregation disbanded, 17
  description of, 13
  educational activities, 15-16
  fire destroys, 17
  gate entrance, 7, **8**
  marriages performed, 17
  religious activities, 14-15
  summer camp meeting, 15

Stanford, Lemerles (wife of Thomas Stanford), 7, 12, 13, 17
  assets of, 16-17

Stanford, Mr. & Mrs. Wilson B.

home destroyed by 1953 tornado, 142

Stanford, Thomas (circuit rider), 7, 12-17

  assets of, 16-17

  biography, 12

  curator for Southwestern University, 16

  education and academics outreach, 15-16

  friendship with E.R. Barcus Sr., 14

  personal demeanor of, 16

  photographs/illustrations, **13**, **16**

  Stanford Chapel and, 13

Stearns, Gustave (pastor), 102

Stermas, Angelo (brother of Chris), victim of tornado, 156

Stermas, Chris (owner of Chris's Café), 156

Stermas, Vic (brother of Chris), victim of tornado, 156

Stevenson, Coke (governor of Texas)

  protests gas rationing, 119

  sets up local tire rationing boards, 116

Stewart, Earl (Baylor University student)

  letter published about student protests, 230-231

Strain of Violence (Brown), 56

Strawbridge, Robert (circuit rider), 11, 12

Sturgeon, I.P. (commissioner of education), 165

sugar rationing during WWII, 122-124

  number of ration books issued, 123

  rationing books, 122-124

  violators, how punished, 123

Summers, Grace, 31

Surratt, Marshall (Sank Majors case trial judge), 60

Suspension Bridge (Waco)

  suggestion to rename "Freedom Bridge", 245

  Waco tornado and, **150**, 164

Swayne, Joe (store owner), 65

T

Taylor, Carrie (student), 248

Taylor, H. L. (Waco doctor), 49

Taylor, J.W. (county attorney), 57

Teixeira, Antonia

    illegitimate pregnancy of, 44

    Rufus Burleson's accusations against, 44

Terrell, W.E. (chairman gas rationing board), 118

Texas Department of Public Safety, 172

Texas Office of Price Administration (OPA), 116, 119, 127

    coffee rationing and, 127-128

    issues gas rationing books, 119

    set rules and regulations on gas rationing, 119

Texas Penal Code, 58

    ambiguity of, 58

    justification for mob violence, 58

Texas Power & Light Co., **162**

    efforts to provide power following tornado, 163

Texas State Patrolmen, assigned to Waco following tornado, 168

Texas State Technical College (Waco)

    present campus (formerly Connally Air Force Base, 192

Texas State Technical Institute, 213

Texas Tornado Conference, 172

Thomas Goggan & Bro., 30

Thomas, Isabella (madam), 35

Thomas, Jesse

    shooting death, 210

    wrongly accused of murder, 209-210

Thompson, Eva (madam), 26

Thornberry, Homer (judge)
  issues order to desegrate public schools in Waco, 197

Tilley, G.W. (sheriff), 59, 60

Tilley, J.A. (deputy sheriff), 60

Time magazine, coverage of Waco tornado, 170

tires and rubber rationing (World War II), 116-118
  buying new tires, complications of, 116-117
  Firestone advertisement, **117**
  McLennan County Tire Rationing Board, 116, 118
  retread and used tires as an alternative, 117-118
  scrap rubber drives, 117
  state-wide speed limit reduced, 118
  truck drivers impacted by, 117
  violators of rationing, how punished, 118

Tom Padgitt Building, devastated by Waco tornado, 148

Torrence, William C. (Waco city manager), 115, 127

Townsend, May (prostitute), 25

Travis County Jail, 59

Tucker, Anna, 31

Turner, Charles D., 217
  recollection of grandfather Osa Turner, 167
  recollection of Vietnam era draft-dodging, 229

Turner, Osa (City of Waco employee), and tornado, 167

Turner, Thomas (newspaper correspondent), 190, 212

Tweedy, Josie (madam), 27, 35

Two Street (The Reservation), 21-40. *See also* prostitution
  1870 census, 32
  1880 census, 32-33, 35
  1886, number of madams operating on, 26

1889-1895 (number of prostitutes), 23-24
1900 census, 34, 35
1910 census, 35-36
1916 street directory, 36
1917 street directory, 36, 37
1921-1922 street directory, 37
African American residents and, 34
age trends of women, 32-33
changing social landscape of, 32
demographics of, 32-36
end of the red-light district, 36-38
ethnic makeup of surrounding neighborhood, 33, 34
guidelines for operating brothels on, 23-24
Hispanic immigration to the neighborhood, 35, 36, 37
immigration patterns of neighborhood, 34-35
interracial mingling between 1860s-1880s, 33-34
madams operating brothels in 1886, 26
Mollie Adams (most famous madam), 25-37
moral crusaders closing the red-light district, 38
mulatto prostitutes, 32, 33-34
photographs, **22**, **24**
racial segregation and, 35-36
transient nature of neighborhood, 32, 34, 35
why named, 23
working class residents living in neighborhood, 32, 34
Tyree, Hattie (madam), 26-27
    sister stabbed to death, 27

U

U.S. Army

all-black regiment, 81-83

   arrive in Waco, 81

   Camp MacArthur Riot, 80-83

   removal of all black troops from Texas, 83

U.S. Army Corps of Engineers, and Waco tornado, 165, 171-172

U.S. Constitution

  First Amendment and the press, 198

United Service Organization (USO) club, 211

   Negro USO, 211

Universal Atlas Cement (Waco business), 195

V

Valentine, Q.Z. (eyewitness to tornado), 152

Valley Mills (TX), 65

Vass, Paul (eyewitness to tornado), 156

Vaughn, Anderson (lynching victim), 57

Veterans Administration (VA)

  challenge of integrating cafeteria, 197

Veterans Administration Hospital, 195

Veterans for Victory (pro-war group), 233

Vick, Pat (jury foreman), 60

Vickers, Annie, 31

Vickers, Ophelia, 31

Vietnam War and Waco, 250

  1964 (students and faculty response), 228

  1965 (students and faculty response), 228

  1966 (students and faculty response), 228

  1967 (students and faculty respond), 234-235, 236

  1968 (students and faculty respond), 235-236

  1971 (Waco-to-Paris committee), 238-245

anti-war protestors and Baylor University, 227-236
Baylor students and response to, 227-228
campus efforts to show support for troops, 228
Christian view on, 231-232
Christmas audio cards sent to troops, 228
Committee to End the War in Vietnam (CEWV), 235-236
draft-dodging efforts by students, 229
endnotes, 251-253
military draft instituted, 228-229
peace vigils on campus of Baylor, 229-236
petition signatures collected and sent to the PRG, 238
PRG (provisional government of South Vietnam), 236
prisoners of war from Waco area, 236-237
    Waco-to-Paris committee, 238-245
    "Write Hanoi" campaign, 237-238
protests turn violent, 232-233
public debate on, 233-234
Tet Offensive, 235
Veterans for Victory, 233
Waco Delegation to Paris, 238-245
Young Americans for Freedom (YAF), 232-234
Young Republicans and, 234
Villa, Pancho (Mexican bandit), 84

W
Waco (TX), 85, 106, 109
army camp, requirements for, 79
atonement plaque, 71-**72** (photo)
Camp MacArthur boosts the economy, 79, 102
Camp MacArthur historical marker, 77

cattle boomtoom, 21, 23

celebrations at war's conclusion, 106-107

City Beautiful movement and, 206-209

City Charter changes brought about by lawsuit, 194-195

city council adopts single-member districts, 194-195

commercial development, 141

Community Race Relation Coalition, 72

cotton harvest festival, 101

county seat of McLennan County, 206

dining establishments integrated, 194

economic past during 19th century, 21

Great Depression and, 124-125

historical description, 55

integration of James Connally Air Force Base, 192

Jesse Washington lynching, 66-71

nicknamed "Six Shooter Junction," 41

police department and, 45-46, 49, 50

post World War II economy, 139-141

prominent employers in the late 1950s, 195

race relations in 1910, 203

race relations in the 1950s, 185-186

reputation for violence, 41, 55-60

residents entertained by pilots, 102

Sank Majors lynching, 58-61

segregation in, 183-185

soldiers parade in Waco, **101**

urban renewal and, 213-214

World War II home front, 113-137

Waco Army Air Field, 211

Waco Chamber of Commerce, 81, 106, 119, 125

bi-racial subcommittee established, 192, 193

call for integration of public facilities, 193-195

and Camp MacArthur, 79, 81, 106

Committee of Fifty, 186-187, 193, 195-197

Community Relations Committee, 195

dining establishments integrated with help from, 194

Inter-Racial Sub Committee, 186-187

promote job opportunities for African Americans, 195, 197

relief efforts and the Waco tornado, 160, 168

role in integration efforts of 1950s-1960s, 186-199

specialized committee formed to tackle integration, 186-187

Waco Chiropractic Society, and Waco Tornado, 159

Waco Cider Extract, 30

Waco City Council, 72

  passes resolution condeming lynching, 72

Waco City Square (downtown)

  and Waco Tornado, 149-150, 158, 171

  photograph of, **149**

Waco Civic Theater, stages play about William Brann, 52

Waco Club (bar), 81

Waco Convention Center, 245, 248, 250

Waco Creek, used as dump site after tornado, 166

Waco Daily News, 42

Waco Disaster Fund, and Waco Tornado, 160

Waco Female Academy, 16

Waco High School (Municipal Stadium), 166

  Baylor Field, 166

  damage done by Waco tornado, 166

  Kiwanis Field, 166

  location was part of Rich Field, 108

Waco Hilton Hotel, 248

Waco Indians

  conflict with Cherokees, 204

  history of the tribe, 203-206

  legend of Lovers' Leap and, 204, 206

Waco Independent School District, 187

  integration and, 198

Waco Lions Club, 125

Waco Morning Times-Herald, 48

Waco News-Tribune

  coverage of Waco tornado, 142, 157-158, 171

  refrain from printing articles about protests, 188

  reporting on cost of tornado, 159

Waco Pastors' Association, 71

Waco Pirates (baseball team), 142

Waco Public Schools, desegregation of, 196, 197-198

Waco Regional Airport, origins as Rich Field, 107

Waco School Board, 148

Waco Suspension Bridge. *See* Suspension Bridge

Waco Times-Herald, 81, **171**

  coverage of the *Brown* decision, 183

  coverage of Freedom Fountain, 246

  coverage of Jesse Washington trial, 60, 62-63, 65, 66, 69

  coverage of Waco tornado, 170-171

  refrain from printing articles about war protests, 188

Waco-to-Paris Committee (efforts to help POWs), 238-245

  background on, 238-239

  delegation meets with North Vietnamese officials, 242-244

  efforts to set meeting with North Vietnamese Officials, 241-242

  fail to meet with PRG in Paris, 244-245

Freedom Fountain, idea of born from trip, 245-250

group attends Easter Service in Paris, 240

legacy of trip, 245

members of committee (Waco Dozen), 238-239, **249**

objective of group, 239

petition presented to North Vietnamese officials, 241

photo album as gift to North Vietnamese officials, 24, 244

photographs of group members, **239, 241**

political support for the group, 239

propaganda given to delegation members, **244**

telegrams sent to North Vietnamese officials, 240-241

trip to Paris, 239-245

Waco Tornado of 1953, 139-179

2nd Street and Bridge St., **149**

5th Street and Austin Ave., **140**, 152

2009 view, **140**

aftermath and damage assessment, 157-159, 170-173

Alico Building (Amicable), 139, 150, 152, 158

Austin Ave., damages to buildings, 152, 158

automobiles damaged, estimates of, 167-168

Baylor Theater, movies shown on day of, 142

Bell's Hill, path of tornado, 143, 158

Billy Graham speaks at memorial for dead, 173

blood drives, 160

Bridge Street and East Waco, 150, 158

bridges, how they held up to tornado, 164-165, 169

building codes, call for stricter codes, 171-172

buildings downtown, damages to, 157-159, 163-164

bus and train service following, 165

businesses encouraged to rebuild, 168

churches, damage done to, 165

communication and utilities, aftermath of, 162-163

cost of, 159-160

dangers from gas fumes, 157

deaths reported, 141, 170, 171, 172, 173

debris dump sites implemented, 166-167

donations received, 173

endnotes, 173-179

eyewitness accounts, 150-157

final death toll, 172

flooding following tornado, 157

funeral homes overwhelmed in aftermath, 161-162

garbage collection efforts following, 166-167

Hewitt and Lorena, path of tornado, 142-143

hospitals overwhelmed in aftermath, 159-160

impact on community for several years, 172-173

initial storm front, 141-142

injuries, 173

insurance companies and, 159-160, **167**

Katy Park, 143, **166**

locals help in cleanup efforts, 168

media coverage in U.S. and abroad, 169-170

military relief efforts in the aftermath of, 161

national disaster relief efforts following, 160-161

Operation Cleanup, 168-169

post office deluged with mail following, 163

Professional Building, damage to, 148-149

public response in the aftermath, 160-161, 168-169

public schools, damages to and aftermath, 165

R.T. Dennis Building, devastation of, 147-148

rainfall in record numbers, 157

reclaiming displaced property, 167-168

relief efforts by volunteers, 161

rumors spread about atomic bomb blasts cause of, 172

safety measures implemented after, 172

structural damages, number of, 173

switchboard circuits overloaded, 162-163

toll in damages and lives lost, 141

urban legend revolving around Jesse Washington, 172-172

victims, 141, 152, 154, 156

Waco Square (downtown), **149**-150

weather bureau staff cut after, 172

weather predictions prior to, 142

Waco Tribune-Herald, 71

  article about Freedom Fountain, 248

Waco Weather Bureau, 172

Waco Weekly Tribune

  account of Brann-Davis Shootout, 52

Waco Zoo, 218

Wade, Mariah (anthropologist), 206

Walker, George (saloon owner), 35

Walker, Virgil (president of Behrens Drug Co.), 187, 193

  works with committee to avoid protests, 187-188

Walmart stores, 113, **114**

Walton, John C. (Deputy Sheriff), 60

war bonds (World War I), **97**, 148

war bonds (World War II), 114-115, 120-122

  advertisements for, **121**

  cost of war bond stamps, 120

  interest earned on war bonds, 120

popular slogans, 122

promotions and pledge drives to sell, 120-122

sales quotas and goals, 122

what funds were used for, 115

war rationing (World War II), 114-116

challenges for the government to institute, 116

gasoline rationing, 117, 118-120

legal justification for, 115

Office of Price Administration and, 116, 119, 127-128

sugar rationing, 122-124

tires and rubber, 116-118

Ward, Joe, Jr. (president Waco Chamber of Commerce), 187, 195

develops strategy for avoiding sit-ins, 187-188, 192

role in integrating James Connelly Air Force Base, 192

statement on desegregation, 193-194

Ward, W. H., 50-51

business manager of William Brann, 50

charged with murder of Tom Davis, 52

present at Brann-Davis fatal shootings, 50

Warren, Earl (Chief Justice), 183

Warren, Homer (dairyman), tornado witness, 142

Washington Avenue Iron Bridge, and tornado, 164

Washington, Henry (Jesse Washington's father), 66

Washington, Jesse (lynching of), 62-72, 80-81, 83

accountability by town officials in lynching of, 69-70

atonement plaque and, 71

charred body of, 56, **69, 70**

confession of, 63-64

crowd at the lynching **67, 68** (photo)

estimated size of crowd at lynching, 69

    innocence, likelihood of, 71

    lynching of, 56, 66-71

    makeshift gallows and pyre, **67, 68**

    police stand by and do nothing, 69-70

    seized from courtroom by mob, 66

    significance of alleged Lucy Fryer rape, 64

    trial of, 65-66

    United States Senate resolution apologizing for lynching, 71

    urban legend surrounding path of Waco tornado and, 172

    Waco's image suffers in aftermath of, 80-81, 83

Washington, Martha (Jesse Washington's mother), 66

Washington Post, coverage of Waco tornado, 169-170

Week's Events, The (magazine), cover of tornado, 170

Welter, Jo (Waco Community Race Relation Coalition), 72

West, Decca Lamar (historian), 204, 206

West, Lucy (prostitute), 34

West Texas, 65

Western Hatcheries and 1953 tornado, 149-150

Western Union and 1953 tornado, 163

  efforts to help with communications, 163

 Wesley, John (Reverend), 9, 11

  rise of Methodism in America and, 10

whitecapping

  defined, 57

  examples of, 57-58

  purpose of, 57

Wild, Mark (historian), 33

Wiles, Dr. W. W. (Waco resident), 49

Wiley, Sallie (madam), 34

Wilkerson, Howard (eyewitness to tornado), 169

Wilkes, Dr. W. O. (Waco resident), 49

Williams' Drug Store (drugstore), 187, 191

  African American students plan protest, 194

Willis, Jimmie (Life photographer), 170

Wilson, William H. (historian), 206

  coins the term "environmentalists", 206

Wisconsin,

  Camp MacArthur troops originating from, 84

Wolf, Ralph (mayor) and 1953 tornado efforts, 167, 169

Wolters Air Force Base (Mineral Wells)

  relief efforts in the aftermath of Waco tornado, 161

Wood, Anna, 31

Wood, Sam (reporter for *Waco News-Tribune*, 171

Woolworth's (department store)

  integration of, 181, 191-193

  modern street view, **182**

  targeted for protests, 187

Working Boys Club, 125

World War I

  Armistice, 96, 106-107

  Congress declares war on Germany, 77

  Jenny (aircraft), **85**

  purpose of American soldiers, 110

  Richfield veterans offer help after tornado, 160

World War II

  challenges to the American economy, 115-116, 129-130

  cost of the war, 129

  federal policies limiting civilian clothing markets, 115

  Japanese aggressions toward the U.S., 115

  military recruitment form, **130**

shortage of workers at beginning of war, 116

World War II Home Front (1942-1943), 113-137

air raid drills and blackouts instituted, 115

coffee rationing, 127-128

defense industry jobs, 124-125

demand for war materials increases, 114

dilemma of toys during the war, 130

endnotes, 131-137

factories need for new workers, 115-116, 124-125

farm life, 128-129

gasoline rationing, 117

grocery store shelves during, 113-114

hurricanes spur storm hysteria, 131

meat rationing, 128-129

product recycling, 127

scrap drives, 114, 117, 125-127

war bonds, 114-115, 120-122

war rationing, 114-116

wartime civil defense measures, 115

wartime propaganda, **126**

women working in factories, 124-125

Write Hanoi campaign

American Red Cross enlisted to help with, 238

Wacoans efforts to help prisoners of war, 237-238

Y-Z

Yarbrough's Grocery, tornado and, 143

YMCA Elks (football team), 215

Young Americans for Freedom (YAF), 232-233

rival protest organization, 232-233, 234

Young, Florence, 31
Young, John (opinion page editor), 222
Zachry, Woody (eyewitness to tornado), 157

Acknowledgments

Bradley T. Turner

Thank you, Andrea, for your patience, support, and love during this project. You are always there to offer your care, editing skills, and encouragement when I do not feel very motivated, and are always standing by with treats while I work — you are wonderful. Thank you, Charlie and Brenda Turner (my mother and father), for being my cheering section, loving me, and for allowing me to remain at home while I was in college — had you not, this book would not be here. Thank you, Luther and Nell Lavender, and Osa David and Virginia Turner (my grandparents), your stories of old Waco, pictures of yesteryear, and help guided me into channels of information I did not know of; thank you for being so proud of me. Thank you, Paul and Sharyn Nourse (my father and mother-in-law), for providing feedback on your thoughts of the book and helping encourage Andrea to co-write the tornado chapter with me — your support and respect are important to me. Thank you, Wallace and Jackie Lavender (my great-uncle and aunt), for providing me with several stories of your teenage years — they were greatly appreciated. Thank you, Jerry and Polly Johnson, for being good friends, encouraging people, and for being excited about this project — I really appreciate that.

Thank you, Melody Flowers, for introducing me to your husband, Mark Long, and helping get this idea off the ground. Thank you, Mark Long, for taking a chance on this book, helping make me a published author, doing an awesome job on arranging my manuscript, cover, and design, and for putting so many resources into this project — you are a fine publisher and I look forward to other projects together soon. Thank you, Grace Arsiaga, for helping make my book look fantastic! Thank you, Melanie Peterson, for always lending a helping hand to me whenever I needed it. Thank you, Sheila Boggess, for helping me take my book to new places and to new people. Thank you, Wes Lowe, for making LVR one of your job's priorities. Thank you, Carly Kahl, Kayla Allen, Dr. Jim Usery, Michelle Graye and Katharine O'Moore-Klopf, for editing the manuscript. Thank you, Steve Tiano, for providing my book with a good layout. Many thanks are due to SoroDesign for the fantastic cover. Thank you TSTC Publishing, for making LVR one of the coolest things I have ever done.

Thank you, Andrea, Rick, Mark, and Amy, for contributing your magnificent chapters to this project. Your research, time, and sleep-deprivation provided me with the opportunity to include important topics that few Wacoans understood.

I hope that this book helps showcase the brilliance you all exhibit and I look forward to reading more pieces by each of you in the future. Thank you, my dear friends!

Thanks, Dr. T. Michael Parrish, for writing the introduction to this book and for helping me understand the beauty of local, public, and social history. I hope we make you proud with this book, especially since it was you who pointed many of us in this direction. Thank you, Dr. Patricia Ward Wallace, for helping me in graduate school and for helping set the bar of expectations for local history — your research, support, and help has been appreciated. Thank you, Ellen Brown, for locating new resources for my work and for being so helpful with my research endeavors. Other thanks goes to the many other people at the Texas Collection, Dr. Thomas Charlton, Michael Toon, Geoff Hunt, Tiffany Sowell, Amie Oliver, and Kathy Hinton, for always being happy to help me find whatever I need. Thank you, David Lintz, for being such a tremendous help during this project and opening your wonderful archives to me at the Red Men Museum and Library, your knowledge of "all-things-Waco" is irreplaceable. Thank you, Kathryn Stallard, of the A. Frank Smith, Jr., Special Collections and Papers at Southwestern University, for helping me locate highly specialized research that I did not know existed. Thank you, Waco History Project, for providing such wonderful primary resources and research online.

Thank you, Cullen Smith, for providing me with helpful feedback on my Vietnam chapter and for being patient with me — your kindness made the quality of my research much better. Thank you, Paul Marable, Jr., for providing me with such helpful information about Waco in the 1960s. Thank you, Kyna Saul, for providing me with good opening scriptures on several chapters. Thank you, Robyn Bean and Kevin Brady, for your wonderful thesis work on Waco and Baylor's history — it inspired portions of my book and taught me many things about my hometown. Thank you, Ross McNew, for providing me with great feedback on my chapters and for teaching Waco history in a public school's classroom — it was a pleasure to work with you.

Thank you, Withrow Family, Bob McEachern, Sr., of the Barcus Family, Margaret Blanton of the Stanford Chapel Cemetery Association, Dan Pennington, Jeannie Fair, Bill Caldwell, Bob Templeton, *Waco Tribune-Herald*, *Dallas Morning News*, NAACP, and Cullen Smith, for providing me with such wonderful images and information for my book.

Lastly, thank you, McLennan Community College, for being supportive of this project and its editor/compiler.

Richard H. Fair

I would like to thank Brad Turner for the opportunity to contribute to this exciting new addition to Waco's history. I greatly appreciate his friendship and support over the years. On a similar note, I would like to thank Mark Long and all our friends at Texas State Technical College Publishing for the hard work put into making this project an exceptional study in local history. I especially want to thank my wife, Jean (Jeannie) Fair for the tireless hours of work she spent offering helpful suggestions and editing my work. I want to thank my precious son, Derek Pierce Fair, for providing me with the perfect distraction from my work. I look forward to sharing my work with him as he grows, and letting him know how he inspires me to be a better person and a better father. I want to thank my parents, Wayne and Lois Fair, for supporting me through my educational endeavors. I owe this opportunity to their never-ending patience and love, and the many times they encouraged me to continue pursuing my goals when I felt like giving up. I would like to thank my MA thesis director, Dr. T. Michael Parrish, for his guidance, support, and encouragement. I could not have finished this degree and contributed to this book without his careful and concerned instruction. He has taught me more about local history than I ever thought I could master, and constantly pushed my limits to make me a better historian. I would like to thank Dr. Thomas L. Charlton and Ellen Brown at the Texas Collection for their gracious support and help throughout my continued research in local history. I would like to thank the McLennan Community College History Department for their continued support in my teaching and professional endeavors. I would like to thank Robert "Robby" Smith for his continued friendship and helpful suggestions in my writing and thank Robert "Robbie" Fletcher for his friendship and support of my academic endeavors. Finally, I would like to thank the National Association for the Advancement of Colored People for their assistance and images that greatly contributed to one of my chapters.

Amy S. Balderach

I would like to express my gratitude to Brad Turner for giving me the opportunity to be part of this wonderful collection. I am indebted to Michael Toon for giving me the idea of writing about Waco's bawdy women. I also extend a hearty "thank-you" to T. Michael Parrish and Rebecca Sharpless, both of whom served on my thesis committee and offered ample suggestions for my research on Waco. The stewards of the McLennan County Archives were also exceptional, and the project simply would not have been the success that it was without Kathy Schwartz and Trudy McGuire. Much gratitude goes to Nali Hilderman for her initial edits during the thesis phase in Waco. I also recognize Russell Martin for his advice and encouragement. Last, I thank my parents and siblings (Lori, Ron, and Mindy) for putting up with me and inspiring my creativity throughout the years. This work is dedicated to my nephews and niece: Jacob, Andrew, Dillan, Alexa, and Adam. I will tell them all about the women of Two Street one day — when they are much older.

Mark Firmin

I would like to acknowledge my parents, Sally and Trigger. Thank you to Liza for her patience and unfailing love and support. Thank you to Dr. T. Michael Parrish and Dr. Thomas L. Charlton, who have been invaluable teachers and sources of support for this and other projects. Thanks to Dr. Stephen M. Sloan, Becky Shulda, Dave Sikkema, and the rest of the staff at the Institute for Oral History at Baylor University for their assistance and guidance with oral history. Thank you to Ellen Brown, Geoff Hunt, Michael Toon, Amie Oliver, Tiffany Sowell, and Kathy Hinton at the Texas Collection and to Sandie Polk and Patricia Ervin at the City Secretary office for their tireless efforts to accommodate my research needs. Thanks to all of the interviewees who shared their memories of Cameron Park. Thanks to Rusty Black, Sharon Fuller and the rest of the City of Waco Parks and Recreation Department. Thank you to Bradley Turner for this great opportunity and his passion for the history of Waco. Finally, thanks to the family of William Cameron for their beneficent gift of Cameron Park to the people of Waco.

Andrea R. Turner

I would like to thank my fabulous husband for inviting me to participate in this exciting project and for all of his love and support. In addition, I would like to thank my loving family for all of their support and my mom for sharing her memories of the tornado with me. I would also like to thank Baylor University Libraries for providing such rich resources and for the help of friendly staff and librarians. The production of this book has proved to be an exhilarating journey, and I feel blessed to have been granted this opportunity.

About the Authors

Bradley T. Turner, a seventh-generation Wacoan, teaches at several educational institutions in the local area and works as a writer. Turner holds degrees from McLennan Community College, the University of Mary-Hardin Baylor, and Baylor University in the fields of political science, American history, and environmental studies.

Mark Firmin was born and raised in Waco, Texas. He received bachelor's and master's degrees in history at Baylor University. He is the author of *Cameron Park: A Centennial History* (2010). He is a candidate for a master's degree in Information Systems (MSIS) with a focus in Archives and Special Collections at the School of Information at the University of Texas at Austin.

Amy Balderach credits her parents for nurturing her lifelong passion for "old stuff." After graduating with a bachelor's degree in history from Westminster College, she attended Baylor University, earning a master's degree in American Studies. Balderach also earned a master's degree in history from Rice University. She resides in Pennsylvania and continues to write about sexuality and gender.

Richard H. Fair received an associate degree from Texas State Technical College, and bachelor's and master's degrees from Baylor University. He is pursuing further graduate work at Texas A&M University. He teaches at several educational institutions throughout the local community and also works as a writer and an audio preservationist.

Andrea Turner, a native Wacoan, serves as the acquisitions unit leader of Baylor University Libraries. She graduated *magna cum laude* from Baylor University with a bachelor's of business administration degree in business journalism and accounting. She loves serving in the children's ministry at First Baptist Church of Hewitt, and adventuring with her husband.